ONE MAN'S DESERT

One Man's Desert

The Story of Captain Pip Gardner, VC, MC

REX WOODS

WILLIAM KIMBER · LONDON

First published in 1986 by
WILLIAM KIMBER & CO. LIMITED
100 Jermyn Street, London, SW1Y 6EE

© Rex Woods, 1986

ISBN 0–7183–0612–0

Typeset by Grove Graphics, Tring
and printed in Great Britain by
The Garden City Press Limited,
Letchworth, Hertfordshire, SG6 1JS

One Man's Desert is dedicated to the memory of all those who fought in the Western Desert but did not return – in particular to the author's five brother-officers of the 4th Battalion of the Royal Sussex Regiment who were killed in action at the Battle of El Alamein on the night of 27/28 October 1942. Their names are:

Lieutenant-Colonel Ronald Murphy
Captain John Harrison
Captain Dick Parkinson
Lieutenant Tony Lyle
Lieutenant Hubert Willett

Contents

List of Illustrations

Maps and illustrations in the Text

Acknowledgements

In chronological order the list of people to whom sincere thanks are due for help in the preparation of *One Man's Desert* starts with Lieutenant-Colonel Robert (Tug) Wilson, DSO and Bar, who first introduced me to Pip Gardner during the research for his own book, *Special Commando*.

At an early stage with work on *One Man's Desert* I was fortunate enough to visit Lieutenant-Colonel Alan (Bertie) Roberts, MC and Bar, and he kindly started me off with information about the 4th Royal Tanks in general and Pip Gardner in particular, for which I am most grateful. Likewise, my thanks go to Lieutenant-Colonel Jack Prichard, DSO, MC, who also provided authentic and interesting information, particularly concerning the launching of Pip on what turned out to be his VC mission in the Desert.

Colonel S. I. Derry, DSO, MC, and Lieutenant-Colonel John Furman, OBE, MC, are warmly thanked for their help, not only for the facts contained in their respective books (*The Rome Escape Line* and *Be Not Fearful*), but also for personal interviews which proved both interesting and extremely enjoyable. Additional thanks go to Sam Derry for kindly providing a good batch of photographs from which to choose some of those that appear in this book.

I am also most grateful to Mrs Susan Hands, the youngest daughter of Percy Gers, for lending me part of an account written by her late father covering his walk-out from Fontanellato Camp, as well as an interesting prisoner-of-war notebook that he managed to bring home with him.

Following a visit to the Tank Museum at Bovington in order to examine all the types of tanks that were likely to be mentioned in this story, useful help was willingly supplied on several occasions on important technical points by the Curator, Lieutenant-Colonel George Forty, and the Librarian, David Fletcher. To both of them I am most grateful.

To the Imperial War Museum, too, thanks are rendered for supplying copies of Tobruk photographs and for permission to include them in the book.

Above all, I want to thank Pip and Renée Gardner for receiving me at their house in Sussex and for making the effort of a return visit to Devon in connection with the book. I would like to record my thanks (albeit posthumous as far as the recipient is concerned) to Pip's late father, Stanley J. Gardner, for the loan of his magnificent wartime scrap-book of press cuttings and Pip's letters home from the Desert, into which I was able to delve over forty years later.

R.W.

'But that's another story . . .'

One Man's Desert is the fourth in a chain of true wartime escape books, each of which has lead most conveniently to the next. The chain started in 1982 with the publication of *A Talent to Survive* – the wartime exploits of Lieutenant-Colonel Richard Broad, MC, Légion d'Honneur, Croix de Guerre avec Deux Palmes. The story told of his unique feat in not only evading capture himself at St Valéry in June 1940, but also bringing back seven of his Seaforth Highlanders with him, via Honfleur, Paris, Marseille, the Pyrénées and Spain. The book goes on to relate his subsequent missions for SOE in Madagascar and the Haute Saône. In the course of the latter there emerged a dashing Commando officer, Lieutenant Sherard Veasey by name, who had managed to escape from a cattle-truck in the Brenner Pass in 1943 and reach Switzerland and happiness – thus forming the central figure in *Night Train to Innsbruck* (1983). This story in turn unearthed another Commando escaper, Lieutenant-Colonel Robert ('Tug') Wilson, DSO and Bar, whose most unusual and eventful war, from which he was lucky to return, formed the subject-matter for *Special Commando* (1985).

While I was gathering and checking material from Tug Wilson for his book, he ran into a slightly misty patch when recalling certain events that befell him while he was on the run and in hiding in Rome. At Tug's suggestion, I contacted his friend and one-time fellow fugitive in 1943/44, Captain Philip ('Pip') Gardner, VC, MC, to find out whether he could help us to establish various facts and dates. He most certainly could, and seemed only too pleased to do so.

In so doing, he touched on other events which, though immediately of interest to me, were not directly concerned with Tug Wilson's book. Pip Gardner would cut short these incipient digressions, adding, 'But that's another story'. After a couple of these asides, I began to realise that he, too, probably had a virtually untold escape story in him, quite

apart from his Victoria Cross and Military Cross won for valour in the
Western Desert.

Consequently, when Tug Wilson's book was completed, with Pip
Gardner's timely help, I felt the urge to visit the latter – the fact that
he now lives in my own Sussex birthplace, serving as an added
inducement. I wanted to find out what his full story was and, equally
important, to discover whether he would be prepared to let me write it.
The idea was agreed by Pip himself and enthusiastically accepted in
principle by my publishers. Thus was born escape book number four,
One Man's Desert, thereby continuing the remarkable chain of events
which has led from one story to another.

The way in which this progression has come about prompts me to
ponder whether there is a common denominator which runs through
the above-mentioned non-fiction war books – or possibly more than one
such denominator. It strikes me that all four of them have one salient
feature, above all others, in common. Each tells the overdue story of a
resourceful and surviving central figure – as opposed to a daring but dead
hero. It is always sad to read a tale of great gallantry or endurance,
only for the hero or heroine to end up with an executioner's bullet
in the nape of the neck in, say, Buchenwald, or perhaps blown up by a
mine or a shell in the Ardennes, with the end of the war in sight.
Obviously for anyone writing true wartime stories which end in tragic
death, there is no way of avoiding a sad ending when such was in fact
the case. But one of the greatest pleasures for me in compiling these four
wartime escape stories that I have been fortunate enough to unearth
one after the other, is the fact that not only the central figures, but also
the subsidiary escapers whose varied adventures have been deemed
worthy of inclusion, have all survived to tell their respective
tales. This fact has made research so much easier and all the more
enjoyable.

Another common denominator is the fact that all the subjects of the
four books are essentially modest matter-of-fact men when it comes to
their wartime achievements. This doubtless accounts for the fact that
by the time I met them, in succession, their stories were still largely
untold – for the simple reason that they were reluctant to bore people
with tales of their own bravery. Fortunately, when given an undertaking
by me that there would be no attempt at hagiography or at sensationalis-
ing events, but that I would merely gather the facts and let the readers

draw their own conclusions, they were all prepared, in their individual amusing ways, to tell me their stories.

In each case I have not considered it my province to give my personal pronouncement on their valour, and thereby risk damning with faint praise on the one hand, for fear of piling on the praise too thickly, so that it cloys, on the other. Suffice it to say that I wouldn't be interested in writing about the conceited or the controversial – however brave. Nor did I seek or desire permission from my subjects to analyse or dissect their characters. Letting deeds speak for themselves, I have preferred to gather the facts and write the story, leaving readers to form their own judgements over character and courage, rather than risk ramming pre-digested opinions down their throats.

Apart from the enjoyable opportunity to meet and work with the four central figures in question, as well as the subsidiary escapers whose adventures have lent variety and have enhanced each book, the research required has led me to France, Italy, Switzerland and Germany, re-visiting old familiar places, as well as following new trails and meeting some of the gallant French and Italian people who risked so much in order to offer humanitarian help to Allied servicemen on the run.

In the case of *One Man's Desert*, it has not proved possible, and probably wouldn't have proved profitable, to pay a recent visit to the scenes of Pip Gardner's acts of outstanding gallantry in the Libyan Desert with the 4th Royal Tanks. Instead, I have relied on the fact that at least I was in the Western Desert myself in 1942 – and thankfully not in a tank! I also followed him into 'the bag' in Italy, and reluctantly preceded him to Germany – the reason for the latter fact being revealed as his story unfolds, as we follow him through the peaks and troughs of his fluctuating fortunes in *One Man's Desert*.

Seaton, Devon 1986   Rex Woods

'I'm no Soldier!'

'I'm no soldier!' may seem a strange opening sentence for a story about someone who was destined four years later to win his country's highest award for valour – the Victoria Cross. But these were the very words that Philip John Gardner used when he told his mother that he felt it his duty to volunteer for military service in the Territorial Army, and that he was joining the Westminster Dragoons as a trooper.

This was in September 1938, at the time of the Munich crisis, which was when it dawned on many young men in Britain of military age and patriotic inclination, from all walks of life, that war with Hitler's Germany was inevitable – as was abundantly proved a year later, with the invasion of Poland followed two days later by the start of World War 2 on 3rd September 1939. The fact that Pip Gardner was prospering in what was bound, in the event of war, to become a reserved occupation giving exemption from military service, didn't shake his resolve or deter him from taking active steps towards doing his duty. Nor did the fact that he was engaged to be married.

'Pip', as he was widely known by family and friends, was twenty-three at the time.

Before moving into his wartime story, it is necessary to go back to the beginning, in an attempt to discover the background of an army officer whose war was to include some high peaks of achievement and acclaim, as well as some grim troughs of despair and degradation as he experienced the vicissitudes of war, first in the Western Desert and later as a prisoner-of-war in Italy and Germany – all of which he was able to survive with the aid of Fate and his own background and upbringing.

*

The logical starting point of Pip Gardner's story is 25th December 1914. This was the first Christmas of World War I – and not the last, as so many optimists predicted at the start of the war. It was also the day on which Pip Gardner entered the world, thereby adding himself to a family that already numbered two daughters. His arrival caused great rejoicing all round and there was never the slightest question of his feeling unwanted. He proceeded towards a very normal and happy childhood at his parents' home in Sydenham in the South London suburbs – well cared for but not spoiled. His elder sisters helped see to that!

His father, Stanley J. Gardner, was Chairman and Managing Director of the family engineering firm with works at Beckenham. It had been founded in Bermondsey in 1873 by Pip's grandfather. The firm specialised in the manufacture of equipment for the ventilating and air-conditioning industry, and from early childhood Pip received every encouragement, without undue pressure, to interest himself in the family firm. He was also encouraged, but again not unduly coerced, to attend services in the Mission Hall which his father and some friends ran in Catford. Pip's main contribution to the proceedings was to pump the organ. He thus had a religious background which was to stand him in good stead, but by no stretch of the imagination could he be described as pious – in the slightly derogatory sense sometimes ascribed to the word.

He received his education as a day-boy at Dulwich College, where his best subjects, fortunately enough, were mathematics and science. This enabled him to study engineering practice and technology – when his other outside pursuits permitted! These included involvement with the Officers' Training Corps, where as sergeant in charge of the bugle band he found he could enjoy some degree of responsibility, coupled with a little scope for showmanship.

He also took part enthusiastically in school games and other activities – preferring rugby to cricket, finding the latter too slow for his mentality. In fact, as an alternative to cricket, he took up rifle-shooting. This had the added advantage of taking him on Wednesday afternoons to Bisley, where, after shooting on the famous ranges, he also learned where and how to procure and consume a sly pint of beer – obtainable at the back door of the Surrey hut.

Pip's only school prizes were for shooting and for his services in the Officers' Training Corps, but he had received a good all-round education, including the subjects that he needed most for his chosen career.

The choice was entirely of his own volition, with parental approval and encouragement, but never any coercion. He had to make up his own mind. But it really seemed that he was bred for the engineering career that lay within his grasp. His talents had always tended in that direction – a state of affairs that many an undecided youth of his age would surely have envied. From a very early age he had spent much of his time in the holidays playing in the factory, creating both amusement and at times annoyance for the employees who, however, were kind and well-disposed in their treatment of the boss's son. They instructed him in engineering practices at an early age, with the result that when he left school he had already acquired a considerable knowledge of the activities associated with the family company.

Leaving school at seventeen, he was grateful for what he had learned there but was now ready to move on. He started on the shop floor of J. Gardner and Co Ltd, working alongside men whom he had already known for many years. They now instructed him without hesitation in the engineering practices of their respective trades. So the transition from school to workshop floor was made relatively smooth for him. There was much to learn and he felt lucky to be able to get straight on with something practical in such welcoming company.

After a year at the Beckenham works of J. Gardner and Co, Pip graduated to the drawing office at Dock Head, Bermondsey. This move widened his knowledge and his horizons. In the first place he got to know London – always an asset for a young man. Then he began to spread his wings, with journeys further afield, accompanying senior draughtsmen to start with and later on his own, in connection with the firm's contracts in many places all over the country. He thus gained valuable experience at an early age of many different industries.

Pip found this work most interesting and fulfilling and it wasn't long before he was carrying out simple contracts on his own. He survived several near catastrophes, caused by his inexperience, from which he was saved, without having to face an irate customer, by the timely support of his father and colleagues in the drawing office. Thus experience was being gained at not too dear a price!

By January 1934, at the age of nineteen, Pip was working as draughtsman in charge of a large building in Oxford Street, London, known as the Mount Royal. It consisted of a number of flats with inside kitchens and lavatories – an arrangement which was at that time an innovation. These required full ventilation. Here Pip met Fred Hubbard, the engineer in charge of mechanical services, and this encounter started a friendship which Pip regarded as the basis of much of the good fortune that was to follow him through life. He had met not only a personal friend, but also a business client who helped him and his company to prosper for many years.

Pip spent many happy months at the Mount Royal site and, although he had already become accustomed to drinking (and holding) pints of beer at the Dulwich Rugger Club (after an early introduction at Bisley!) he completed this side of his education under Fred Hubbard and the builder's agent after business hours. This training in the consumption of beer was to stand him in good stead, without fear of disgracing himself.

When he had acquired a certain amount of experience at a comparatively early age, he received a surprise telephone call from his father, starting with an enquiry whether he would like to go to China? What Pip at first took to be some sort of a joke, turned out to be a serious suggestion. One of the firm's best clients had undertaken the job of air-conditioning the Hong Kong and Shanghai Bank, in Hong Kong, and required a draughtsman to go out there to measure and engineer the air-ducting required.

Such an opportunity had never entered Pip's head, but he at once realised that this was an experience not to be missed. Accordingly he arranged to visit the Managing Director of the company concerned, together with his father, that very afternoon.

The Managing Director, Mr Nelson Haden, of G. N. Haden and Sons, explained that his firm was carrying out the installation of air-conditioning in the Hong Kong and Shanghai Bank, which was a fourteen-storey building and was the first building in Hong Kong to be fully air-conditioned. It was also, at that time, the highest building erected on the island.

Owing to the distance from England, it would be necessary to manufacture all the required air-ducting locally in Hong Kong and for this purpose a draughtsman and sheet-metal foreman would be needed on site to deal with the drawing and manufacture. After some discussion, in which Pip's father queried whether, at nineteen years of age, he was perhaps rather young to be entrusted with the drawing work, Mr Haden decided that, although Pip's previous experience had been limited,

he felt nevertheless quite confident that under the management of
Mr Michael Mead, their site engineer, he would be able to perform
the duties required.

Accordingly, after a hectic week spent in visiting tropical clothing
shops and saying goodbye to family and friends, Pip Gardner found
himself sailing from London Docks in May 1934 aboard the *Kaiser I
Hind*, a rather old but dignified ship of the P and O Line. With already
a fair amount of experience for a young man of his age, Pip Gardner
was about to have his horizons considerably widened in the Far East.
Not surprisingly he felt that the world was his oyster.

*

For all the confidence of youth, things happened rather quickly for
young Pip Gardner and at first it all seemed somewhat strange for a
nineteen-year-old embarking on such a big adventure. But he soon
became friendly with some other young men who were travelling out
to the tin mines in Kuala Lumpur and Penang.

The ship's first port of call was Marseille, to which some passengers
travelled overland across France to avoid the swell of the Bay of Biscay.
The rest of the route was via Malta, Port Said, through the Suez Canal
to Aden, Ceylon, Penang, Singapore and finally to Hong Kong.

Pip soon started to enjoy himself – rather too much so, when he went
ashore for a few hours on Malta. The attractions of the island proved
rather too much for him and his recently-acquired young mining
friends. When they returned to the jetty to board the boat to take
them back to the ship, they found that they had arrived just in time
to see their ship steaming off to the Far East without them, leaving the
disconsolate young men behind, without passports or belongings. Pip
thought his visit to Hong Kong had come to an abrupt end, through
his own folly, before he had even got there.

Galvanised into action by such embarrassing thoughts, they rushed
around and managed to charter a fast motor-launch which raced at full
speed after the disappearing ship. Following much shouting and waving
from the launch, the ship's captain hove to and lowered a jacob's ladder
for the young men to climb ignominiously up. Not surprisingly, the
whole experience had proved somewhat traumatic and was followed,
naturally enough, by a subsequent dressing-down in well-chosen words

delivered by the captain. A chastened Pip learned a lesson that has ensured that he has never again been late for a ship, plane or train! It was for him a salutary lesson, fortunately learned at no great cost, as it turned out.

After this scare, Pip's voyage continued on a more even keel. His knowledge of the Far East was still very limited and amongst his purchases before leaving for tropical climes, he had been persuaded to invest, at no small expense, in a sola topee. His was white, with a tin-foil lining to ward off the penetrating rays of the tropical sun. But when he paraded his new topee on his first encounter with the hot sun of the Eastern Mediterranean, his new friends, who had already been out that way before, were vastly amused. They suggested that he looked like a Royal Marine, or perhaps someone from Mars. Pip rectified matters by buying a modern light-weight model in Aden. He later found a use for the much-ridiculed original topee as protective headgear for walking round a building-site. In fact on one occasion it saved him from what could have been an unpleasant accident, when a red-hot rivet dropped on to his head from six floors above.

As well as his mining friends, Pip also found some congenial female company on the voyage – notably a charming young girl from Perth in Western Australia. After spending many happy hours in each other's company, they parted with mutual protestations of love and promises to write. But this shipboard romance went the way of many another and nothing further transpired once dry land was reached.

After passing through the Suez Canal, down to Aden, and on down to Ceylon (before it became Sri Lanka), Pip had his first experience of swimming in a warm sea and gazing at the wonderful scenery of a tropical island. After further interesting stops at Penang and Singapore, the five-week voyage ended at Hong Kong.

There he was met off the ship by the firm's site manager, Michael Mead and his wife, Lesley, who took him under their wing. They had arranged for him to stay at a small private hotel in Kowloon. Here he resided for two months, before meeting a young man of his own age, Laurie Kilbee by name, who lived with his parents in a very pleasant flat on the Peak. His father was the Marine Superintendent for Jardine Matheson, the well-known Far Eastern trading company. The Kilbees invited Pip to go and live in their spacious flat, an offer that he readily accepted.

He welcomed the change of residence since, despite being frequently entertained by Michael and Lesley Mead, he had at times felt rather lonely in his hotel. But with Laurie Kilbee and his parents, he was soon treated like one of the family and was asked out to dine with Laurie's friends. He also became a member of the local rugby and cricket clubs and met lots of people. This enabled him to settle down most comfortably to enjoy his work and his play on the island.

Although he was employed to undertake the drawings necessary for the air-conditioning installation, it soon became essential for air-ducts to be manufactured immediately, and Michael Mead asked Pip if he could set up a small factory in order to produce the sheet metal work entailed. Although a skilled sheet metal worker was supposed to have been sent out from England, this had not yet been arranged. So it was left to Pip to find an excellent Chinese foreman to start up a factory. Eventually a staff of over a hundred Chinese workers was built up, without the aid of anyone else from England. Besides manufacturing the air-ducting, it was also necessary to recruit a team of fifty erectors to install it as the building progressed. It was all a great challenge for a young man of Pip's age to be heavily involved in such a project.

During the last six months of his eighteen-month stay in Hong Kong it became necessary to have men working in shifts day and night. Excellent though most of the Chinese staff were, Pip still found it advisable to visit the site at night on occasions to see that all was well. Sometimes he would do this after dining out at a hotel and would arrive on the site in the early hours of the morning in a dinner jacket – much to the surprise and consternation of the Chinese workers, some of whom he found asleep until they grew wary of his nocturnal habits.

Pip's time in Hong Kong passed very happily as he thoroughly enjoyed his work and also had time for a very full and exciting social life. He joined the Hong Kong Volunteers as a member of the Armoured Car Section – shades of things to come! – and although they only had two old Rolls Royce cars, they managed to carry out their training and duties in a reasonably efficient manner. They toured the areas around Kowloon which bordered on China, which thus enabled him to see a great deal of the hinterland.

His friend Laurie Kilbee was an officer in the Volunteer Naval Defence Force, which had a small naval vessel moored off the harbour, which was used as a training headquarters. Each night an officer was appointed Officer of the Watch and had to spend the night on board. After training hours the Officer was allowed to invite guests for dinner. This gave Pip great pleasure when Laurie was on duty. Pip would arrive at the quay with two of their girl-friends, where they would be met by the ship's boat and duly taken out to the *Cornflower*, as the training ship was named, where they would be piped aboard.

After an unhurried dinner the mixed foursome would continue merrily until it was time for the guests to return. Pip would escort the girls ashore, leaving Laurie to keep watch for the rest of the night. Little did either of them realise then that a few years later Laurie would be a prisoner-of-war under the Japs on the mainland, while his wife Evelyn and their two children were interned on the island for the duration of the war – nor, for that matter, that Pip would become an unwilling guest of the Italians and the Germans, after winning the MC and the VC in the Libyan Desert.

After working, swimming, sailing and enjoying himself enormously for eighteen months in Hong Kong, Pip was there for the completion of the work at the Hong Kong and Shanghai Bank – an event which was celebrated with amply-flowing champagne. It also signalled the time for his return to England in November 1935, having completed a very exciting and happy phase of his life. Having worked (as well as played) throughout his stay in Hong Kong, he decided to make his way back to the other side of the globe by completing a circuit of the world. So he booked his passage home via Shanghai, Peking, Japan, Honolulu, San Francisco, Los Angeles, the Panama Canal, Cuba and New York.

After sad farewells to all his many friends in Hong Kong, he set sail for Shanghai. He spent three days sightseeing and sampling the night life, which for a young man in 1935 was an experience never to be forgotten – nor too often repeated! Pip discovered night spots where one bought a book of tickets, which enabled one to dance with beautiful partners of many nationalities, Shanghai being one of the most cosmopolitan cities at that time.

From ship he changed to train, on a forty-eight-hour journey to Peking. In the absence of any Europeans on board, he found the train journey somewhat tedious, and he found himself rather wishing that he hadn't embarked on such an undertaking. But his flagging morale was much restored next day when, on arrival in Peking, he found an excellent Chinese guide and spent a memorable day seeing the sights of the city, including the Temple of Heaven.

His journey then took him on by train for three days through Manchuria (Manchukuo as it then was), down through Korea to Pusan, glimpsing the Great Wall en route. Arriving at a station close to the Great Wall on the borders of China and Manchukuo, the train stopped to take on some Japanese Customs officials, who passed along the train examining passports in a most officious manner. As they reached Pip, an elderly Englishman, who was accompanying them and appeared to have some authority, introduced himself.

Finding that Pip was English, he said that he was the Superintendent of the Manchukuo State Railway, and asked if he had seen the Great Wall of China. On Pip's replying that he hadn't, he said : 'Come with me and I will show it to you.' Without more ado they walked on to the platform and mounted a foot-bridge across the railway and there, in full view, was the Wall. Pointing to a large gate with towers on either side, the Superintendent explained that, according to local legend, in each tower there was a Chinese god with jade eyes focussed on the gate. While these existed China would be safe from invasion. 'But', added the Superintendent, 'I have been here many years and I can tell you that it is me and my diplomacy that ensures the safety of that gate!' Pondering on the superstitions of the East, and grateful for his grand-stand view of the famous Wall, Pip continued on his way.

Changing trains at Mukden involved a lengthy wait at the station, where a White Russian befriended him and took him to a small German private hotel. Despite having one eye on his watch, still mindful of being late for the ship at Malta and not wanting to take any chances with the train, Pip enjoyed the hospitality and duly returned to the station with time to spare. Just before the train left he was asked by the conductor of the sleeping-car whether he would mind another male passenger in his compartment, as they were over-booked. Feeling that he had little option but to agree, he was somewhat taken aback when from behind the conductor there appeared a Japanese traveller. Pip was fearing a language problem. But he needn't have worried, as the Jap was a multi-lingual businessman, travelling with a trade delegation. Pip soon found himself being entertained by the whole delegation in the observation car to lunch and dinner, which passed the time enjoyably to Pusan, at the southern tip of Korea.

On arrival at the port, they all embarked on a ship for the crossing to Shimonoseki in Japan. The trip took eight hours and the sea was very rough, but Pip managed to sleep the whole way and only woke up in the calm waters of the harbour in brilliant sunshine.

There followed a train journey from Shimonoseki in the West over to Yokohama in the East, the large port near Tokyo from which Pip was due to sail to Honolulu. The train had small wash-basins in the corner of the sleeping compartments and Pip failed to realise that these basins tipped up and threw the waste water outside the train. The result was that he lost his razor and toothbrush somewhere in the middle of Japan. Apart from this unexpected loss, the journey proved enjoyable. It went through some beautiful scenery, the highlight being a grand view of Mount Fujiyama, looking most impressive with its covering of snow with the winter sun glistening on the top of it.

He spent one night in Yokohama in a magnificent hotel, waited on by two attractive Japanese girls in national costume who wouldn't even let him serve himself with tea or butter. Bidding this lotus-eating life goodbye, before it took a hold on him, he set off to board the *President Hoover*, bound for Honolulu. But before leaving Yokohama he went shopping for a coffee set, a tea set and several pieces of Satsuma porcelain to take home. All these were carefully packed for him and he took them with him back to England without a single piece broken. In fact they have survived to this day.

The call at Honolulu included a visit to the Dole pineapple factory where one could drink glasses of ice-cold juice out of running taps, which struck a hot and parched Pip as a useful form of technology. And so to San Francisco, where there was time for a quick tour of the city, before catching a Greyhound bus down to Los Angeles where he visited the Chinese Theatre, where leading film-stars had left their foot-prints in the cement outside. He also went to the famous Hollywood Bowl. But his search for film-stars in the flesh proved unsuccessful – probably not helped by the fact that he was unable to afford the kind of restaurant that they no doubt frequented.

After this brief glimpse of Hollywood in its heyday, it was time to board yet another ship, the SS *Pennsylvania*, which was to take him through the Panama Canal to Cuba and New York. Again an enjoyable shipboard romance came Pip's way, with an American girl. The romance spilled over on to dry land this time and at New York he stayed for five delightful days, with his new girl-friend acting as his private guide to the sights. Their lavish round of pleasure included a visit to Radio City, which had just been completed and was the largest cinema and amusement centre in the world. They went to the famous Rainbow Room high up on the Rockefeller Center skyscraper, for the then fashionable pastime of dancing to the band of Ray Noble, to hear that 'Love is the Sweetest Thing' from the composer's own orchestra. To the languid tones of his 'Goodnight Sweetheart' they swore to see each other again, etcetera, but after one letter on his return to England, Pip found that the novelty of this early love affair was waning, mainly because he wasn't old enough, or wealthy enough, to pursue this enjoyable experience. He soon had other fish to fry !

A mid-winter Atlantic crossing in the *Aquitania* landed him safely back in England on December 23rd. He was thus able to be home in time for his twenty-first birthday on Christmas Day 1935, bearing gifts for his family from the Far East. Though at his tender age he could hardly claim to be a man of the world, he could at least say with truth that he had been round it by twenty-one – something which, in the pre-jet era, was an opportunity granted to few young men of his age.

*

After spreading his wings in the Far East for nearly two years, Pip found it rather strange at first re-starting work in the family firm in London, but he soon made the adjustment. With money saved while working in Hong Kong, he bought himself a second-hand MG Magna, which became the pride of his young life. It also gave him the mobility of which he now felt in need, and he lost no time in looking up two school-friends of Laurie Kilbee, his friend in Hong Kong. They both lived in Folkestone – Norman Franks a solicitor, and Gordon Norris a hotelier. He was immediately glad that he did so.

Then for a summer holiday in 1936 he took his MG down to Torquay, where he stayed at a hotel right on the sea-front. On the first morning he was sitting in the garden, wondering what to do on his own, when he heard someone talking on the terrace about him, saying : 'Go and ask him if he would like to join us.' The next moment he was approached by a very attractive girl of about his own age, who asked him whether he would join a party of guests at the hotel, who were going out in a motor-launch to follow the 'J' class racing yachts which were assembled in Torbay. He gladly accepted the invitation to join the party – a state of affairs that continued for the whole of his two-week holiday.

The chief attraction for him was the charming girl who first approached him. She lived at Bedford and was an only child, whose father owned a factory for making high-quality panelling and staircases. This friendship, unlike his previous shipboard romances, continued to flourish on dry land – despite the fact that Pip never managed to beat her at golf, at which she excelled.

Fortune continued to smile on him, because his work took him north to Leeds in the autumn of 1936. This enabled him to call at Bedford on his journeys to and fro between Leeds and head office in London. His job consisted of undertaking the drawing and supervision of the ducting installation for the Queen's Hotel in Leeds. He soon fancied himself to be in love.

With life in general going so well, Pip decided to buy himself a new car, and he became the proud possessor of a 'T' type MG – the first new car that he had owned. This smart-looking vehicle was to have a considerable bearing on his and other people's lives, in a manner that will soon emerge. After early teething trouble, in the shape of a five pound fine for driving with his friends from Folkestone, Norman Franks and Gordon Norris, aboard without due care and attention. This aberration was closely followed by a ten pound fine for passing a police car at sixty miles an hour in a thirty-mile limit, before he drove the black MG to what was to prove a fateful rendezvous.

Despite the arrival in Leeds, as manager of the Victory Hotel, of his new friend Gordon Norris, Pip found that he was rather lonely at times living in a small hotel. At the suggestion of his sister Molly, who had lived for some time in Doncaster, that he should follow up an invitation to visit the Sherburn family, who lived in the same road as Molly, he rang them up. The elder daughter, Muriel, answered the phone and at once asked him over for Sunday lunch. Pip accepted with alacrity.

Arriving in his black MG, he was introduced to her younger sister, Renée. Pip was immediately captivated by the very slim and attractive girl before him, and she in turn was equally impressed with Pip's new MG. She didn't need asking twice when Pip offered to take her for a spin in his new car. The trap was baited and sprung! There followed a succession of dates in Leeds, where Renée was conveniently attending a beauty course. The result was that Pip's attention was diverted from Bedford and transferred to Doncaster and, for better or for worse (doubtless for better, seeing that they are still married forty-seven years later) Philip Gardner and Renée Sherburn became engaged in 1938.

But by September 1938 war clouds were gathering ominously over Europe. In fact they had been gathering since 1931, when Adolf Hitler rose to power in Germany, though most people in England tended to ignore this fact, preferring to get on with their own lives. But when Hitler, having already annexed Austria in 1936, succeeded in acquiring half of Czecho-Slovakia in September 1938, without having to go to war, and was making threats in the direction of the rest of Czecho-Slovakia and Poland, with insistent demands for *Lebensraum* in the east, it finally dawned on most people in Britain that war in the near future was inevitable. Neville Chamberlain, the Prime Minister, did not achieve his hoped-for 'peace for our time'. The best he could manage was to buy a breathing space – at Czecho-Slovakia's expense.

This was the time when young men of military age, but not necessarily of military inclination, such as Pip Gardner, flocked to join the Territorial Army and other volunteer services in their spare time. In view of his aptitude for matters mechanical, as well as his liking for fast cars, it wasn't surprising that Pip elected to join an armoured unit of the Territorial Army, the Westminster Dragoons. At five feet eight he was also a convenient size to fit into the cramped interior of a tank or armoured car.

It was at the army medical examination that Pip first met Jack Kempton and discovered that the latter had lived in Bedford. He soon identified Pip as the owner of the black MG sometimes seen in those parts – and as the purloiner of his one-time girl-friend! But this didn't prevent them from becoming firm friends, whose paths were to cross in some surprising places during the war.

On 3rd June 1939 Renée and Pip were married in Doncaster, with a large reception at the Danum Hotel. Norman Franks was best man and Gordon Norris a groomsman. They just had time for a honeymoon in Paris, before settling into their first home at Beulah Hill, Upper Norwood, where they were delighted to find that their next-door neighbours were Pip's old school-friend Geoffrey Gardner (no relation) and his wife Betty. Then Pip had to go off to his first Territorial camp in

August at Warminster. He had only just got back and was sent to Corsham in Wiltshire, on a ventilating job for some underground explosive dumps. A Captain in the Royal Engineers, who handled the explosives strictly in accordance with Army Regulations – in marked contrast to the comparative disregard of precautions with which they had been handled by the civilian storemen – remarked to Pip that by the time he got home he would probably find his call-up papers waiting for him.

This was precisely what happened – the date being 3rd September 1939. Married bliss had been suspended and war, for Pip and millions of others, had now begun.

CHAPTER TWO

Venison Galore

Following Neville Chamberlain's dramatic radio announcement on Sunday morning, 3rd September 1939, telling the nation what had been regarded as inevitable, namely that Britain and France had declared war on Nazi Germany after the unprovoked invasion of Poland two days earlier, Pip Gardner duly reported to the depot of the Westminster Dragoons in Elverton Street in London. Four days later he found himself at Blackdown barracks, near Fleet in Hampshire. In this rather sandy and barren area, better suited to army manoeuvres than the growing of agricultural crops, he was to start his training to become an officer in the Royal Tank Regiment.

When tanks first appeared on the military scene, more than half-way through the First World War, as a new addition to the existing infantry, artillery and cavalry forces, the new units thus established were known collectively as 'The Tank Corps'. The battle of Cambrai in 1917 marked their first significant use, which caused considerable havoc and trepidation amongst a surprised enemy on the Western Front. In 1923 the prefix 'Royal' was bestowed and from then until 1939 reference was made to 'The Royal Tank Corps'. In 1939, on the outbreak of war, The Royal Armoured Corps was created. Its two components were, on the one hand, the existing Tank battalions (which soon increased in number, as fast as the ordnance factories could provide more tanks off the production lines) and, on the other, the mechanised cavalry units which began to replace the former horsed-cavalry and Yeomanry regiments, bearing the same famous names. Both components were grouped together to form The Royal Armoured Corps.

During his three months of basic training in and around Blackdown barracks, Pip distinguished himself by landing a training tank axle-deep in a bog on Fleet Common. This occurred in front of one of his senior instructors, Major Jack Prichard, a regular soldier who was destined

Captain Philip John Gardner, V.C., M.C., in 1945.

A marriage that endured. Left: Pip and Renée Gardner at their wedding in Doncaster in 1939.

a mere two years later to prove instrumental in Pip's VC-winning exploit in the Libyan Desert. He was, however, by no means alone in perpetrating such an error of judgement – Fleet pond being more than once the receptacle for an out-of-control armoured vehicle whose driver was unable to negotiate the bend in the road and ended up in the water. However, it wasn't Pip's error of judgement, but someone else's clerical error that nearly caused him to fail the course. There were two cadets by the name of Gardner and the other one was regarded as pretty useless. Only a last-minute correction of initials saved Pip from a premature end to his prospects as a Royal Tank Regiment officer !

On 1st January 1940 Pip moved to the Royal Tank Regimental Depot at Bovington in Dorset for his driving and maintenance course, followed by a short move to Lulworth for gunnery. At both Bovington and Lulworth Pip was able to find accommodation locally for Renée, and it wasn't long before he obtained a sleeping-out pass – a highly-prized document indeed. Renée stayed in a beautiful old house right in the middle of Thomas Hardy country, called Woolbridge Manor, which featured in his *Tess of the D'Urbervilles* and was reputed to be haunted – though after some of the evening parties that took place there any lurking ghosts must surely have been exorcised !

In March came a return to Blackdown for the wireless and collective training course, at the end of which Pip was commissioned as a Subaltern in the Royal Tank Regiment and was ready for action, after the thorough training he had undergone. After some leave with Renée, he reported to the Depot at Bovington on 1st June 1940. But there was one snag – although he was now a trained tank-officer, there were no tanks available for him to man.

Suddenly on 10th May the so-called Phoney War in France had erupted overnight into the now famous Blitzkrieg, during which the German panzers thrust their way through Holland and Belgium into France. There they were opposed by a woefully under-equipped British Expeditionary Force, alongside a French army in which the emphasis had been placed much more on infantry than on tanks. The result was that the panzer spearheads were able to drive a wedge and achieve a breakthrough, which enabled them to push for the Channel ports of Boulogne, Calais and Dunkirk. The units of the British Royal Armoured Corps opposed the rampaging panzers to the best of their limited ability, but were outnumbered and out-gunned, and consequently out-fought and at times nearly annihilated. The result was that by mid-June, when the depleted remnants of the British Expeditionary Force had been obliged to evacuate from France, first via Dunkirk and later via other ports further west, such as Le Havre, Brest and Bordeaux, the numbers of tanks and armoured cars that were retrieved from the débâcle were extremely few. A mere skeleton force had been kept at home for the defence of Britain against the anticipated German invasion that appeared bound to follow. It seemed that only the Royal Navy ships and the Royal Air Force fighters stood in readiness to repel the enemy – unless kindly Fate were to play a part and divert Hitler's attention elsewhere, which miraculously occurred. As for the Army, which needed time to re-group and re-arm after the return from France, there were simply not the tanks into which to put newly-trained officers such as Pip Gardner.

Consequently, instead of moving against the enemy in a tank, for which he had been trained, Pip found himself on an anti-aircraft site near Wareham in Dorset, not far from Bovington. The date was 10th June 1940, the day on which Mussolini joined in the war on what he now reckoned must be the winning side, and thus started the war in the Western Desert and in North-East Africa. After ten days mainly on the alert at Wareham, Pip was sent to Lulworth gunnery school nearby.

At the beginning of July, with the tanks lost with the British Expeditionary Force not yet replaced, rather than hang around indefinitely, Pip and several other Royal Armoured Corps officers in his position answered a call emanating from Winston Churchill himself for volunteers for action 'of a hazardous nature' against the enemy. Pip was thus one of the first volunteers for these newly formed Commandos, as they were soon to be named. Number 4 Commando was being formed at Weymouth, in Dorset, under the command of Lieutenant-Colonel C. D. P. Legard, and Pip's offer to volunteer was readily accepted.

As was to be the custom in the Commandos, the personnel were accommodated in hotels and digs in and around Weymouth. Pip and some of the other officers stayed in the Oxford Hotel on the front, and Renée was able to join her husband there.

Pip assisted in the recruiting of the men for 4 Commando. This was done by visiting local units and interviewing volunteers. Steering well clear of misfits, but selecting those men who, like Pip, wanted to join a unit where they would have a good prospect of striking at the enemy, rather than wait passively on coastal or inland defence, they sought men who could cover five miles across country in quick time in gym shoes and could also swim – since from the start the role of the Commandos was expected to be amphibious.

With the selection made, the immediate task was to train the officers and men. With only a limited array of weapons available at first, the main emphasis was on physical fitness and endurance. The day would start, in the lovely summer of 1940, with a dive off the end of Weymouth pier each morning at six-thirty. On the first day, it was immediately discovered that not all the volunteers who had claimed to be swimmers could actually swim. Such was their enthusiasm to be accepted for the Commandos that several of them who were, in fact, unable to do so, had nevertheless volunteered. Even this didn't deter three or four of them from jumping into the sea when given the command! After some unscheduled life-saving had been performed, the problem arose of what to do with these brave but misguided volunteers. Some were given a crash course in swimming, in cases where there seemed some prospect of success. The rest had to make a reluctant return to their units.

One night, as Pip and some fellow-officers were leaving a party in the Gloucester Hotel, one of his troop came running to him with the news that a German invasion was expected that night. This was announced by the pre-arranged code-word 'Cromwell'. Pip, who had had a convivial evening after a hard day's training, failed at first to grasp the full significance of the code-word, and said : 'Who the hell is Cromwell?' The runner replied : 'You know, Sir – *Cromwell!*'

Suddenly Pip woke up with a jerk to its full import, and it meant that they all had to report to various places along the beach to defend the area. Pip's first action was to present Renée with a hand-grenade for protection and told her to return to the Oxford Hotel, while he went off to join his men in manning the beaches, ready to repel the foe with rifles and pistols. Fortunately for them all the invasion never took place and at dawn they solemnly marched back to their hotels for breakfast. Renée and another officer's wife had been up all night, looking out of the window with considerable anxiety and they were overjoyed when they perceived through the early-morning mist that the echoing footsteps in the road were those of their valiant husbands – and not those of jack-booted German invaders. Renée was only too glad to return the hand-grenade!

July gave way to August and, in glorious summer sunshine, the Battle of Britain began to take place in the skies above them, mainly in the south-east of England. At the beginning of September Pip was sent on a four-week course at the Irregular Warfare School on the west coast of Scotland, at Lochailort. There Captain The Lord Lovat was in charge of the fieldcraft course, which included covering long distances over the mountains at high speed with full packs. Pip found himself becoming fitter than he had ever been – with a healthy appetite to match. His diet consisted mainly of fresh venison (tasty but tough), which appeared stewed for lunch and roasted for dinner.

He also found that, whereas at Bovington Depot the saying was: 'If it moves, salute it – if it doesn't move, paint it', at Lochailort, where a very effective explosives course was run, the saying became: '. . . if it doesn't move, blow it up'. Pip certainly did his share of demolition of railway-lines and bridges for practice.

He also found time to indulge in some deer-stalking and fishing (by a variety of methods, including hand-grenades), with some lighter pursuits at week-ends. The latter included an outing on foot in company with two other subalterns on the course, for a Sunday meal at a pub some ten miles away from Lochailort. They set off in a light drizzle which soon turned to the heavy rain which is so familiar in those parts. When they reached their destination they were absolutely soaked to the skin. But the kindly Scottish woman who ran the pub welcomed them into a room with a large log fire burning and, brushing modesty aside, she made them take off all their clothes so that she could hang them up to dry. She produced some blankets for them to drape round their wet bodies, while their soaked clothes steamed away in front of the fire. A friendly cat ventured into the room and soon tried to snuggle under Pip's blanket, until the Scots woman chased it away, saying: 'Awa' wi' ye! You're no' safe in here.' An excellent hot meal was soon produced and, after that, Pip and his companions slept while their clothes dried out. They were woken up with the arrival of a huge Scottish tea, with baps and scones and oatmeal cakes. They were able to face their return journey to Lochailort well rested, fortified with nourishing food and grateful for their sample of real Highland hospitality.

Pip returned to Dorset after a month's training and toughening-up, only to find that on 1st October he and the rest of 4 Commando were being sent up to Inverary, in Scotland again. Soon after their arrival they were put on board a specially equipped commando ship, HMS *Glengyle*. They naturally assumed that they would soon be sailing to carry out a raid, probably on the German-occupied French coast. From the *Glengyle* they went ashore on several night operations. On one occasion four men, missing the gangway in the pitch darkness, stepped into the oily water between the ship and the shore – a mistake that they took good care to avoid in the future!

After two weeks of being quartered aboard the *Glengyle*, they were transferred ashore and were billeted in hotels and digs in Ayr and Troon.

At the beginning of December, instructions were received that trained Royal Armoured Corps personnel would be recalled to their units. Now that replacement tanks were starting to arrive in significant numbers, officers and crews were needed to man them. Pip thus returned and reported to the 52nd Battalion of the Royal Tank Regiment at Bovington. His commando days were over and he was about to revert to what he had been trained for – tank warfare. Little did he realise what excitements and achievements lay ahead of him.

CHAPTER THREE

Foot-drill in the Sand

After the threat of invasion had abated in England during the autumn of 1940, thanks to the heroic resistance by the fighter squadrons of the RAF against Goering's powerful Luftwaffe, the way was clear for an outstandingly bold and far-sighted decision, made by the Chiefs of Staff – with ample prompting from Churchill. The decision was that, limited though they were in number, tanks and armoured cars of the Royal Armoured Corps should be sent where they were now most needed, and where they could best mount an immediate attack on Axis forces – in the Middle East.

With Italy now at war against Britain and her staunch Commonwealth allies, the Middle East had automatically become an active war-zone. After a cautious start, the Italian army under Marshal Graziani had advanced eastwards from the Libyan–Egyptian frontier to a fortress at Maktila, east of Sidi Barrani and only seventy miles from Mersa Matruh. General Wavell, as Commander-in-Chief of Middle East Forces, had perforce to bide his time with his Western Desert troops of the Army of the Nile, the title of 'Eighth Army' only being adopted later – not until 26th September 1941, in fact, by which time General Auchinleck had assumed command.

At the same time the Italians were intent on expanding their hold on their new colonial acquisitions in Abyssinia, thus posing a threat, from Italian Somaliland and Eritrea as well, to the British colonies of Kenya, British Somaliland and the Sudan, besides endangering the Suez Canal. To meet these widespread threats, General Wavell had deployed his British and Commonwealth troops in both directions – westwards towards the frontier between Egypt and Libya, and southwards towards Abyssinia and Eritrea. Meanwhile timely help was arriving via Kenya from South African and Rhodesian forces attacking the Italians in Abyssinia in a northerly pincer movement.

Only when the bold decision was made in the autumn of 1940 to send tanks to the Middle East, despite the urgent need of them for home defence against possible invasion, could Wavell move to the offensive in the Western Desert. These reinforcements were obliged to travel round the Cape in order to reach the Middle East, under strong Royal Navy escort. Previously it had been possible to dash through the Mediterranean to Egypt, but by late 1940 this was no longer possible, owing to the presence of the Italian navy and German submarines.

Thus it was that when Pip Gardner returned in December 1940 to the Royal Tanks depot at Bovington, he and several of his fellow-officers were detailed to go on draft to the Middle East, where they would be used as replacements in the tank regiments that had preceded them in that direction. There was just time for embarkation leave and Christmas and, in his case, birthday celebrations with Renée. Following family farewells, he boarded the *Highland Princess* at Avonmouth, before moving up to Gourock on the Clyde. From Gourock the troopship sailed on 3rd January 1941 across to Belfast, to pick up more troops, whence the convoy, escorted by destroyers with the flagship HMS *Barham*, sailed well out into the Atlantic. Having thus managed to avoid the German long-range bombers and the lurking U-boats, the *Highland Princess* put into Freetown, in Sierra Leone on the west coast of Africa. Luckily for Pip and his fellow-passengers she was considered the best ship in the convoy. She normally plied the South American run, and was very well provisioned with food and alcohol.

They lay at anchor off Freetown in steaming heat for five days, with almost non-stop entertainment from local ebony-skinned youngsters diving for coins thrown from the ship by the troops. The divers retrieved the coins with seldom a miss. Some of the ships lowered their boats into the water, so that the crews and the troops could stage rowing races to pass the time and amuse the onlookers. But when it was time for the convoy to re-form and continue the journey southwards, there were no regrets from the troops on board. They were anxious to get to their destination in time to join in Wavell's successful advance into Libya, encouraging reports of which had been received by radio. They were keen not to arrive too late – little knowing that a further two years of desert fighting still lay ahead !

The convoy continued its way down the African coast and round the Cape. Some of the ships docked in Cape Town, leaving the others, including the *Highland Princess*, to sail on into the Indian Ocean and up the coast to Durban. Here a magnificent welcome greeted them, such as was to be accorded to numerous Allied convoys that followed in their wake. Fleets of private cars were awaiting them as they stepped ashore, with their owners anxious to drive them around and take them into their homes. It was a welcome that most of them never forgot and was the last taste of home life that many of them were to enjoy for several years – or, sadly in some cases, ever again.

Also awaiting Pip was a disappointment. He was transferred to HMS *Orbita*. If the *Highland Princess* had been considered the best passenger ship in the convoy, he was about to discover which was the worst – the *Orbita*! Apart from being generally filthy, with little to offer in the way of food or drink, she was laden with rotting potatoes. Pip and his fellow-passengers had to console themselves with the thought that two-thirds of their voyage had already been completed. Furthermore the news to hand concerning the fighting in Libya was still buoyant, with Benghazi in British and Commonwealth hands. What might have been taken as ominous news, namely that a German force under General Rommel had landed in Tripoli, was ignored for the simple reason that scarcely anyone had heard of him – yet! Rommel had, of course, led his tanks with great dash and skill as the spearhead of the German forces in the Blitzkrieg through France in May 1940, but that was a fact that only became known to most people after he had continued his havoc across the Western Desert.

Pip's journey now took him up the Mozambique Channel, past the large island of Madagascar and past Dar-es-Salaam and Mombasa without calling. Finally they docked at Port Tewfik, near Suez, on 10th March 1941.

After receiving something of a shock on seeing miles and miles of sand, with hardly any vegetation (though there were plenty of water-melons for sale, which boded ill for the unwary consumer!) they were transported by train to Cairo and quartered briefly in Kasr-el-Nil barracks, where they had their first introduction to bed-bugs waiting to make a meal of them. The bugs seemed to prefer tasty newcomers! Two days later they moved to the Base Camp at Abbasia, saying 'Good-bye' to dozens of bed-bugs and 'Hullo' to millions of flies.

Pip Gardner summed up the fly situation in a letter written soon after his arrival to the staff of his family firm. He wrote to them :

'Flies are the chief pest in this part of the globe. There are simply millions of them and they continually settle on your face and even on your mouth, although you are always brushing them off. They have a nasty habit of infecting the food and, although you take all the precautions possible, you find yourself upset pretty badly from time to time in spite of everything you do.'

Nearly all the troops who arrived in Egypt at that time had to undergo an attack of 'Gyppo Tummy' at least once, and Pip was no exception. The blame was put squarely on the flies.

At first there was little for the new arrivals to do and they were allowed to see the sights of Cairo and its surroundings – notably the Pyramids and the Sphinx, as well as numerous night clubs only too willing to relieve the troops of their boredom and their money. It was difficult for the newcomers to grasp the fact that a war was actually taking place only a few hundred miles of mainly flat desert away. Just when the fleshpots were proving a trifle expensive for them all, they were taken on a desert navigation course – an outing which was to prove both interesting and beneficial. Pip Gardner described it vividly in a letter written to his father, dated 28th March 1941. He wrote :

'Well, I expect that this will be the last letter from here. As you will see by the address, I have now been posted to a tank battalion and expect to go and join them wherever they may be within the next few days.

'I don't know if I told you in my last letter, but I have just been on a navigation course and, apart from the actual knowledge obtained, we also had an opportunity of seeing sights in our trucks on an all-day trip out into the desert. On the way, we passed quite close to the Pyramids and we worked our way about fifty miles straight into the desert. During all that time we didn't see a living soul. For miles around us there was nothing but flat soft sand, into which your wheels sank if you didn't keep going. In finding your way about a spot like that, you have to rely entirely on your compass and the mileage shown on your speedometer to give you your position. Without these you would get absolutely lost, as there is not a single landmark to guide you for perhaps fifty to a hundred miles.

'Several times we came across the skeletons of camels, whose bones were dried and bleached white in the sun. We also saw many fossilised trees lying on the sand. They must have been there for thousands of

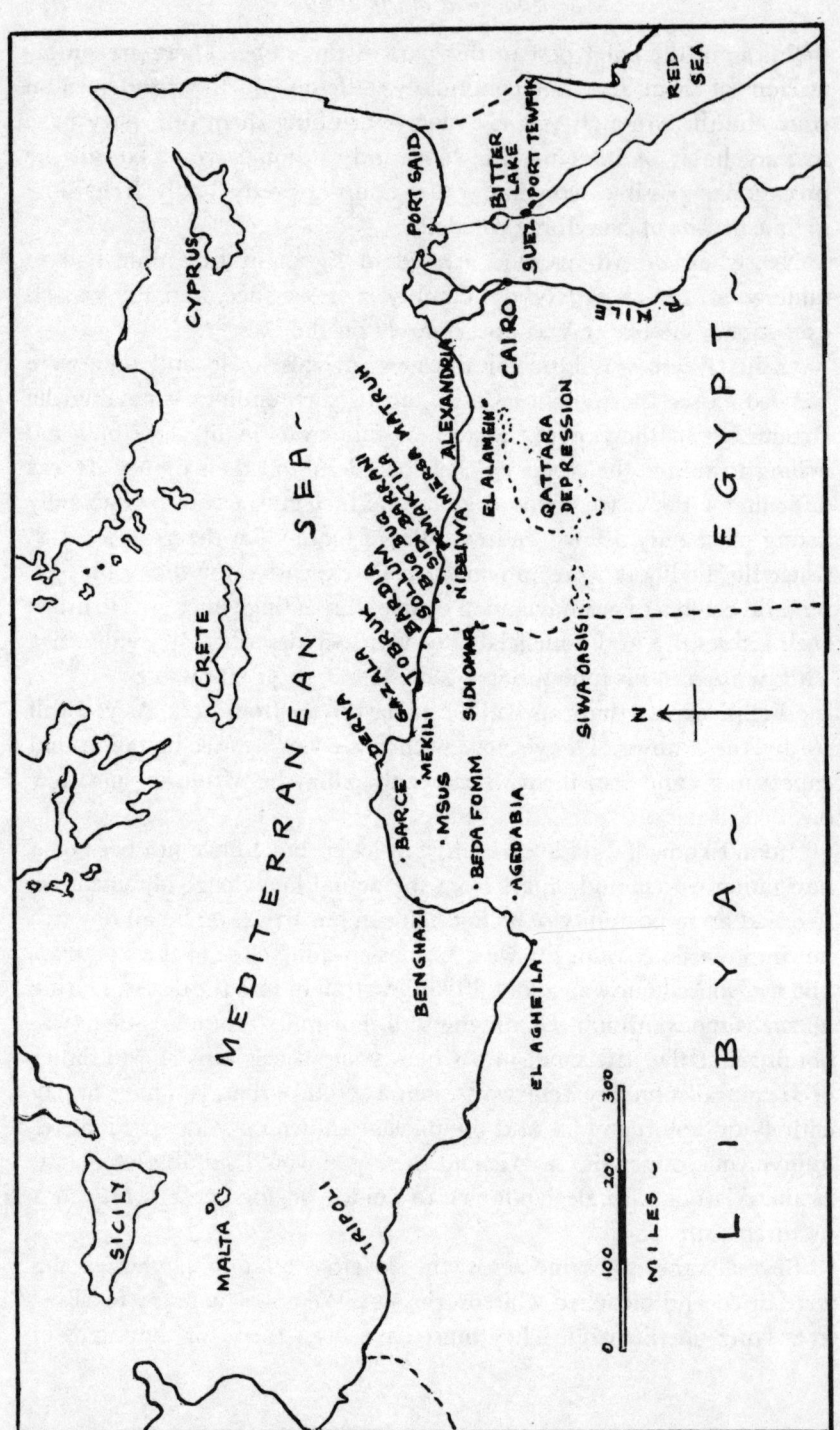

The Desert Scene, 1940/43

years, as they were quite big ones and no such trees ever grow in that part of the desert now. All over the sand you find sea shells, showing how once the sea must have covered the place, although it is difficult to imagine how it got so far inland. We also came across a salt lake, which proves that it must have been there at one time.

'About four in the afternoon we suddenly came across a monastery, set away out in the desert, miles from anywhere. It was surrounded by a white wall about thirty or forty feet high and, as our six lorries approached, there was no sign of life about at all, although we must have made a lot of noise and clouds of dust. After discovering the door, we also found there was a large bell which was rung by pulling a long rope which was hanging from the top of the wall. In reply to our ringing an aged monk opened the door to us and our instructor, who speaks Egyptian, asked him if we we might be allowed to go in and have a look round. Sure enough we were very welcome there and were at once ushered inside and shown all over the place. These monks are the true-blood Egyptians, unlike most of the people you see about the town, and they are also of Christian faith, which surprised me.

'The monastery is about fifteen hundred years old and some of the monks, of which there were about thirty, have been there for thirty or forty years without going outside. The interior is divided up into a number of little churches, all not much bigger than your office, and each one is dedicated to a different saint, such as St Patrick and St Peter, etcetera. In one of these I noticed some large eggs hanging over the altar and one of the monks, who incidentally spoke very good English, told me that these were ostriches' eggs. He said that when the ostrich lays an egg it buries it in the sand and watches it all the time until it hatches, but if it looks away, or goes away from the egg, she will probably lose it and it will not hatch. The monk likened this to ourselves who, like the ostrich, if we don't keep looking to God all the time, will lose sight of Him and so go to Hell, as he said; but if we keep looking to Him, everything will turn out all right. I thought that this might be a good little story to tell your kiddies on Sunday. Of course you can make much more of it than I can tell you.

'In another place was the grave of some monks who were murdered when the Arabs attacked the monastery about seven hundred years ago and killed everyone in it. There was also a secret hiding-place for their treasure (if any) and an old biblical-type wine-press; but that is not used in these days, as they don't get any grapes. We also saw the bakery and the place where they eat. They feed practically entirely on a very hard bread and some meat. But in Lent they eat nothing but the bread, and water, although, as my friend told me, "Each pleases himself whether he fasts or not, and no one will think the worse of him if he doesn't."

'Each monk has his own little room, but they don't have any beds, although he told me that they had had many offers to buy them some. They absolutely begrudge themselves any comforts whatsoever, and are really most devout old gents. One thing that amazed me most was the little garden that they have got to grow around the well in the middle of the monastery, and here were a number of small birds all chirping away. In the middle of all that waste of dried-up sand to find a few little birds was a real sight to see. A most ingenious lock was on the front door, and this was all made of wood. The lock itself was about eight inches square and slid to and fro through a box in which were a number of plungers which dropped into holes in the lock, and could only be held up by using a massive key which one of the monks looks after. You can probably decipher how it works from the sketch. Rather after a "Yale", isn't it? And invented hundreds of years before, too.

'After showing us all round they gave us some small cups of Turkish coffee which, although very thick and full of grounds, didn't go down too badly, if washed down with a glass full of water, which is the correct way to drink it.

'After many farewells and many blessings from the monks we all shook hands and went on our way back home. Oh, just one thing I forgot was that they had a massive bell inside, which they said was the largest bell in Egypt, and it certainly sounded like it when they started ringing it in the middle of that walled-in place.

'This really was a most interesting day, and a sight that you would never see in the ordinary way. A tourist to this part of the world would never get a chance to see it, as without a vehicle like we had you could never get across the soft sand.

'Last Sunday afternoon Jimmy, a friend of mine, and I went out to see the Pyramids, as we both had "Gyppo Tummy" when all the other chaps went, and we were not able to make it. Anyhow, on reaching there we chartered a couple of camels and a guide and set off round the Pyramids. They certainly are a wonderful sight – so well preserved, after all these thousands of years. It is incredible to think that these terrific Pyramids were built by human hands without all the knowledge and machinery that we have to-day. The largest Pyramid is about four hundred and fifty feet high and some of the slabs are anything up to fifteen feet long and five feet square. It is very difficult to imagine how they ever got them up there. The guide told us that it took thirty-three years to build and that fifty thousand slaves were employed every month. We also went inside and climbed up small stairways, in which you had to bend yourself double, until we came to the King's Chamber, which was where the mummies were put. We also saw the Sphinx, as you will see by the enclosed photo. It certainly is some size. There are also the remains of various temples, all made of black granite and alabaster, which, when you strike a match, sparkles like diamonds. It was altogether a great trip and one I wouldn't have missed for worlds.'

In the same letter Pip Gardner continued :

'Last Monday we went out for a two-day trip on our navigation course and took all our provisions with us, including a cook to do the work. We started early and travelled all day over the most terrible rough ground, over hills and valleys, until eventually we reached the sea. Here we made camp for the night. We were terribly dusty and sunburnt after driving hard through the heat of the desert, and so we all had a swim in the lovely cool clear water, before getting down to steak and chips, which our very able cook produced. About eight thirty we all turned in for the night, it being too dark to do anything, and before very long we were all asleep, with only the starry blue sky as our shelter.

'The next morning we were up early and all had a hot bath in a sulphur spring, which was almost too hot to get into. This was followed by a fine egg-and-bacon breakfast. Unfortunately we had a spot of trouble with one of the vehicles and so had to make our quickest way home, which was across a desert track and so on to the main road. I had a grand time driving along absolutely flat out, with clouds of sand rising everywhere, and skidding all over the place. When we got on to the road I had forty miles of dead straight and practically flat road to drive on. As you can imagine, I fairly made the old tub shift. We drive on the right of the road here, and the other chaps in my bus were afraid that I was going to forget myself and pull over to the wrong side of the road every time something came the opposite way. But as you can imagine, this didn't occur.

'So you can see that altogether I have had a pretty good time so far, but I think that it won't be long before I have to do some real work for a change.'

*

At the beginning of April, Pip was posted to a Royal Tank regiment with two of his friends, 'Bon' Cole and 'Percy' Gers, both subalterns. 'Percy' Gers from the Westminster Dragoons was really Ronald Gers, but was known as 'Percy' owing to a close resemblance to Percy Fender, the well-known Surrey and England cricketer. (One can safely assume that the resemblance was far closer than that of the actor who was selected to portray Percy Fender in a laughably mis-cast TV play on the famous Body-line controversy.) The origin of 'Bon' Cole's unusual name remained obscure – but if, as some people thought, it was short for 'Bonhomie', then it could hardly have been more appropriate. As a fellow-officer he, like Percy Gers, was exceedingly good company. His initials being R.M., he was also known as 'Ready Money' Cole, as he was always ready to lend money to his friends.

Together they were posted to a regular Tank unit, the 4th Royal Tanks, at El Tahag on the sweet-water canal, near Ismailia. The 4th Royal Tanks had only arrived in the Middle East shortly before Pip, having sailed from home in December 1940. Their tanks had been sent ahead in a slower convoy which left from Newport in Monmouthshire, after they had been loaded under the supervision of A. G. ('Bertie') Roberts, the Technical Adjutant, who was a Second-Lieutenant (Acting-Captain) at that time. Despite a brush, which could well have proved disastrous, with the 10,000-ton German cruiser the *Admiral Hipper*, off the Azores on Christmas Day, the convoy carrying the troops was able to reach the Middle East ahead of the tanks, and Bertie Roberts was able to supervise the unloading at Port Tewfik. The Battle of the Azores, as the encounter became known, was quite an affray, resulting in serious damage to the escorting British cruiser HMS *Berwick*, and the issue of the order for the convoy to scatter. Fortunately the presence of three other escort vessels induced the *Admiral Hipper* to withdraw, thus enabling the *City of London*, which was transporting

the personnel of the 4th Royal Tanks, to reach refuge off Gibraltar –
despite the uncomfortable discovery that she was the slowest vessel in
the convoy. Off Gibraltar the convoy had to be re-constituted in order
to continue the journey round the Cape, which was completed without
further encounters with the enemy.

Consequently, when Pip joined them, the 4th Royal Tanks had yet
to experience battle in the desert, but under an outstandingly fine commanding officer in Lieutenant-Colonel Walter O'Carroll everybody was
ready for action. They hadn't long to wait.

The arrival of a new intake of officers failed to arouse any great
enthusiasm. In fact Second-Lieutenants Pip Gardner, Percy Gers and
Bon Cole were by no means amused when, soon after their arrival, they
were ordered to report together to RSM Jock Armit, who was a noted
footballer and boxer in the regiment, for some smartening-up (and
doubtless deflating!) foot-drill which was conducted, for want of a
better surface, in the desert sand – and in the desert heat, with myriads
of desert flies in attendance.

After this early taste of regimental life, Percy Gers and Bon Cole disappeared from Pip's orbit for a while, as all three of them were posted
to different squadrons. Percy's squadron was sent to Eritrea, and Bon's
was moved to Mersa Matruh. Pip, meanwhile, joined 'A' Squadron,
under Major Ian Banks and was moved to a place, hitherto unknown
to him, called Buq Buq, between Sidi Barrani and Sollum.

For the first time he was given command of a troop of Matilda tanks.
He had never even been inside a modern tank – all his training in
England having been done in First World War vehicles.

He was soon to get to know the inside of a Matilda extremely
intimately!

CHAPTER FOUR

Wavell's Push

Before joining Second-Lieutenant Pip Gardner in his own particular desert, it is necessary to review the events that had gone before and had produced the situation to which he was about to lend his presence.

'Wavell's push', as the campaign soon became known, was essentially a combined effort planned and executed by all three fighting services in the Middle East, under the direction of General Sir Archibald Wavell, Admiral Sir Andrew Cunningham and Air Marshal Sir Arthur Longmore.

The RAF prepared the way in early December 1940 by strafing the Italian aerodromes of Libya from Derna eastwards and causing considerable havoc in the rear echelons of supply. On 8th December, ships of the Royal Navy moved westwards along the Mediterranean coast and heavily bombarded the enemy's easternmost positions at Maktila and Sidi Barrani. Immediately it was the turn for Wavell's Army of the Nile, a title favoured by Churchill to denote the British and Empire forces in Egypt, to move against the positions held by Marshal Graziani's Italian army, which had been occupied in the latter's initial advance in September 1940.

Since that time, Graziani had been at pains to consolidate his gains and to strengthen his lines of communication behind him by extending his Libyan road – a task at which the Italians excelled. He also set about improving his water sources and establishing large depots of supplies, preparatory to making his next advance into Egypt to Mersa Matruh. Fortunately for Wavell, Graziani's preparations proved somewhat prolonged, while he appealed to Mussolini for reinforcements and better equipment. Mussolini was more concerned with his commitments in Greece, where things were not going well for his army, and he merely pressed for immediate action from his army in Libya.

Graziani was about to comply, if somewhat hesitatingly, with Musso-

Captured Afrika Korps soldiers on the coastal plain near Sollum Bay, with the Halfaya escarpment beyond—the scene of Pip Gardner's first battle honour, the Military Cross, in June 1941.

A near miss from a Stuka bomb in the desert.

November 1941. Brigadier A. C. Willison, Commander of 32 Army Tank Brigade, explaining his break-out plans at Fortress HQ in Tobruk during the siege. Pip Gardner is front right, holding a map.

December 1941. A change of name (only temporary) for Rommel's Tobruk by-pass.

lini's demands for action, when he was pre-empted by the suddenness of Wavell's thrust. This pre-empting of impending attacks from the enemy by means of a sudden offensive of one's own was to become a regular feature of the war in the desert – the tactic being adopted by both sides, under different generals, as will be seen later.

The delivery of this sudden blow was entrusted by Wavell to General Sir H. Maitland Wilson, who was commanding the Army of the Nile, although the campaign was usually referred to as 'Wavell's push'. The actual fighting in the desert was led by General Richard O'Connor, under the direction of General 'Jumbo' Wilson, with the overall strategy conducted from Cairo by Wavell, as Commander-in-Chief for the whole of the Middle East. This large area included his forces in action in North-east Africa, where they were engaged in liberating Abyssinia and reinstating King Haile Selassie, whom the Italians had ousted in 1936 in the quest for a larger empire. Wavell's campaign was to prove the source of a much-needed boost for morale in the winter of 1940/41 in beleaguered Britain, as maps appeared, altered almost daily, in the newspapers showing the sensational gains made by the advancing British and Commonwealth troops spearheaded by General O'Connor. It certainly warmed the cockles of many a heart at a time when Britain stood alone against the might of the hitherto all-conquering Axis armies. It was their first taste of success on land.

Wavell had at his disposal a truly Empire and Commonwealth force, consisting of troops from Britain, India, Australia, New Zealand, Rhodesia and South Africa, as well as some small but gallant units of Free French and Polish comrades-in-arms. Graziani had deployed his forces into several large well-defended but separate camps – a policy which, though rendering them safe against enemy raiding-parties, left them unable to give each other the necessary mutual support against a concerted attack with encircling pincer movements. These fortresses were thus liable to defeat and capture one after the other, which was precisely the fate that befell them.

The first to fall, on 9th December 1940, was the fortress of Nibeiwa, situated some fifteen miles due south of Sidi Barrani, followed a few hours later by the capture of the easternmost stronghold of Maktila on the coast. For the capture of Nibeiwa the main honours went to the 4th Indian Division, and for the taking of Maktila on the same day, by British and Australian land forces, much credit also went to the

15-inch guns of the Royal Navy, which so scared the Libyan levies that they deserted their Italian officers and fled helter-skelter along the road to Sidi Barrani.

With the camps of Tummar East and Tummar West, to the immediate north of Nibeiwa, also captured, the way was clear on 10th December for a concerted assault on Sidi Barrani. Here the defence included Blackshirt regiments under General Gallina and these Italians stuck to their guns and fought well against a British attack converging from all four points of the compass, including a bombardment from the north by the Royal Navy again. RAF co-operation, too, helped tip the scales in favour of the attackers. General Gallina was captured, along with 15,000 Italian troops, to add to the large numbers already taken in the capture of the fortresses all round Sidi Barrani, the fall of which was announced by British General Headquarters in Cairo in a special communiqué of 11th December.

With this big opening success completed, the way was now clear for a continued push along the coast beyond Buq Buq to Sollum, which lies below a steep escarpment leading via Halfaya Pass up to Bardia. The Italian retreat then developed into a rout. The total number of prisoners now rose to 30,000, as the Italian army was thrown out of Egypt and back into Libya. In their hurry to get away, they left an enormous quantity and variety of stores and equipment to fall into British hands, ranging from guns and ammunition to macaroni and Chianti – with even what seemed to be a hastily evacuated mobile brothel, judging by the lingering smell of perfume! The sheer number of prisoners taken created a problem which was only alleviated by the general desire of the captured to say a farewell to arms, as they were marched towards the coast to be evacuated by ship to Alexandria.

Sollum was stormed by British armoured units and taken on 16th December after the frontier forts of Sidi Omar and Capuzzo had been entered by the British. Thanks to a preliminary softening-up by bombardment from the Navy and aerial attack by the RAF, Bardia fell on 5th January 1941, the final assault being made by Australian infantry under General Mackay, a veteran of Gallipoli, supported by British tanks. An enormous quantity of heavy, light and anti-aircraft guns was captured, along with another large haul of prisoners. Of Graziani's original estimated force of 250,000 men, at least a third were now out of the struggle, the majority of them having been captured.

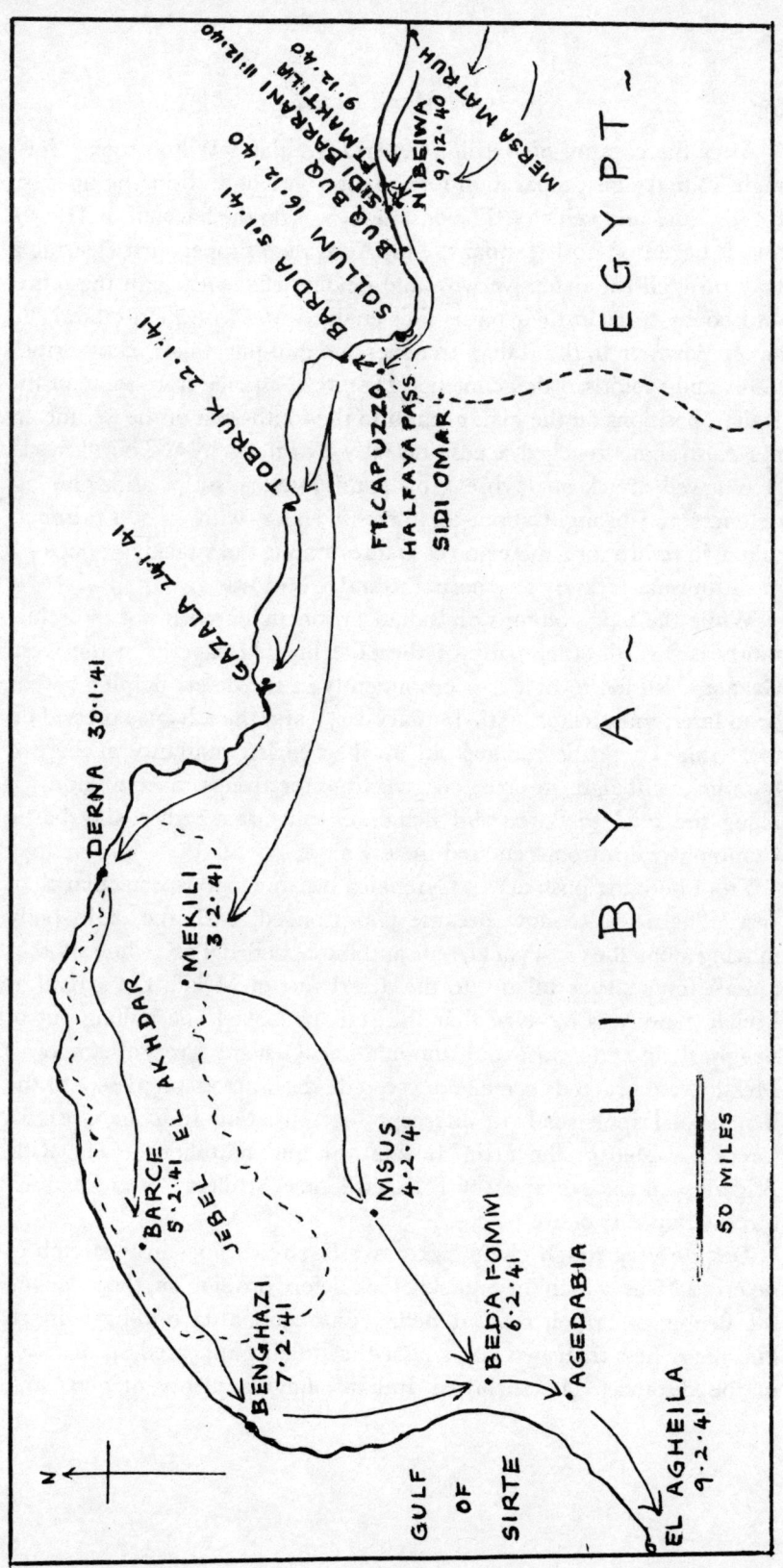

MERSA MATRUH

NIBEIWA 9·12·40

BUG BUG
SIDI BARRANI 9·12·40
FT. MAKTILA 11·12·40

SOLLUM 16·12·40

BARDIA 5·1·41

FT. CAPUZZO
HALFAYA PASS
SIDI OMAR

TOBRUK 22·1·41

GAZALA 24·1·41

DERNA 30·1·41

BARCE 5·2·41

EL AKHDAR

JEBEL

MEKILI 3·2·41

BENGHAZI 7·2·41

MSUS 4·2·41

BEDA FOMM 6·2·41

AGEDABIA

GULF

OF

SIRTE

EL AGHEILA 9·2·41

LIBYA ~

EGYPT ~

N

50 MILES

Wavell's Push, 1940/I

After the capture of Bardia, General Maitland Wilson took a fortnight to make his preparation for the next onslaught, bringing up fresh
troops, guns and vehicles. The onslaught was on the harbour of Tobruk
and it began on 20th January, with Australian sappers first clearing a
way through the defensive wire and dealing efficiently with the mines
and booby-traps in their path. This enabled the Australian infantry to
sweep down on to the Italian trenches and gun-pits, followed by British
tanks and motorised detachments. Despite resistance from some of the
Italian positions on the high ground to the south-west of the perimeter,
the Australians reached a position only two miles from Tobruk itself.
A renewed attack at daybreak on 22nd January swept aside the last
defences and brought about another surrender, with 15,000 prisoners
taken, in return for a mere 500 casualties among the attacking troops – a
most unusual ratio by any normal standards of war.

While the long columns of Italian prisoners marched not too reluctantly eastwards, the Army of the Nile hurried eagerly to the west.
Gazala, destined to figure so prominently in the desert fighting a year
or so later, soon fell on 24th January 1941 and the advance pressed on
to Derna. There the Italians put up their stiffest resistance of the two
months' campaign, in order to give time for troops to be withdrawn
along the road to Barce and Benghazi; but after a three-day battle
Commonwealth troops entered the town.

From here the push across Cyrenaica became more spectacular than
ever. The advance now became two-pronged, with the main body
moving along the coast via Cyrene and Barce to Benghazi, while another
mobile force struck inland, to the desert fort of Mekili. On arrival at
Mekili, news was received that the Italians looked like pulling out of
Benghazi, in order to avoid annihilation. General Creagh's forces at
Mekili were ordered to make a 150-mile dash across the desert to the
Benghazi–Tripoli road, to intercept the retreating Italians. Creagh's
forces consisted of the 11th Hussars, the 2nd Battalion of The Rifle
Brigade and the 4th and 106th Royal Horse Artillery – a mechanised
force with plenty of fire-power.

Despite very rough going across a rock-strewn and dusty stretch of
desert to Msus, which they quickly took before pressing on, they reached
the Benghazi–Tripoli road at Beda Fomm just after mid-day on 5th
February. Less than two hours later the Italians appeared on the road
in the distance. The surprised Italians, having plenty of guns and

armoured vehicles with them, in a column stretching about ten miles back along the road from Benghazi, had no option but to stand their ground and attempt to fight their way through to Agedabia. Creagh's guns held them up. Meanwhile the vanguard of the main British force, hurrying on past Benghazi, attacked them in the rear and on the landward flank. The battle lasted until the second afternoon, as the trapped Italians desperately tried to force their way south. But a commendably firm stand by the 2nd Rifle Brigade held fast, and 20,000 more prisoners and an enormous tally of guns, tanks, and lorries were duly 'bagged'.

Meanwhile, in the rear the Australians had reached Benghazi on 6th February and entered it the next morning, to the cheers of the local population – cheers which were to be repeated on four more occasions, twice to welcome each side, when the town changed hands as the tide of desert warfare ebbed and flowed over the next two years.

By 9th February, General O'Connor's advanced mechanised units had occupied El Agheila, and this was to prove the high-water mark of General Maitland Wilson's advance and virtually the whole of Cyrenaica was now in British hands.

This was the healthy situation when Pip Gardner was on the high seas – and doubtless itching to land and be able to jump on the bandwagon of success. Alas, by the time he had landed in Egypt, the situation was about to undergo a very considerable change. For six weeks after the vanguard had halted at El Agheila, there was no change in the position in Libya – on the surface, at least. But behind the scenes an ominous event, not fully appreciated at first, had occurred. In late February, reports were received of the recent landing in Tripoli of an 'Afrika Korps' under the command of General Erwin Rommel. On 24th March an Italian–German force had re-occupied El Agheila. To the consternation of those who had cheered the spectacular successes of Wavell's push, whether from the cold comfort of an armchair in wintry Britain, or from the comparative warmth of an office desk in Cairo, not only was El Agheila evacuated by the troops of the Army of the Nile, but one by one in alarmingly quick succession the towns and fortresses so dashingly captured by Wavell's forces only a few weeks before were once again in enemy hands.

Rommel, it was thought, had been sent to Libya primarily to bolster up the crumbling Italian resistance, and was technically under the orders of Marshal Graziani, with instructions to prevent further loss of territory, rather than carry out any aggressive action at this stage. Rommel, who had received this promotion in recognition of his dash displayed while commanding the 7th Panzer Division in France, was in no mood to hang around and miss the opportunity for one of his lightning thrusts for which he was already famous at home, and was about to repeat with startling success in the Western Desert.

After action at Msus, Barce and Mekili, he recaptured Benghazi on 3rd April 1941 and led his spearheads on further across Cyrenaica. Derna fell on 7th April, Bardia by the 12th, Fort Capuzzo on the 14th. Before the end of April his panzers had taken Sollum, and Wavell's army was back on the Libyan–Egyptian border. But there remained one serious thorn in Rommel's flesh – Tobruk. As his leading panzers dashed past in their hurry to reach Bardia, Halfaya Pass and Sollum, Rommel by-passed Tobruk, intending to turn his attention to it later. The garrison of Tobruk, consisting mainly of Australian troops under General L. J. Morshead, made good use of the large stocks of captured weapons and ammunition which the Italians had recently left behind. They defended a thirty-mile perimeter, protected by mine-fields, with every intention of denying this important harbour to Rommel. This area, as will be seen, was to prove a hectic battlefield for the 4th Royal Tanks, where many of their officers and men were destined to distinguish themselves in the fighting – not least Pip Gardner.

There were those who, far removed from the scene, were surprised that Wavell had stopped at El Agheila instead of pressing forward along the coast to Tripoli, thus ridding the whole of North Africa of Italian forces, before they could be reinforced and stiffened by the arrival of the Afrika Korps. The plain fact was that the headlong pursuit of the enemy across Cyrenaica had brought its own inevitable problems of supply over a vast distance, and of replacement of worn-out tanks and men. Furthermore, troops commanded by General Maitland Wilson also had to be supplied by Wavell from his widely stretched Middle East resources in order to go to the aid of Greece and Crete.

Less plausible at the time, though possibly more acceptable in retrospect, was the assertion of a British official spokesman in Cairo advancing the theory that in desert warfare it was not the policy to capture towns or vast expanses of 'useless desert', but to prevent armies from being scooped up, as Marshal Graziani's had been by General Wavell. The object, rather, was to fight on ground of one's own

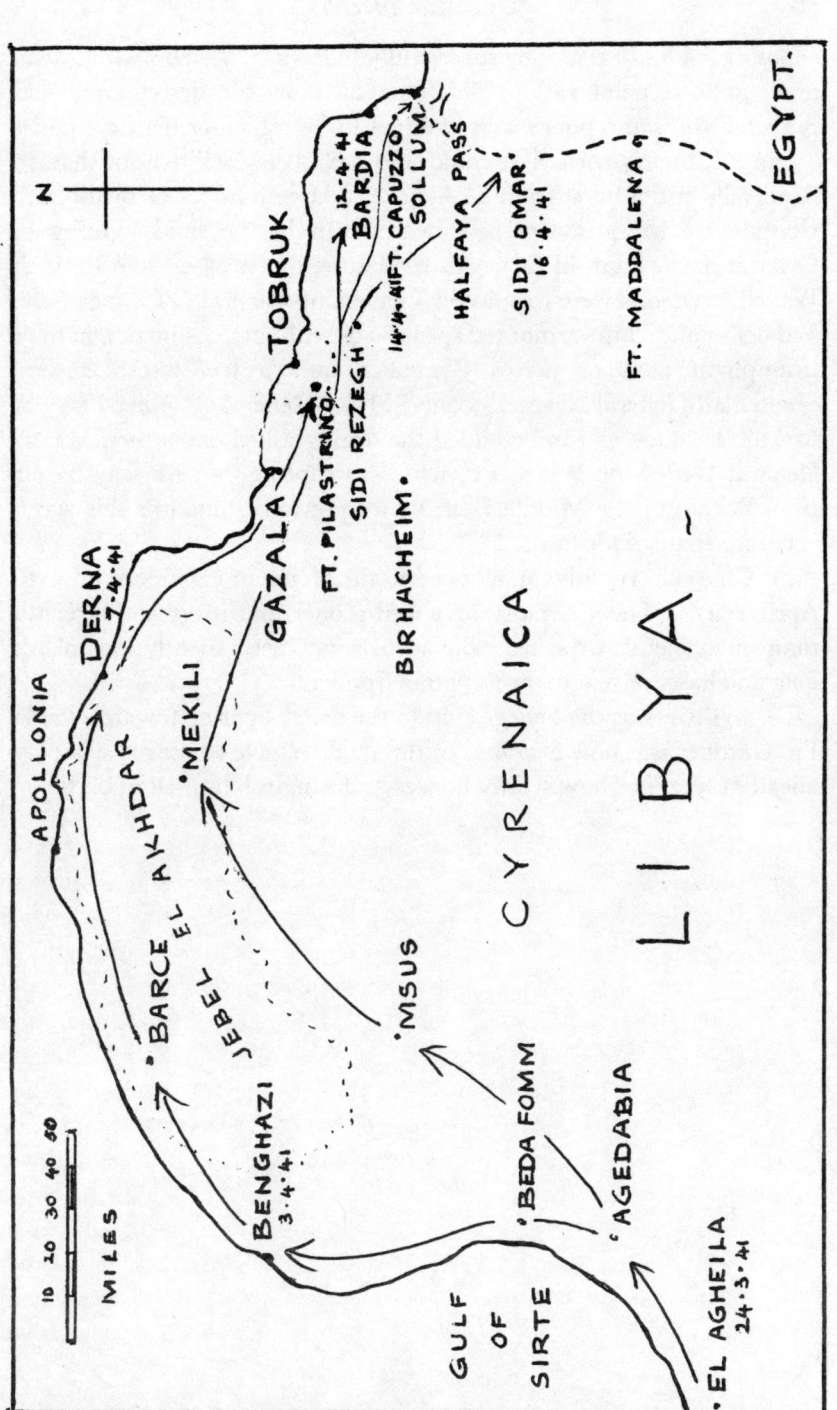

Rommel's First Thrust, 1941

EGYPT.

LIBYA ~

CYRENAICA

TOBRUK

GAZALA

DERNA
7·4·41

APOLLONIA

BARCE

JEBEL EL AKHDAR

•MEKILI

•MSUS

BENGHAZI
3·4·41

•BEDA FOMM

•AGEDABIA

GULF
OF
SIRTE

•EL AGHEILA
24·3·41

FT. PILASTRINO•
12·4·41
SIDI REZEGH•
BIR HACHEIM•
14·4·41 FT. CAPUZZO
BARDIA
SOLLUM
HALFAYA PASS

SIDI OMAR
16·4·41

FT. MADDALENA

N

10 20 30 40 50

MILES

choosing, as had been done successfully following Wavell's withdrawal in 1940 to a point east of Sidi Barrani. Now the desert army was pursuing the same policy and claimed to be inflicting high casualties on an advancing enemy. It could also have been pointed out that, in Rommel's initial burst from El Agheila, a large number of British and Commonwealth prisoners had been taken in the fluid fighting in Cyrenaica. So fluid, in fact, was the battle, that no less than three of Wavell's generals were captured : Lieutenant-General O'Connor (who had commanded the armoured spearheads with such distinction in their triumphant advance across Cyrenaica only a few weeks earlier), Lieutenant-General Neame, vc, and Major-General Gambier-Parry at Mekili. To these had to be added the distinguished one-armed Major-General Carton de Wiart, vc, who was captured on his way by air from Britain to the Middle East. By all previous standards this was a very large haul of top brass.

As Churchill ruefully announced to the House of Commons on 27th April 1941 : 'The Germans advanced sooner and in greater strength than our generals expected.' But all was not permanently lost in this long and hasty retreat to the Egyptian frontier.

Such, then, was the background to the desert fighting towards which Pip Gardner was now heading. Little could he have envisaged what lay ahead of him, nor how swiftly he was to distinguish himself in battle.

CHAPTER FIVE

Military Cross

Pip for his part was anxious to join the fray, as can be seen from a letter that he wrote to the employees of his family engineering firm J. Gardner and Co. He wrote :

'You are probably thinking to yourselves that I am pretty lucky to be wintering in a warm climate, where the sun is always shining and the skies are forever blue. Perhaps I am, if it means being away from air-raids. But when you take all the other disadvantages into consideration, it isn't really so wonderful after all. . . . Here I am sitting in my tent in the middle of the desert with nothing but miles of sand and absolutely nowhere to go and nothing to do in your spare time.

'Every now and again we have terrific sand storms that sweep across the desert like a fog and drive in everywhere, and for the rest of the day you find yourself eating quantities of sand in all your food. When you lie down to sleep on your camp-bed, it's like lying on sandpaper.

'The weather now is approaching the hottest that we have, but somehow for the last few days it has gone all to pieces and, although I wear shorts during daylight, I have been very glad to wear a thick pullover to keep myself warm. The nights, too, are very cold and I have been using four or five blankets lately.

'I was pleased to hear in my last letter from Father that you are still keeping busy and that you are now assisting to make equipment for us mechanised forces. I only wish that I were at home with you assisting on this work, instead of sitting here waiting to do something. But still I suppose my hour will come quite soon enough, and then I shall have added my contribution to the job of work we all have in hand.

'Whereas you, I expect, could do with a rest, I on the other hand am yearning for some real work to do, instead of the continual waiting which I have been doing for so many months now. Anyhow I don't think it is going to be so long a war as some think and I am sure that before we know where we are, I shall be up in the general office trying to find out why a 2-inch hexagon nut costs 30 shillings to make, or something of the sort.

'Please accept my kindest regards and best wishes for a speedy return to normal days once again.

'Yours very sincerely,

'Philip J. Gardner.'

*

It wasn't long before Pip's desire for activity was to be gratified – even if his forecast for a speedy return to normal days was to prove a trifle optimistic! He would have needed a very clear crystal ball to see Pearl Harbour, Singapore, and Stalingrad all looming in the distance. In fact Hitler hadn't yet sealed his own ultimate fate by attacking Russia, and Rommel, though on the warpath, hadn't yet become a legend. But for Pip Gardner in the desert things were about to happen.

Wavell was under strong pressure from a disappointed Churchill to make every effort to relieve the garrison at Tobruk and return to Cyrenaica. His first aim was to attack Fort Capuzzo, which barred the way initially to Bardia and ultimately to Tobruk. Rather against his better judgement, at a time when he would have preferred to build up his forces for a decisive blow at Rommel, Wavell mounted in early June 1941 an ill-starred operation, in an effort to achieve what was being demanded of him.

As part of this plan, it was intended to use the 4th Indian Division for a frontal assault on Halfaya Pass, while the main force worked its way round the left flank towards Capuzzo and Sidi Omar. Tank support was required for the 11th Indian Brigade in their frontal assault on the escarpment. Two troops of tanks were sent up from Buq Buq to provide this support. Each troop of three tanks was under the command of an officer, of which Lieutenant Tom Rowe was the senior, and Second-Lieutenant Pip Gardner was the other.

As the six Matilda tanks moved forward in the direction of Sollum, at intervals along the coastal road, it wasn't long before they were spotted from the air. Very soon the inevitable Stuka dive-bombers arrived, making a crescendo of noise as they swooped down to attack.

Plenty of bombs landed in the desert and made big holes as they threw up vast clouds of sand all around. This proved to be a foretaste of things to come.

When they had reached the plain below the escarpment leading up to Halfaya, the tanks spread out in line abreast to await further orders over the wireless. Pip took the opportunity during the halt to spread out his tailor-made officer's greatcoat, which he had worn the previous night, on the ground next to the tank, while the customary brew of tea was being hurriedly made by one of the crew. Tank-crews seldom missed a chance of a quick brew-up – nor anyone else in the desert, for that matter! Just as Pip was having his first sip of strong tea, a Messerschmitt swept over the horizon and strafed the tanks with machine-gun fire. It was all over so quickly that there wasn't time to be scared and no personnel were hit. But when it came to picking up his precious greatcoat, Pip was in for a great shock. The coat, for which he had had more than one visit to his tailor, to make sure that his first officer's garment really fitted him, was riddled with bullet-holes and resembled a colander! But fortunately no serious damage had been done to the tanks, and Pip was able to carry on into battle next morning, wearing his well-ventilated greatcoat.

At dawn the six Matildas crossed the start-line and advanced towards an unseen enemy across the flat desert ahead. Pip was about to have his first experience of battle. Though not scared, he was somewhat apprehensive about the unknown, when suddenly a strange figure appeared on the track, all huddled up in a blanket and waving to him. For a moment Pip thought that the figure was a woman in that unlikely place, but he at once realised that it was an infantryman from the 11th Brigade of the 4th Indian Division whom they were supporting. The soldier had wrapped a blanket round him from head to foot to ward off the early-morning cold. Oddly, Pip felt encouraged by this surprise encounter, and it banished all his apprehension over the unknown, as the figure waved him on.

Very soon, as it began to get light, the tanks came under heavy fire as they made their way forward. For a while all hell was let loose as they returned the fire in the direction from which it was coming. They were in the thick of the fray so quickly that there wasn't time to feel scared. Unfortunately they hadn't been warned that a minefield lay ahead of them and suddenly when the tanks all hit the mines, as they advanced in open formation, they found themselves immobilised, with their tracks blown off. There they were, like sitting ducks on a pond, unable to move.

They were, however, still able to fire their weapons, which included a two-pounder gun on each tank, as well as machine-guns. They were also still in wireless contact with headquarters and they received orders to hold the plain against a counter-attack on the Indian Brigade. For some hours they managed to keep up a spasmodic gun attack with their two-pounders, against targets which they were unable actually to see. They were forced to act more like pill-boxes than tanks, now that they had lost mobility, but their role, though restricted, seemed to be effective.

As far as Pip's tank was concerned, it eventually received a direct hit from the front, which unfortunately killed the driver and put the two-pounder gun out of action. Worse was soon to follow.

Tom Rowe, who was the senior officer in charge, got out of his tank and ran across to Pip to find out if it might be possible to repair the broken tracks and thus regain mobility. He went on to the next tank to issue similar orders, but when he was half-way across he suddenly fell to the ground. Pip realised at once that Rowe had stepped on a mine. He jumped out of his tank and, disregarding the shells and machine-gun fire from the enemy, he followed Rowe's footprints in order to avoid a similar fate. He found that the latter was seriously wounded in the leg, body and one eye. He was in fact mortally wounded. Retracing his footsteps hurriedly but carefully, Pip got out the first-aid kit from his tank and returned to Tom Rowe with the idea of giving him some morphia tablets; but regrettably he was already dead and Pip could do nothing for him.

This casualty now left Pip in charge of the six tanks still marooned and under intermittent fire. Carrying out Rowe's orders, they struggled all afternoon to repair their tracks. But they were all too badly damaged. As daylight faded and the firing died down, Pip decided that they must leave their battered tanks and make their way back to headquarters on foot.

By shouting orders and signalling to the survivors in the other tanks, telling them to walk back along their tracks with care, in order to avoid treading on more mines, he safely led them back to assemble under an escarpment in rear. They all managed to pick their way like cats on hot bricks in gingerly fashion – having witnessed what had happened to the luckless Tom Rowe. Once they had all rejoined Pip, he led them for another mile or so, until they managed to find their way in the dark to their headquarters, where they were given some badly needed food and hot tea. It had been a harrowing day for all of them.

Next day, as soon as it was light, Pip decided that he must make sure that all the guns on the tanks were properly immobilised, to prevent their capture and use by the enemy. This he did by walking along the tank tracks with utmost care, just as they had on the previous night. He also collected a few small items of identity from those who were dead in or beside the tanks, so that they could be sent home to their next-of-kin. This naturally took a considerable time and called for a great deal of nerve on Pip's part. He felt that as officer-in-charge it was up to him to perform this task himself.

He and his surviving tank crews were sent back, in several stages, with lifts in various vehicles, to base camp near Buq Buq. This attempt to relieve Tobruk, though it helped to stem any further advance by Rommel's troops, failed to achieve its purpose, despite some determined fighting with infantry and tanks in the area from Halfaya to Capuzzo and Sidi Omar. The operation was officially known by the code-name 'Battleaxe' – a fact which many of those taking part, including Pip, only discovered afterwards. At the time, it resulted in very fierce fighting and a heavy loss of British armour. This time Rommel had scored a success, not so much with his thrusting panzers as with skilful siting and use of the 88 mm anti-aircraft gun in defence against the British tanks, which were vulnerable to it from the flank. The timing of 'Battleaxe' was not of Wavell's choosing, and merely resulted in further heavy losses of men and equipment at a time when he really wanted to build up his resources after setbacks in Greece as well as the Western Desert. Pressure from home had ruled otherwise.

Th crews of the 4th Royal Tanks were assembled at base near Alexandria for re-equipping with new tanks. In early July Pip had seven days' leave in Alexandria, and on his return he was pleasantly surprised to learn that for his handling of a tricky situation in his very first engagement with the enemy, beneath Halfaya Pass, he had been awarded the Military Cross – quick work by any standards. His wife, Renée, was proud and delighted with the news, but, knowing Pip, she wasn't really very surprised.

Having failed, for the present, to reach Tobruk by a frontal attack on land, the 4th Royal Tanks were about to make a back-door entry to the beleaguered port by sea. Pip Gardner and his regiment hadn't by any means seen the last of Tobruk.

*

For a week or so in early April the troops in Tobruk, from the higher points inside the defensive perimeter, had watched Rommel's armoured columns sweep past in the desert in hot pursuit of Wavell's retreating army. The latter had withdrawn across Cyrenaica with somewhat indecent haste, in order to take up defensive positions along the frontier between Libya and Egypt – almost back to their starting-point in the previous December. After the fall of Derna to the west on 7th April, and the capture of Bardia to the east by 12th April, followed at once by that of Fort Capuzzo to the south, Rommel felt that he was now in a position to deal with Tobruk. Nor did he anticipate much trouble in doing so, judging from the fact that it had only taken a day and a half for the British and Commonwealth troops to oust the defending Italians when they had advanced westwards only four months before.

General Morshead and his resolute garrison, however, thought otherwise. As soon as the decision had been taken to hold Tobruk against any attack by land, and to supply and reinforce the garrison by sea, thanks to the supremacy of the Royal Navy, Morshead's troops set about manning and strengthening the defences along the thirty-mile perimeter, which enclosed an area round the harbour of about the size of the Isle of Wight.

Morshead's garrison consisted largely of his own Australian sappers and infantry, well supported by Royal Artillery gunners, a squadron of the King's Dragoon Guards, alongside a battalion of machine-gunners of the Northumberland Fusiliers and a squadron of Indian cavalry. To these were added units of the Royal Army Service Corps, the Royal Army Ordnance Corps, and men of the Royal Tank Regiment, eventually amounting to more than a brigade. The defenders set about converting to their own use much of the weaponry and ammunition left behind by the Italians when they had surrendered. The sappers were very active in mining the perimeter, even to the extent of making sorties by night in order to purloin and use some of the mines that were put down by the enemy.

Rommel's panzers, supported by Italian infantry, made their first attack on Tobruk on 13th April and the siege of Tobruk may therefore be said to have begun on that date. The attack was made from the south-west and some twenty tanks were reported to have penetrated the perimeter, but were met with such heavy artillery fire that they were driven back with substantial losses in tanks and infantry. The defensive position was soon retrieved and the enemy infantry in support of the tanks were repulsed by the determined Australians. Three days later, on 16th April, another attack was made, with the same result. Two days later a similar attack was launched from the direction of Derna and was again resolutely driven back with heavy losses in tanks, leaving the Italian infantry in no position to enter the battle.

General Morshead's policy was far from one of passive defence. He was insistent that while the surrounding enemy troops were making life uncomfortable for those inside the perimeter, his night patrols in their turn would, by almost nightly sorties, make matters very uneasy for the enemy. For this policy he had just the troops for the job, in his own Australians and Indians well-versed in North-West Frontier fighting. The consequence was that some spectacular hauls of surprised prisoners were brought inside the perimeter to which they had hoped to force a more victorious entry.

Further German–Italian attacks were made from the south-west on 24th and 30th April, and though the latter resulted in several days and nights of fluctuating fighting at close quarters round Fort Pilastrino, heavy artillery fire finally forced back the enemy tanks and the Italian infantry were obliged to give up the ground that they had initially succeeded in winning. The Imperial forces lost no time in strengthening their defences in the south-west sector of their outer perimeter. For the time being Rommel realised that in Tobruk he had found a hard nut to crack, and there was something of a lull in his repeated assaults.

This however didn't mean that there was any cessation of the continual bombardment by enemy artillery by land and by Axis planes from the air. The fierce retaliatory fire from the guns of Tobruk resulted in a noisy time, day and night, for all those within the perimeter – particularly in the harbour and the ruins of the town itself.

The Royal Navy's sustained effort to keep Tobruk's defenders in touch with the outside world was prodigious. Between 12th April and 10th December 1941, it conveyed 29,000 troops into Tobruk and evacuated 23,000, as well as running in 34,000 tons of supplies and food during that period. At first the transport was provided by a scratch assortment of vessels, including mine-sweepers, and later by destroyers, notably those of the Australian Navy in support of their besieged fellow-countrymen. Because of the danger of air-attack, the ships had to arrive by night, unload their cargo under cover of darkness and be gone before first light. The fact that Tobruk harbour was littered with wrecks, some visible and some submerged, and that the docks had suffered extensive bombardment, greatly added to the difficulty of the Navy's task.

During May and June attempts by Wavell, in the latter of which Pip Gardner took part, to reach and relieve Tobruk were doomed to failure to reach their objective. An insufficient build-up of strength, the relative limitations in speed and fire-power of the British tanks, and the devastating use of the 88 mm gun by the enemy were the main reasons for this failure – which was to result in the replacement of Wavell soon after the end of 'Battleaxe'. He was replaced by General Auchinleck on 30th June. His task was to assemble an army of sufficient numbers and strength for a decisive push in the autumn – later than Churchill urged, but more in line with the situation that Auchinleck found on his arrival in the desert.

Wavell's abortive attacks had, nevertheless, had the effect of lessening the pressure on Tobruk. Rommel's troops were needed elsewhere, in the forward areas, in order to repulse Wavell's attempts to break through. He realised that, with troops of the calibre of the Australians and the Indians guarding the perimeter, gallantly supported by British light tanks and gunners and supplied by the Royal Navy, the siege was likely to be a long one. Yet the presence of the enemy-held territory on his flank greatly irked him – not least because, instead of being able to use the proper coast road past Tobruk, his supplies to his forward troops had to travel across an increasingly churned-up and dusty stretch of desert. Rommel himself found a solution to this major irritation, which was to prove of great benefit to both sides in the months of see-saw fighting that lay ahead. He proposed the immediate construction of a loop road to by-pass Tobruk. The Italians greeted the plan with enthusiasm, and set about their task with a will. This was something at which they excelled, and the road was completed in the space of three

Historic moment—half an hour before winning the V.C. Pip Gardner (left) talking to fellow officers of the 4th Royal Tanks: Lt. Richard Simpkin (later Major-General, M.C. and Bar), Major Alan Roberts (later Lt-Col., M.C. and Bar), and Lt. Paul Gearing (later M.C. and Bar). On the Matilda tank is Sgt. Boniface, M.M., who later died in a POW camp.

Lt-Col. Walter O'Carroll (centre) and officers of the 4th Royal Tanks inside the Tobruk perimeter, at full strength before the break-out in November 1941.

At the Tank Museum at Bovington. The Curator, Lt-Col. George Forty, and Mrs Anne Forty with Pip Gardner by one of the Matilda tanks used in the Western Desert.

months. At a special opening ceremony an Italian general named it 'Achsenstrasse' – Axis Road. German battalions had at first been detailed for the work, but as they were more suitable for, and more interested in, front-line duty, they soon changed places with Italians who were at battle stations. Everyone was happier that way.

Less happy, however, were the German reinforcements who arrived in Junkers 52s at Derna. Troop carriers were waiting at the airfield to meet them, and before they knew where they were, they found themselves in the front-line outside Tobruk. Far from finding the desert palms depicted in the insignia of the German Afrika Korps to which they now belonged, they found themselves dumped in a fly-infested desert, short of water and existing on meagre and monotonous rations. The discomforts of Tobruk were by no means confined to those inside the perimeter. Equally galling for the new arrivals, was the lack of movement in the situation that they found. Instead of being part of what, in that summer of 1941, looked like being a fast-moving and triumphant conquest of Russia, they had landed into a seemingly stalemate position in Libya, all too reminiscent of the trenches in France in World War I.

As the summer wore on, it was decided, against Auchinleck's judgement but in response to political pressure, to replace the Australian troops in stages with British troops. The process was started in September and in place of the Australians there came into Tobruk, by the back door at sea, the British 70th Division, a Polish brigade and a Czechoslovak battalion. This was no easy change-over to accomplish and several ships were sunk or damaged in the process. But the operation was to provide Pip Gardner with a renewal of his acquaintance with Tobruk – this time from the inside.

After his part in Wavell's unsuccessful attempt to relieve the beleaguered port by means of an advance overland, there had followed for him a two-month period of re-assembly and re-equipment with new tanks in July and August. During this time Pip went on a useful Air Liaison course at El Daba with the South African Air Force. He also spent a relaxing week's leave in Alexandria with his friend Percy Gers.

Then in September 1941 he found himself forming part of a plan which was to astonish the enemy by its scale. It involved the insertion into the garrison of Tobruk of a sort of Wooden Horse, ready for an eventual break-out, in the form of the 32nd Army Tank Brigade, under

Brigadier Willison. Included in the brigade was the 4th Royal Tank Regiment. Under Auchinleck the army previously known as the Western Desert Force (or, as Churchill seemed to prefer, the Army of the Nile) was henceforth to become known as the Eighth Army and as such was destined to win great renown – though not immediately.

Thus in September the 4th Royal Tanks were sent by sea to enter the fortress of Tobruk. The tanks were sent separately in tank-landing craft, while the officers and men were transported from Alexandria in the destroyer HMS *Hotspur*. Their journey first took them well out from land through rough seas in a westerly direction, parallel to the coast. It was not a comfortable passage. They were packed like sardines on the decks and were soon subjected to dive-bombing attacks from enemy aircraft which had spotted them. They had no option but to crouch on the decks and pray that the bombs would land in the sea, which providentially they did.

They moved thankfully into Tobruk just before first light and hurriedly disembarked. The harbour appeared strewn with wrecks in various stages of submersion, and the quays had suffered badly from repeated bombing. But despite all the hazards, 4th Royal Tanks and its vehicles were all safely landed and they lost no time in deploying in their allotted sector to the south-east and digging into reasonably sheltered positions, making full use of the ravines and natural rock formations within the perimeter.

Having safely arrived they soon adapted to life in Tobruk under siege. Thanks to the Royal Navy, there was enough food – lacking in variation and fresh fruit and vegetables though it inevitably was. Bully beef in various disguises and specially compounded service biscuits, fortified with calcium, formed their diet. To drink, tea was their mainstay, in the absence of canteens and beer. Pip and a few of his friends managed, however, to lay hands on some stimulating liquor on occasions. Their regimental Medical Officer, Captain John Lipscombe, would visit his friends after dark, bringing with him his bag of 'Medical Comforts', from which he would produce some extremely welcome brandy and eggnog, which did wonders for the morale, Pip found. John Lipscombe was able to find plenty of reasons to visit the docks in order to replenish his 'Medical Comforts'. He also had the right contacts!

The troops guarding and patrolling the perimeter were relieved after every ten days and given two days off, during which they might even get a chance to swim and refresh themselves in the sea. But even this could prove hazardous, with interruptions from low-flying aircraft. Mail was irregular but it managed to arrive spasmodically, and apart from desert sores caused by the restricted diet, the place proved reasonably healthy for those already accustomed to desert life. Contrary to what some subsequent German prisoners seemed to think, the garrison wasn't reduced to eating rats!

For Pip, much of the time was spent in digging in their tanks and keeping their guns free from sand. They also spent a lot of time studying maps of the German and Italian positions opposite them, beyond the perimeter, and in carrying out night patrols. On one occasion he was sent out on patrol under the command of his new squadron-commander, Captain Jack Gough, to try to ambush some enemy tanks which had been menacing one of the forward infantry outposts. Their instructions were to proceed as quietly as possible and be in position to lie in wait for the enemy. But, halfway to their objective, an infantryman suddenly appeared in the dark and told them that another outpost had been overrun. Jack Gough decided to use his initiative and go to the aid of this outpost and the tanks moved off at full speed with him in the lead and with the noise of their tracks now advertising their position. Unfortunately, after a few minutes they came under enemy fire and a shot went through Gough's turret, temporarily blinding him in the process.

He then ordered Pip to take command. As Pip was navigating officer and was in a Mark VI Light Tank, he felt somewhat exposed. He then led the squadron to their original objective, where they waited for some hours without any contact with the enemy. They finally had to return empty-handed and thwarted, as apparently the enemy tanks had been there earlier. As it was, getting back in the dark, through his own lines, proved quite a hair-raising business and Brigadier Willison was amused to hear on the radio a voice saying: 'I am coming in into the middle of the squadron. Don't shoot – it's me, Pip!' They all got back safely, with the exception of their luckless commander, Jack Gough, who was subsequently invalided home.

Round about this time, as autumn arrived, there was some very heavy rain, which added to their discomfort. Rare though rain is in the desert, when it comes it can prove most disconcerting, as Pip and his companions were to find. They had a large tent for an officers' mess, which was well protected by rocks piled up all round it. They normally slept in shelters nearby, in holes in the ground, under pieces of corrugated-iron which were held down by rocks. During one night, the rain poured down so hard that these small individual shelters were leaking badly. So they all took their bed-rolls into the tent for shelter. After about two hours' sleep, Pip suddenly woke up and found himself afloat in a foot of water, which had run down the gully and filled the tent. The surrounding rocks were preventing this unaccustomed flow of water from getting away. Unbelievable chaos ensued as they all tried to get out of bed in the dark, and endeavoured to make an outlet for the water, before rescuing their soaking bed-rolls.

But even this downpour failed to dampen their spirits. They knew that it wouldn't be long before they would be called upon to break out of the Tobruk perimeter, which was the reason why they had been sent there in the first place. It merely made them all the more determined to end the siege and link up with their overland forces once they received the signal to start their break-out.

CHAPTER SIX

Victoria Cross

On 21st November 1941 the eagerly awaited order to break out was received by General Scobie, who was now in command of the Tobruk garrison, following the replacement of General Morshead and his 9th Australian Division, less one battalion which there wasn't time to extricate. Thus this single Australian battalion, along with three British artillery regiments and a battalion of Northumberland Fusiliers had the distinction of going right through the siege from start to finish.

The object and the timing of the break-out were linked to a well-devised plan of attack by the Eighth Army intended to relieve Tobruk and carry on and drive the Axis forces out of Cyrenaica again. The plan was known as 'Operation Crusader' and was launched on 18th November – three days before the planned break-out, which was timed to catch the enemy in the rear and thus enable those breaking out to meet the main attacking troops which General Auchinleck, who had replaced Wavell, had entrusted to General Sir Alan Cunningham as the new commander of the Eighth Army. Cunningham had recently concluded a successful campaign in East Africa and now had at his disposal the 2nd New Zealand, 4th Indian and 1st South African Divisions, in addition to a two-to-one numerical advantage of British tanks over those of the Germans – without taking into account the armour of doubtful effectiveness that the Italians might have mustered since their débâcle of less than a year ago. His intention was that, despite the superiority of the German tanks in fire-power and armoured protection in previous encounters, this time it would prove possible to get within close enough range in large enough numbers to inflict heavy casualties.

Tactically, Cunningham's plan was for part of his forces to pin down the enemy on the Egyptian frontier, while the rest attacked further inland in the south, before swinging north-west to tackle the enemy armour in the suitable tank-battle terrain in the area south of Tobruk, around Sidi Rezegh. It was to join up with this big left hook that the break-out from Tobruk was planned.

Not for the first or last time in desert warfare, the attack by one general succeeded in pre-empting that of another. This time it was Rommel who was pre-empted. He was particularly anxious to mount another surge towards the east, with the Nile Delta and the Suez Canal at the end of his rainbow – if not as yet in his sights – before the Eighth Army under the guidance of the new Commander-in-Chief, Middle East, General Auchinleck, grew too strong for him. But first he must once and for all rid himself of the nuisance on his flank in the form of the troublesome Tobruk garrison. He had tried several times unsuccessfully in April and May to force an entry from the south-west. He had finally planned a renewed assault on the perimeter for late November – but from the south-east this time, hoping to gain access that way. With this end in view he had been concentrating his troops and guns in that area.

His plans were forestalled when Cunningham's troops moved over to the attack on 18th November and pushed up towards Sidi Rezegh as planned. Rommel's tanks were needed to counter this threat, but the concentration of guns and troops opposite the south-east sector of the Tobruk perimeter meant that whoever was chosen to break out at that point would find plenty of enemy opposition there. This was precisely where Pip Gardner and the 4th Royal Tanks, under the inspiring command of Lieutenant-Colonel Walter O'Carroll, were poised to make their move.

The plan for the break-out from Tobruk was devised by General Scobie in consultation with Brigadier Willison, who was in command of the 32nd Army Tank Brigade inside the perimeter. His brigade consisted of the 1st and 4th Royal Tanks, plus one squadron of the 7th Royal Tanks, as well as Brigade Headquarters. The first stage of the break-out was the capture of a series of enemy strong-points outside the perimeter, all familiar by name to the occupants of Tobruk, and the subject of much scrutiny on the map. They bore such names as 'Jack', 'Jill', 'Lion' and 'Tiger', etcetera, which had been given them for identification purposes by the defending troops.

The key-point in the enemy defences was thought to be the strong-point known as 'Tiger', at a distance of nearly three miles beyond the perimeter. On the way, at a distance of a mile from the wire, lay the strong-point 'Jill', with 'Butch' at a similar distance away to the east. 'Jack' and 'Lion' flanked 'Tiger' itself, to the north-east and south-west respectively. These strong-points were assigned to the various squadrons of the 4th Royal Tanks. 'C' Squadron was to attack 'Tiger' from the front, while 'A' Squadron under Major Alan ('Bertie') Roberts was ordered to make a quick dash round the flank to shoot up the position from the rear, to coincide with the frontal attack.

After Sappers had toiled dangerously but skilfully through the night at removing mines and clearing gaps in the wire, it was the turn of the Gunners to subject the enemy strong-points to a softening-up barrage. By dawn on 21st November the stage was set for the Matildas of the 4th Royal Tanks to enter the scene and make their break-out.

Emerging through the prepared gaps along a one-mile section of the perimeter defences, they fanned out across the desert in a south-easterly direction. Pip was in the lead, once again as navigator for his squadron in a Light Mark VI tank. He found it an exhilarating feeling to be on the move at last, after weeks of confinement within the perimeter, as he dashed towards his objective.

As the crews of the 4th Tanks rushed forth across the desert to attack their respective strong-points, some of them saw a familiar figure frantically waving at them. It was Brigadier Willison, who had had his tank put out of action by a mine. The first few to rush past conveniently interpreted his frenzied gestures as encouragement for them to hurry on towards their targets – whereas, in actual fact he was in urgent need of a fresh conveyance into battle. To have stopped to offer him a lift might also have resulted in one's having to hand over one's tank to a senior officer in need of a vehicle. Brigadier Willison believed in leading his troops from the front, whenever possible. Small wonder was it, then, that those in the first wave of the stampede of advancing tanks chose to interpret the brigadier's frantic gestures as encouragement to press on even faster! Eventually, in the second wave, the brigadier managed to stop one of the on-coming tanks and climb thankfully aboard.

Pip, too, had his light tank, put out of action during the advance before he reached his objective. But he was able to transfer to a Matilda and catch up with the rest of his squadron which managed to capture 'Tiger', thanks to the timely intervention of 'Bertie' Roberts with 'A' Squadron in the rear, and the well-judged use of the reserve squadron when very heavy infantry losses by the 2nd Black Watch in the capture of 'Jill' looked like jeopardising the whole attack. O'Carroll's use of his reserve squadron saved the day and turned possible failure into a resounding success.

'Tiger' had been subjected to a heavy artillery barrage, which had had the required demoralising effect on the large number of troops there. It had also contained a big concentration of guns – but fortunately no tanks at the time. They had doubtless been sent elsewhere, to help stem the tide near Sidi Rezegh.

The flanking posts of 'Butch' and 'Jack' were also taken, as well as 'Jill' on the way to 'Tiger'. In all over a thousand prisoners were taken of which half were Germans of the Afrika Korps – an unexpectedly high proportion, which had accounted for the stubborn resistance encountered on the way. The prisoners, Germans and Italians alike, seemed astonished to find such an array of tanks coming at them from inside the perimeter of Tobruk. They found their presence hard to believe – though, of course, they were reckoning without the resourcefulness of the Royal Navy, which had enabled such a surprisingly large number of tanks to be infiltrated and held in readiness to strike. The prisoners were soon to find the Royal Navy on hand once more to evacuate them by sea to captivity.

Having taken their appointed strong-point, 'Tiger', the 4th Royal Tanks set about consolidating their position, in readiness for further action – or for any possible counter-attack that might be launched at them. The following day was spent in preparation for the next phase of the break-out. This consisted of capturing the high ground ahead of them to the south-east. It was a long sausage-shaped ridge known as Ed Duda, some seven miles beyond the perimeter in the direction of Sidi Rezegh and destined to loom large in the annals of the Royal Tank Regiment. If this high ground could be taken and held, then the Tobruk by-pass leading to Bardia – the new Achsenstrasse – would be dominated and effectively cut.

The 4th Royal Tanks, by now considerably reduced in strength by the recent fighting, prepared to spend the night of 22nd November in open laager some two miles south-east of the Tobruk perimeter. Lieutenant-Colonel O'Carroll was called to Fortress Headquarters to receive new orders for the following day, leaving his senior squadron commander Major Jack Prichard in command of the regiment during his absence. He was away for the night and early next morning he sent a signal to Major Prichard, telling him to alert the regiment for an immediate move, probably towards the south.

Major Prichard had summoned the other two squadron commanders in order to pass on the instructions that he had just received. While they were assembled they were approached by an officer of the 1st Royal Horse Artillery in a truck urgently seeking assistance on behalf of two Marmond Herrington armoured cars of the King's Dragoon Guards, which were in difficulties in no man's land in front of them. At first Major Prichard demurred, in view of the fact that the 4th Royal Tanks were due to move off as a regiment at any moment. But when the Royal Horse Artillery officer continued to press the case for the stranded armoured cars of the King's Dragoon Guards and explained that they were just visible on the horizon and were under heavy artillery fire, Major Prichard relented. He quickly ordered Major 'Bertie' Roberts to send someone out with a troop to go to their assistance.

The 'someone' turned out to be Pip. He had just finished breakfasting beside his tank immediately after 'standing to' at dawn and was on hand to receive the orders from Major 'Bertie' Roberts. He was now within half an hour of winning the Victoria Cross!

*

Pip Gardner stood not upon the order of his going – he went at once to the help of the two stranded Marmond Herringtons, which were visible on the sky-line. He took two Matildas with him – his own and another to provide covering fire if necessary. His own Matilda was manned by a crew of three: Sergeant D. M. McTier (gunner), Trooper Richards (wireless operator and loader) and Trooper B. Robertson, MM (driver). In the other tank, under Lieutenant Paul Gearing, the crew included a gunner who rejoiced in the nickname (given to him by his pals) of 'Mickey the Greek' and a description (self-styled) as 'the best f . . . ing gunner in the whole f . . . ing squadron'. He was shortly going to be called upon to live up to his self-styled description!

The two tanks quickly set off towards the stationary armoured cars to investigate the trouble. It was soon obvious that they were under fire from the enemy and Pip immediately summed-up the situation and issued his orders. The following citation from *The London Gazette*, at the start of the Second Supplement dated Tuesday 10th February 1942, gives the official version of what happened next. The citation runs as follows:

'War Office,
'10 February, 1942

'The KING has been graciously pleased to approve the award of the VICTORIA CROSS to

'Lieutenant (acting Captain) Philip John Gardner, MC (132595), Royal Tank Regiment, Royal Armoured Corps (Sydenham).

'On the morning of November 23rd, 1941, Captain Gardner was ordered to take two tanks to the assistance of two armoured cars of the King's Dragoon Guards which were out of action and under fire in close proximity to the enemy, south-east of Tobruk. He found the two cars halted two hundred yards apart, being heavily fired on at close range and gradually smashed to pieces. Ordering the other tank to give him covering fire, Captain Gardner manoeuvred his own close up to the foremost car; he then dismounted in the face of intense anti-tank and machine-gun fire and secured a tow-rope to the car; seeing an officer lying beside it with his legs blown off, he lifted him into the car and gave the order to tow. The tow-rope, however, broke, and Captain Gardner returned to the armoured car, being immediately wounded in the arm and leg; despite his wounds he lifted the other officer out of the car and carried him back to the tank, placing him on the back engine louvres and climbing alongside to hold him on. While the tank was being driven back to safety it was subjected to heavy shell fire and the loader was killed.

'The courage, determination and complete disregard for his own safety displayed by Captain Gardner enabled him, despite his own wounds, and in the face of intense fire at close range, to save the life of his fellow officer, in circumstances fraught with great difficulty and danger.'

*

As one would expect, from anyone as matter-of-fact as Pip, there is a marked similarity as regards the basic facts of this official citation and a letter written to his parents on December 28th, after the action in question – and much more to follow – but before any award had come through. The letter, not unnaturally, conveys more about his personal feelings at the time. He wrote :

'Once again you see your only son has safely returned from the battles and, thanks to God, with great honour again.

'I may as well tell you that I have apparently been put in for the vc this time although it will take a long time before it comes through, if it comes off at all, which is pretty unlikely as there must be a lot put in; but still it's something to be put in for it, isn't it? At the least I expect I shall get a bar to my mc.

'Although this must sound to you like rather a swollen-headed account, I know you will like to hear how it all came about, and what I have been doing this month.

'Last September the battalion was sent up to Tobruk and there we lived under very adverse conditions until the great operations which you have to read about were ready for the word "Go". I was then a reconnaissance officer in my light tank and in the first stage of the attack my job was to follow up the heavy tanks, keeping contact with the Infantry and Gunners. This operation was carried out successfully, although I had one very sticky moment when my tank was knocked out; but I managed to get back OK and the rest of the day passed more or less uneventfully. The second day resulted in more attacks and we now pass to the third day.

'We had spent a very cold night sleeping under our tank (I had taken over a heavy one by this time) and we were just "standing to" at daylight, when I received an order to go and rescue two armoured cars that had run into difficulties about a mile away. I took one other tank with me and set off. When I got near the cars I found that one of the crews had managed to get out and had crawled away to some trenches and were lying "doggo" there, waiting for a chance to make a run for it, as they were under very heavy fire.

'I passed them and went on to the front car, only to be greeted at very short range with heavy anti-tank and machine-gun fire. We managed to back the tank up to the car and I hopped out to get it on tow; I found behind the car a badly wounded officer with his legs off. I seem to have this sort of thing falling to my lot, don't I? I got the chap into his car again and got the car on tow and started off; but as luck would have it the rope broke, and so we had to go back again and get the chap out of the car and on to the tank. During all this we had been under heavy fire and my guns were put out of action, and the tank with me was unable to give us much covering fire, as his guns were damaged.

'Well, I had to leave the car and started off back again, only to discover that, while I had been outside, the top of my turret had been shot away and my loader was dead. Well, to make a long story short, we picked up the rest of the boys on the way back and got out of it. I then found I had stopped a few small pieces of metal in my leg, neck, and arm, but nothing serious.

'So you see how it all happened, and you may be sure I said many a prayer out loud while I was trying to lift the chap off the ground, and God certainly answered my prayers once again, as He always does.

'I was sent back to hospital, but after three days I got fed up with that and went back to the battalion, only to find myself a captain, and I had many more battles before we were eventually relieved by other troops. Now we are back once more at Base, waiting to know what our next job will be. I am going on leave next week and I will drop you another line then. Thank you so much for your cable and also letters which I received yesterday, giving me Xmas Greetings, etc.

'I hope you are still keeping well and happy. God bless you both! My love to everyone.

'Your loving son,

'Phil.'

*

The name of the wounded officer was Lieutenant Peter Beames of the King's Dragoon Guards. Before the war he had been a keen climber. He had joined the Mountain Rangers Club at the age of fifteen, in 1928, and from that time he had devoted much of his spare time to climbing, not only in the British Isles but also in Switzerland and Greece. He was also a poet, and his poems included some written in far-off places, including Tobruk. Unfortunately, despite Pip Gardner's valiant efforts to save him, he subsequently died of his wounds. After the war his father, Lieutenant-Colonel Hewitt Beames, sent a copy of a booklet of Peter Beames's poems to Pip, with the inscription: 'To Captain Philip Gardner, vc, mc, from Hewitt Beames, in everlasting gratitude.' This naturally moved Pip greatly, and made him realise once again how kind Fate had been to him in comparison with so many of his less fortunate colleagues in the desert. He also felt that all honour was due to his worthy crew, of whom Sergeant McTier received a ricochet on the face, as well as a DCM for taking charge of the tank while Pip was endeavouring to recover the armoured car and Lieutenant Peter Beames.

As Pip mentions in his letter to his parents he was taken to 'hospital' in Tobruk to have his wounds attended to. In fact it was little more than a field-dressing station in a rather damp and dark underground room, which served as a hospital in the outskirts of what was left of the town of Tobruk.

After three days in these improvised surroundings, Pip decided that it was time for him to rejoin his unit. With another officer he commandeered a bizarre captured German car. It had huge wheels, which were higher than the sides of the car, and in this they made their way to the battle area. Driving this strange machine proved quite an experience for Pip. Heavy rain during the last two days had made the surface of the desert very slippery in places and time and again the unmanageable vehicle would suddenly turn through a hundred and eighty degrees in the most disconcerting fashion. However, Pip was used to all sorts of vehicles, from MGs to Matildas, and this cantankerous conveyance served its purpose by delivering the two officers back to the fighting.

On reporting back to his squadron, Pip was informed that he had been promoted to Captain and this called for a celebration – the only liquor available being a small tot of rum. When he met Lieutenant-Colonel Walter O'Carroll, he received a very warm welcome back and further congratulations. The welcome and congratulations were punctuated by shell-bursts and other missiles. Pip soon realised that he had arrived back into the thick of things and marvelled at his Colonel's coolness under fire. Where many might have taken evasive action by falling flat on their faces, the most that O'Carroll seemed prepared to do was to lower his head and stoop slightly, as if merely to reduce the target area of his tall body by a few vital inches. By his bearing he certainly set a brave and imperturbable example which Pip, for one, felt bound to follow. In fact he would have been prepared to follow him to the gates of Hell, if ordered to do so. His bearing was reflected throughout the whole of the 4th Royal Tanks in the fighting that still lay ahead of them in the immediate future.

The fighting to which Pip had returned took place on Ed Duda ridge which had been captured in his absence. Of course at this stage there was no certainty of a VC to come, as a reward for his conspicuous gallantry. All he knew was that Major Bertie Roberts, who had sent Pip out to rescue the people in the armoured cars, was ordered by Brigadier Willison and Lieutenant-Colonel O'Carroll to write out a citation for one. Time alone would tell.

The fighting of the next few days would also tell whether the impending award, whatever it might be, would also be posthumous!

CHAPTER SEVEN

Cyrenaica Regained

Though Pip Gardner had missed the advance from 'Tiger' to Ed Duda, which had included the storming of another strong-point, 'Wolf', en route, he had arrived back with the 4th Royal Tanks in time to take part in some fierce and fluctuating fighting that ensued. Ed Duda was seven miles from the Tobruk perimeter. It was a sausage-shaped ridge, three miles long and a quarter of a mile broad, that had to be retained at all costs. Its capture on 26th November meant that the break-out troops had created an elongated bulge into the enemy position. At no point was the bulge a wide one and it was obviously vulnerable on the flanks. The continuous occupation of Ed Duda was based on the arrival of the Eighth Army, to meet whose advance the sortie had been timed.

The action to capture Ed Duda had been a model in its execution. A phalanx of tanks had led the way, followed by the King's Dragoon Guards in their armoured cars and the Northumberland Fusiliers with their machine-guns in small trucks. The enemy, Germans and Italians alike, scattered, abandoning their battery positions. As soon as the high ground had been taken, the lorried infantry of the Essex Regiment arrived to dig in and hold the position. The big snag was that there was no sign of the arrival of the relieving troops of the Eighth Army, despite the fact that the leading elements were known to be as near as four miles away.

The battle joined round Sidi Rezegh had almost from the start proved very confusing, with the area changing hands at least three times. Furthermore, Rommel had made one of his typical bursts through the forces that were trying to surround and destroy his armour at close range. He had thrust among the rear echelons of his opponents and pushed in most alarming manner towards the Egyptian frontier.

This swift and characteristic counter-blow, combined with the recapture of Sidi Rezegh by Rommel's forces, had caused great confusion in high places. It seemed to General Cunningham that a withdrawal to prepared defences back at Mersa Matruh might be necessary in order to re-group. General Auchinleck as Commander-in-Chief would have none of this and he acted swiftly. On 26th November, eight days after Operation Crusader had started, he replaced General Cunningham by General Neil Ritchie. The latter shared Auchinleck's opinion that Rommel had made a desperate thrust which, this time, he would not be able to support with adequate supplies, and that the numbers of serviceable tanks at his disposal, despite a very efficient recovery service, must be running low.

As 30 Corps re-grouped to the south of Sidi Rezegh, 13 Corps pressed on in the north towards Tobruk. On 27th November General Freyberg's New Zealanders managed with difficulty and courage to link up with the Tobruk forces at Ed Duda, as planned. But soon the corridor which was being grimly held on Ed Duda became the scene of repeated German attacks, as the panzers were forced back from the frontier to which they had rushed and were now fighting their way back westwards.

The 4th Royal Tanks were continually required to defend the ridge by day and at night, under Lieutenant-Colonel O'Carroll's vigorous direction. At dusk on 29th November panzers reached part of the Ed Duda ridge but were driven off it by a night counter-attack headed by Major Prichard's squadron of the 4th Royal Tanks, which put the enemy to flight and enabled a battalion of Australian infantry to clear the ridge of the enemy. However, on 30th November the battle took a bad turn for the defenders of Ed Duda. Rommel delivered a concentrated blow against the New Zealanders and drove them back. Thus the Tobruk garrison was again cut off from the relieving troops of the Eighth Army.

But for O'Carroll, who was in charge of the whole situation of the break-out troops, there was no question of withdrawing as the relieving forces receded into the distance, despite the fact that he and his troops, with the addition of two of the leading New Zealand battalions, had been cut off.

On 2nd December the Ed Duda position looked very precarious, with the Essex battalion being severely mauled by the attacking Germans. The 3rd December brought renewed attacks, but still Ed Duda was held. Finally, on 4th December the Germans made their last bid to capture

Riding high in the Desert, 1941. Pip Gardner and friends.

(*Above*) General Auchinleck pinning the Victoria Cross ribbon on Captain Philip J. Gardner, 4th Royal Tanks. Brigadier A. C. Willison is on the left.

(*Left*) Pip Gardner, V.C., striding out with his 'manager' Bon Cole (left) in Jerusalem, 1942.

the ridge, but they suffered tank losses that by then they could ill afford. To the great relief of the defenders, and of the whole of the Eighth Army, on 5th December there were signs that the Axis forces were packing up and moving westwards – and so it proved. The retreat across Cyrenaica was about to start.

A wartime correspondent for the *Daily Telegraph*, Richard Capell, reporting at the time as soon as the battle was over, asked a senior officer friend of his who he thought were the principal heroes of the whole operation. His answer was: 'The Tobrukkers who took and held Ed Duda.' In all, the 4th Royal Tanks had fought twelve distinct tank battles since the break-out, with fifty per cent casualties suffered. Pip Gardner was naturally proud to have been among these Tobrukkers who had stubbornly held out, broken out and held out again.

In what was from the start a very confused overall battle, Pip was personally involved in a particular piece of confusion. Part of Ed Duda had at one stage been captured and occupied by the enemy, but had later been cleared by troops of the Essex Regiment, with the aid of the tanks. Pip's task then became to keep the area under observation from his tank. Two seemingly undamaged German lorries had remained on the high ground at one end of the ridge, left behind when the enemy withdrew in haste. At dusk Pip discerned a dim figure walking towards one of the lorries. Thinking that it must be a German returning to collect his lorry, and feeling disinclined to let him have it, Pip let him have a burst of machine-gun fire instead. The dim figure made off in a hurry, without his lorry.

Only several days later, when Pip was visiting a wounded friend back in Tobruk hospital, did he unravel the mystery of the man at the German lorries. In the next bed to his friend was an officer of the Essex Regiment with a wounded arm. The latter greeted Pip rather half-heartedly, adding: 'I'm not really speaking to the Tanks.' He went on to explain that he had been fired upon at long range by one of his own tanks while examining some enemy vehicles on Ed Duda ridge. He was by no means pleased! Pip had the uneasy feeling that this must be the figure he had fired upon in the semi-darkness a few days previously. He felt bad about it – but was somewhat relieved when the wounded officer added, more cheerfully, that he was going to be sent down to South Africa to recuperate.

By 8th December Sidi Rezegh had been once again recaptured, and with it a New Zealand divisional dressing station which had been over-run when the enemy had rushed the position a fortnight earlier. Seven hundred wounded New Zealanders were still there. The siege of Tobruk was finally and completely raised on 9th December, when patrols operating out of the perimeter to the south-west joined up with South African and Indian troops advancing westwards at El Adem, where the important airfield was captured and soon put to good use.

By 11th December Rommel's forces were in retreat across Cyrenaica, a situation that the new Eighth Army commander, General Ritchie, was determined to exploit to the full by using his mobile forces, coupled with full air force co-operation. It was vital to regain Cyrenaica, particularly in order to relieve the pressure on Malta by denying the airfields to the German and Italian air forces. In addition, with Cyrenaica cleared, there could be no more supplying reinforcements to the Axis forces by German Junkers and Italian Savoias at convenient airfields such as Derna, or by sea at Benghazi. Future supplies would have to revert to their original port of Tripoli, with Allied submarines out of Malta able to take a constant toll of Axis shipping on the longer run.

To hasten Rommel's departure, now that he was on the move, and to harass his protective rear-guards, General Auchinleck had created some special desert Commandos, known as 'Jock columns'. They were so named after their leader, Brigadier J. C. ('Jock') Campbell, whose sustained aggression and gallantry had reached a peak in the fighting at Sidi Rezegh on 21st and 22nd November and had stemmed the tide at a crucial time. It had also earned him a VC. Jock columns were designed to counter Rommel's dashing and successful tactics of using small cells of tanks to circulate in the desert, like raiding-ships at sea. They varied in size and composition, but a typical Jock column would consist of a few tanks, several armoured cars, a few powerful field guns, some batteries of anti-tank and anti-aircraft guns, plus a detachment of lorried infantry to attack troublesome gun-positions by night or to round up prisoners by day. Jock columns were thus designed to be fast moving, with plenty of fire-power. All the vehicles were self-contained, with enough rations, water and petrol to last for seven days. These Jock columns contained a large number of South Africans – which Auchinleck considered appropriate, since the name 'Commando' was derived from the Boer Commandos in the South African War.

Gazala was taken on 17th December by the New Zealanders, who

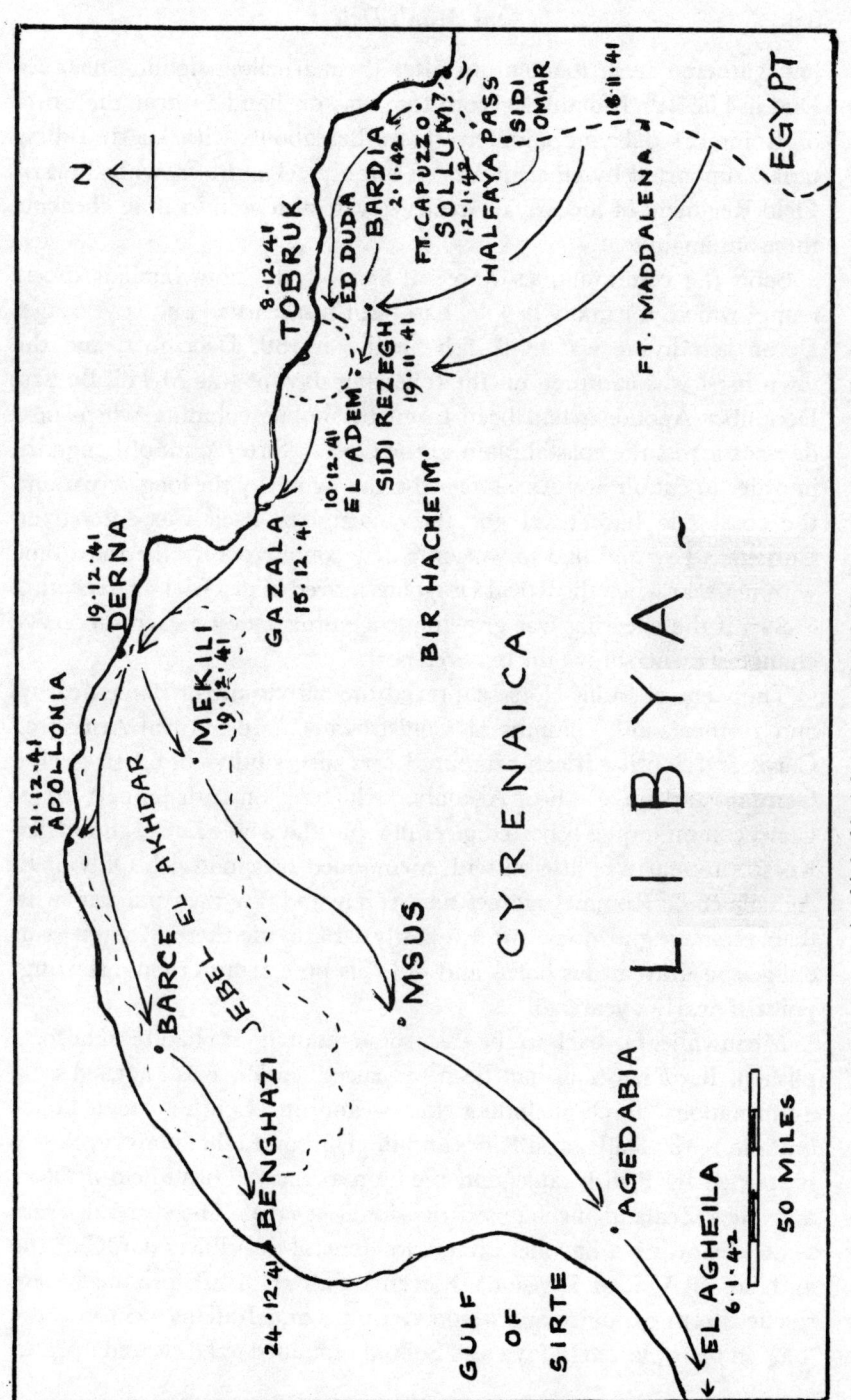

Auchinleck's Advance to El Agheila, 1941/42

had gathered fresh momentum after their gruelling fighting near Ed Duda. The 4th Indian Division, too, was on hand to bear the brunt of Rommel's delaying counter-attacks hereabouts with his dwindling tanks, supported by efficient lorried infantry. The Buffs, with the 21st Field Regiment of the Royal Artillery, were also prominent in checking these onslaughts.

Soon the communiqués were rattling off the now familiar desert names which, for many people, had been first learned only a year ago. Derna aerodrome was in British hands on 18th December, and the town itself was captured on the following day, as was Mekili. By 21st December Apollonia had been taken by mobile columns, which next day cut across the coastal plain to the Gulf of Sirte, south of Benghazi, in order to cut off any Axis forces that had gone by the long way round the coast and hadn't yet got away. Benghazi itself was entered on Christmas Eve and had to welcome new conquerors for the third time within a year when the Royal Dragoons moved in to a friendly reception – even if the cheering was growing less enthusiastic on each successive change of ownership of the battered port.

The Central India Horse captured the aerodrome of Barce nearby, and further south columns of Coldstream Guards, Royal Armoured Corps and South African armoured cars successfully cut off straggling Germans and Italians near Agedabia, which fell on 12th January 1942. Cairo communiqués reported gleefully that the whole line of the Afrika Korps's retreat was littered with abandoned war matériel. Only at El Agheila could Rommel's forces turn at bay and face their pursuers with their remaining armour. After a costly tank battle there, Rommel was obliged to draw in his horns and bide his time at his original starting-point of nearly a year ago.

Meanwhile, far back to the east, some mopping up had been accomplished. Bardia, which had been by-passed earlier, was attacked by a multi-national force, including the 1st and 2nd South African Police battalions, the Kaffrarian Rifles and the Durban Light Infantry, closely supported by British tanks and medium artillery, Polish field artillery and New Zealand mechanised divisional cavalry. The surrender was made, following a bayonet attack, to General de Villiers (GOC of the 2nd South African Division). Eleven hundred British prisoners were rescued from captivity and 7,000 Germans and Italians went into the 'bag' in their place. Halfaya and Sollum remained to be cleared up, and after shelling from the Royal Navy, accompanied by bombing by the RAF and Free French planes, Sollum fell on 12th January. This followed an attack by the 2nd South African Division, with the Transvaal Scottish figuring prominently. Five days later, on 17th January, the Axis troops at Halfaya finally surrendered, yielding 5,500 prisoners, including two Italian generals to balance the trade in 'top brass' that this desert warfare seemed to generate.

Thus with Cyrenaica cleared of the enemy, Operation Crusader, which had started in such confusion and fierce fighting at places such as Sidi Omar and Sidi Rezegh, had developed into a full-scale retreat across the desert, with both sides racing hell for leather for the bottleneck at El Agheila. However, Rommel might be out of Cyrenaica and licking his wounds, but he wasn't yet by any means out of Africa, as he was soon to demonstrate.

Meanwhile General Auchinleck could justifiably claim that Rommel had suffered his first-ever defeat in battle, and that he himself had been the first British general to win a victory over a German counterpart.

*

The 4th Royal Tanks had been in the thick of the fray from their break-out on 21st November to the conclusion of the fierce fighting on Ed Duda on 8th December. After their exhausting exertions they could hardly be expected to join in the westward dash in pursuit of Rommel, tempting though the prospect must have seemed. The chase was entrusted to fresher and more mobile units, spearheaded by fast cavalry regiments.

The survivors of the 4th Royal Tanks were only allowed to advance towards Gazala before being recalled and ordered to hand over their remaining battle-worthy tanks, some of which had been retrieved by the busy recovery units several times over. The crews were told to get themselves back to rail-head about a hundred miles back, near Mersa Matruh.

In order to reach rail-head, the officers and men of the 4th Royal Tanks commandeered as many lorries and other captured vehicles as they could procure and set off. On arrival at rail-head they found an assortment of battle-weary troops from other regiments waiting for transport to take them back to Alexandria. A friend among the Railway

Transport Officers organised the onward journey by rail for Pip and the 4th Royal Tanks survivors aboard cattle-trucks in which they jogged along for the next two days. In the absence of scenery to look at, apart from unlimited sand, most of the time was spent in much-needed sleep. They reached Alexandria on Christmas Eve.

On arrival they were driven to a rest camp just outside Alexandria where they first wallowed in the unaccustomed luxury of hot showers, before receiving new clothes to replace those that they had worn in Tobruk and on Ed Duda. Then came the reintroduction to beer in the canteens and good food in the messes. There were also cinemas with Betty Grable and Alice Faye to help them unwind. It was a far cry from the desert rat existence that they had been leading, and all ranks were glad to have survived to savour this civilised living after the confinement and squalor of Tobruk. Their enforced economy during their months in the desert now meant that they had accumulated the necessary cash to be able to enjoy the leave that soon followed. Pip spent his seven-days' leave in Alexandria, where he revisited old haunts and ran into a surprisingly large number of friends and acquaintances from various phases of his pre-desert existence.

On his return to Amiriya, he was transferred to the 32nd Army Tank Brigade staff as a liaison officer, under Brigadier Willison, who treated Pip like an aide-de-camp. Pip thus found himself on a few occasions being driven to the races in Alexandria with the Brigadier in his staff-car. These outings always included dining in style at the Turf Club – a procedure to which Pip was by no mean averse. In Cairo and Alexandria, those just back from the 'blue' (as the front was called – wherever it might happen to be!) tended to grab the good life where and when they could find it – in the certain knowledge that they would soon have to return to the 'blue'. Some of them said that the 'Gabardine Swine', as the permanent desk-wallahs clad in service-dress were generally called by those who actually did the fighting, knew no other life. Pip certainly believed in grabbing his relaxation while he could.

In early February 1942 the 32nd Army Tank Brigade, including the 4th Royal Tanks, moved to Palestine by rail. While waiting at the station in Alexandria for the train to arrive and disgorge its passengers who had just returned from Palestine, Pip was delighted to see Gordon Norris who had been a groomsman at his wedding. There was just time for a quick chat before Pip had to board the train in the opposite direction.

On arrival in Palestine, they were stationed under canvas at Hadera, on the coast between Tel Aviv and Haifa, and near Caesarea. Just as they had during Wavell's push the previous year, they listened to the communiqués for news of Auchinleck's progress in Cyrenaica, with General Ritchie commanding the Eighth Army's westward thrusts. They had been in many ways sorry to miss taking part in the pursuit across Cyrenaica, but they knew that they were being prepared for further battles against Rommel's panzers, which, though harassed and temporarily depleted, were now holding their position at the El Agheila bottle-neck. Pip knew that his turn for further action would come, as soon as his brigade had been reinforced and re-equipped with new tanks.

It was shortly after their arrival in Palestine that one evening they were listening to the radio when, out of the blue, the announcer said that the Victoria Cross had been awarded to Captain Philip J. Gardner for an act of bravery outside Tobruk on 23rd November 1941. This sudden announcement came as a great surprise to everyone, despite the knowledge that Pip had been put in for the award. Only the day before there had been the announcement of Brigadier Jock Campbell's VC, and now Pip felt that he was indeed in honourable company. Those round Pip at the time all went mad with jubilation over his award. It was an honour for them all to help celebrate. Brigadier Willison, who was encamped nearby, called on Pip, and this was the start of a party that lasted into the early hours.

Next day Pip was allowed to set off by truck to Jerusalem, with his friend Bon Cole, to try to find a medal ribbon. After trying all the likely places, they had to settle for a ribbon dyed in ink to approximate to the genuine maroon colour of the VC. The fact that the colour was only an approximation didn't make much difference, as Bon Cole appointed himself Pip's manager and in every hotel they entered, including the famous King David Hotel, he would announce to all and sundry that Pip was a VC. This invariably resulted in an invitation to drinks all round – some of which Pip or Bon paid for – before they lurched their way back to camp.

When Pip woke up he was still in a daze. The following letter of congratulation from General Auchinleck arrived, to dispel all doubts as to whether it was all a dream ! The General wrote :

GHQ. MEF.
10th Feb. 42.

'My dear Gardner

'I am delighted to be able to tell you that I have just received a cable from the War Office informing me that His Majesty the King has conferred on you the Victoria Cross for most conspicuous bravery and outstanding devotion to duty in the Western Desert on 23rd November 1941.

'The award will be announced in the London Gazette to-day.

'I can assure you that it gives me the greatest personal satisfaction, and I send you my warmest congratulations on receiving so signal an honour.

       'Yours sincerely,

            'C. J. Auchinleck.

'Captain P. J. Gardner, M.C.,
'4 Royal Tanks.'

A letter written by Pip to his parents on 14th February 1942, when the celebrations had subsided, throws interesting light on his state of euphoria at the time. He wrote :

'I expect that by this time you have read of the great honour conferred on me by the award of the VC. It really is marvellous and I can hardly believe it is true.

'I hadn't heard anything about it when suddenly one night over the radio they announced it and even then for a second or so we couldn't believe our ears, and then of course everyone went mad.

'The Brigadier came in, and the Regimental Sergeant-Major, and then ensued the most terrific celebration, which went on until 3 or 4 o'clock in the morning. During the proceedings a despatch-rider arrived hot-foot with a message from the King, and of course he was dragged into the Mess for a drink – and so it went on.

'The next night I had a special party in the Sergeants' Mess and they made a great fuss of me, as you can imagine, and so it goes on day after day. I can't think it is ever going to stop.

'I am now the only member of the Tanks to win the VC and be alive, as only five others have been awarded to the Tanks in the last war, and they were all posthumous awards.

'I do thank God for another great delivery and honour; he really is

GHQ. MEF.

10 Feb. 42.

My dear Gardner

      I am delighted to be able to tell you that I have just received a cable from the War Office informing me that His Majesty the King has conferred on you the Victoria Cross for most conspicuous bravery and outstanding devotion to duty in the Western Desert on 23rd November 1941.

      The award will be announced in the London Gazette today.

      I can assure you that it gives me the greatest personal satisfaction, and I send you my warmest congratulations on the receiving of so signal an honour.

Yours sincerely

Auchinleck

Captain P.J. Gardner, M.C.,
4 Royal Tanks.

Letter from General Auchinleck

good to me, isn't he? I think it must be because I have such good parents and such a good little wife, that he does all this for me.

'I have had masses of telegrams from the Regiment and various people in Egypt, etc., and to-day I had a special letter from General Auchinleck himself; so I am doing very well.

'I received the cigs from Mr Chalmers last week, and also Uncle Harold, and of course I have written to both of them.

'Well, God bless you both and look after yourselves.

'Your loving son,

'Phil.'

While he was in Palestine Pip had the good fortune to be sent on a reconnaissance trip to Syria and Lebanon. In 1941 British forces in the Middle East under General Wavell had conducted a successful and at times bloody campaign, with the aid of Australian and Free French troops. The whole force was under the command of General Sir Henry Maitland Wilson, who had conducted Wavell's push to El Agheila with such skill and dash. The object of the Syrian campaign had been to rid Syria of German agents who had infiltrated the Vichy-controlled state, which was already allowing German and Italian planes to use air bases at Damascus and elsewhere, thus endangering British-controlled Cyprus as well as the area of the Suez Canal.

Now in 1942, with the Germans thrusting their way in the southern-most sector of the Russian front, there loomed the danger that they might strike further south, through hitherto neutral Turkey or Persia and thence down into Syria and Lebanon, with the Suez Canal as their ultimate goal – the aim being to link up with Rommel's forces which were still hoping to reach Suez from the west, provided that enough reinforcements could be spared from the Russian front, and provided that enough of them were allowed by British submarines to reach North Africa. Though Syria and Palestine were secure for the time being, it remained possible that they might have to be defended against a sudden Axis advance from the north. As a precaution against this happening, certain contingency plans had to be laid and coastal and inland reconnaissance had to be carried out. Hence Pip's reconnaissance assignment in February and March, 1942.

For Pip the assignment meant a chance to see even more of the Middle East than he had seen already. He had never been averse to travel and seeing as much of the world as he could – especially at the Army's expense! His journey took him through Syria, where he visited many ancient fortifications and castles, which were still in a remarkably good state of preservation, dating from the days of Richard Lionheart and the Crusades. He also visited the Great Temple of Baalbek (AD 131–161). His mission also took him via the Cedars of Lebanon as far north as Beirut, which in those days was a beautiful and cosmopolitan city.

While in Beirut, Pip ran into Captain John Lipscombe, his one-time regimental Medical Officer who had kept him supplied on occasions in Tobruk with brandy and eggnog from his medical comforts bag. John Lipscombe was now in charge of brothel inspection in Beirut and one day he invited Pip to accompany him on his rounds. Pip, ever ready to broaden his outlook, cheerfully accepted the invitation – but took care to remain strictly an observer, merely enjoying the champagne provided by 'Madame'.

His free tour took in such places as Tripoli in Lebanon, Homs and Damascus in Syria, and Haifa, Tel Aviv, Lake Galilee and Capernaum on his wanderings through Palestine. When he and his companions had been cooped-up inside Tobruk, he had never dreamed of seeing so much of the Middle East. In fact there had been many moments when he hadn't expected to see any of it!

By mid-April, it was time to return to Egypt in order to take over new tanks at the depot at Amiriya. But before leaving Palestine there was a full parade of the 4th Royal Tanks at which Pip was decorated with the correct ribbon of the VC by General Auchinleck in person. This was naturally a great occasion for Pip, to receive the honour personally from a General who was held in such high regard by his troops. Furthermore, it reminded Pip how fortunate he was to be alive to receive his medal – in sharp contrast to all previous Tanks winners of the VC hitherto. All of them had been honoured posthumously, whereas Pip, who was the first VC in the Tanks in World War 2, was actually alive to receive his medal.

This parade was a ceremony that marked the peak of Pip's fortunes in the desert. More fighting was in prospect, and peaks have a tendency to be followed by troughs – as Pip Gardner was shortly to discover.

CHAPTER EIGHT

The Pendulum Swings

Viewed in retrospect, 1942 proved to be the year of decision in World War 2, but before the two great reverses suffered by the Axis powers at Stalingrad and El Alamein took place, thereby signalling the beginning of the decline in the fortunes of Hitler's Germany and Mussolini's Italy, some devastating defeats had first to be sustained by Britain and her allies. There were hectic struggles on all fronts, and before things could get better they were destined to get very much worse.

In the Far East, following Japan's entry into the war on 7th December 1941, shattering news from Hong Kong at the start of 1942 was soon followed by the fall of Singapore in early February, after a series of almost unthinkable naval losses in the South China Sea. As 80,000 British and Commonwealth prisoners were surrendered wholesale to the incredulous and contemptuous Japanese troops, who regarded all prisoners, whatever the circumstances of their capture, as having *ipso facto* forfeited all rights to humane treatment, the victorious Japanese were left free to swarm all over south-east Asia and the Pacific, and to force their way menacingly through Burma and threaten India. Though the sudden attack by Japanese planes on the American fleet in Pearl Harbor brought the might of the United States right into the war alongside the Allies, thereby sealing the ultimate fate of the Axis powers, including their new ally Japan, at the start of 1942 America was hard put to it to stem the tide of Jap expansion across the Pacific. It was not until June 1942 that the US Navy managed to register a very hard-won victory at the Battle of Midway Island.

Likewise in Russia, by the end of 1941 the Red Army had managed to halt the German advance at Leningrad and only just short of Moscow in the northern and central sectors, thanks largely to the harshness of the wintry conditions that the inadequately clothed German troops had to endure. But the German advance in the southern sector was soon able to gather fresh momentum as the weather relented. In their drive towards the oilfields of the Caucasus, the Germans pushed south-eastwards as far as the industrial city of Stalingrad on the Volga. As the relentless German army swept through the Ukraine and the Crimea, there was little to suggest during most of 1942 that Stalingrad was to prove the easternmost limit of Hitler's over-ambitious advance. In fact there was a very real danger that he might thrust down between the Black and the Caspian Seas towards the Middle East, aiming at linking with his Afrika Korps in the region of the Suez Canal.

Nearer to home, Britain had started the year with the humiliating failure to check a remarkable piece of effrontery on the part of the enemy in bringing off a successful dash from Brest along the English Channel on 12th February 1942 by their battleships, the *Scharnhorst* and the *Gneisenau*, accompanied by the heavy cruiser *Prinz Eugen*, to reach the safety of Wilhelmshaven. Further trouble at sea of an even more serious nature was to ensue, when the ill-fated convoy of ships known as the PQ17 was decimated on its journey in almost continual daylight in early July to Murmansk, with the loss of many lives among the crews of the merchant ships ferrying vital vehicles and equipment to Britain's and America's Russian allies. The submarine warfare, too, was at its height and very much in the balance, particularly in the Atlantic.

These troubles at sea were soon to be followed by another fiasco across the English Channel. On 19th August 1942 the costly raid on Dieppe was carried out, including the unsuccessful landing of tanks, most of which got no further than the beach. The Canadians bore the brunt of the battle in the central attack, to the tune of 2,753 casualties out of the 4,963 men who originally set out by sea from Southampton. Despite subsequent claims that the experience gained at such high cost at Dieppe contributed nearly two years later to the success of the D-Day landings in Normandy in June 1944, the one bright spot in the whole dismal venture was the intelligent and successful use of Commando troops to attack and silence the enemy gun batteries on the flanks – notably by Colonel The Lord Lovat and Major Derek Mills-Roberts (as they then were) with 4 Commando on the right or western flank.

Malta, too, was in a parlous state, with enemy aircraft based in Italy and Sicily taking heavy toll of the supply convoys and their escorts sent to relieve and sustain the vital but beleaguered island, whence the submarines of Number 10 Flotilla managed to function with continued success, though with heavy losses among their much-decorated captains and crews.

Though by the end of 1942 in these various theatres of war the tide was destined to turn, and light was to appear at the end of a long tunnel, some grim struggles lay ahead – not least in the Western Desert, where the pendulum of fortune was poised to swing once again in Rommel's favour.

*

While Pip Gardner had been away resting and re-equipping in Palestine and Syria, after completing almost a year's active service in the desert, the news from the Western Desert, which had been so heartening at the beginning of January 1942, began to sound ominous by the end of the month. Rommel, far from being annihilated or driven out of Libya, was on the attack once more. This time he surprised even his own high command as well as his Italian allies, as he struck eastwards again across Cyrenaica with his 15th and 21st Panzer divisions, supported by his mobile 90th Light Division. This secrecy from his own high command meant that no advance warning was gained by the Eighth Army from Ultra intelligence interceptions, and Rommel's swift move from his defensive position caught everyone by surprise.

As in the previous year when Wavell's push had reached El Agheila, so now the Eighth Army supply line was stretched almost to breaking-point. Fuel, food and water were soon in short supply, because almost all replenishments had to be brought by truck from rail-head, which still only reached as far as Sollum, near the Egyptian frontier. The capture of Benghazi had, in the event, done little to alleviate the situation because it was within range of German planes operating from Sicily, and magnetic mines were dropped in the approaches to the harbour. Furthermore Axis submarines were lurking outside the port for Allied supply ships venturing to use the much-needed but badly-battered landing facilities. Nor could air-supply take place, because winter rains had precluded the rapid establishment of advance landing-grounds by turning much of the desert into a morass of well-nigh impassable mud. All in all, despite their recent spectacular advances and territorial gains in Cyrenaica, there had followed a very trying period for the forward elements of the Eighth Army.

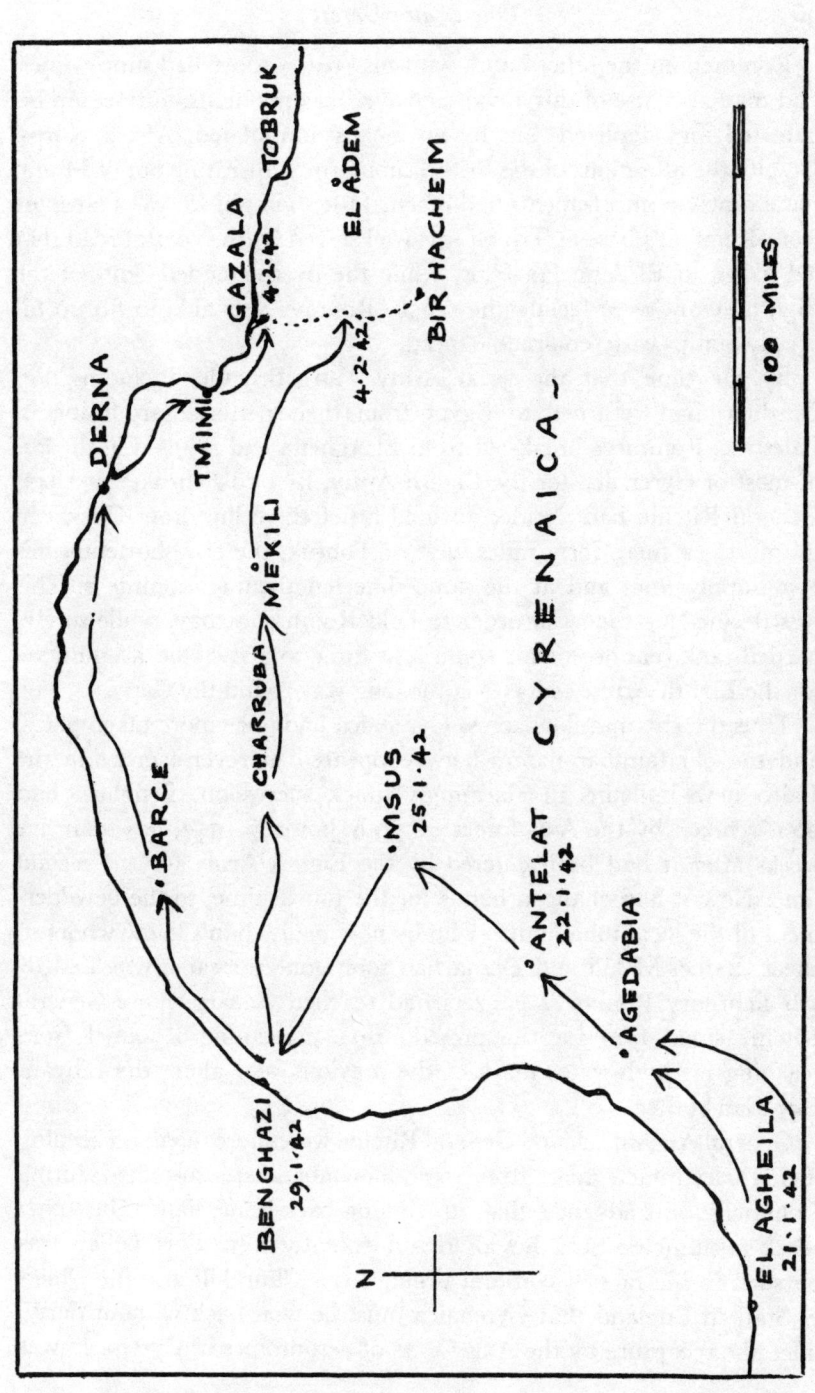

TOBRUK
GAZALA
4·2·42
EL ÅDEM
BIR HACHEIM
4·2·42
DERNA
TMIMI
MÉKILI
CHARRUBA
CYRENAICA
BARCE
MSUS
25·1·42
ANTELAT
22·1·42
BENGHAZI
29·1·42
AGEDABIA
EL AGHEILA
21·1·42
N

100 MILES

Rommel's Counter-thrust to Gazala, 1942

Rommel, on the other hand, with his greatly shortened supply lines, had made full use of this advantage over his opponents, to re-equip his defeated and depleted, but by no means annihilated, Afrika Korps. Despite the attentions of the British submarines operating out of Malta, some timely reinforcements had reached the shores of Libya. Transport from Rommel's base at Tripoli was well served by the coastal road that led along to El Agheila. Thus, while the over-extended units of the Eighth Army were feeling the pinch, Rommel was able to fill up his supply dumps with remarkable speed.

By the time that the 32nd Army Tank Brigade, including Pip Gardner, had returned to Egypt from their period of re-fitting in Palestine, Rommel's break-out from El Agheila had resulted in the loss of most of Cyrenaica for the Eighth Army. By mid-February of 1942, General Ritchie had decided to hold a defensive line from Gazala in the north, a mere forty miles west of Tobruk, thereby shortening his own supply lines and at the same time lengthening Rommel's. This was deemed necessary in order to hold Rommel at bay, while sorely-needed tank reinforcements could have time to arrive and accumulate for the Eighth Army – albeit via the long way round the Cape.

Thus the ebb and flow across Cyrenaica had once more taken place, and the old familiar names had reappeared in reverse order in the Cairo news-bulletins in alarmingly quick succession. Benghazi had been retaken by the Axis forces on 29th January 1942, less than five weeks after it had been entered by the Eighth Army for the second time. Now it had changed hands for the fourth time, to the bewilderment of the local inhabitants, who by now really didn't know whom to cheer. Barce, Mekili and Derna had soon gone the same way and by 4th February Rommel's panzers had reached Gazala where General Ritchie stood firm for the present, thus preventing Rommel from reaching his high-water mark of the previous year along the Libyan-Egyptian border.

General Auchinleck and General Ritchie were more intent on keeping their forces intact, apart from some inevitable losses sustained during Rommel's swift advance, than in winning back immediately the some-what meaningless stretches of desert recently lost. This policy was pursued in the face of constant urging from Churchill and the Chiefs of Staff in England that Cyrenaica must be won back without delay, since the recapture by the Axis forces of aerodromes in Cyrenaica was once again proving a serious threat to the continued survival and strategic use of Malta. Auchinleck was aiming at building up his forces with a view to moving over to the attack by the beginning of June at the earliest – and possibly not until the first of August. He regarded it as being of paramount importance to build up his strength until he felt confident that there was a good chance of being able to sustain his momentum, and not finding himself once more obliged to withdraw and give up his hard-won gains.

In this build-up process he hadn't been helped by the diversion of 18th Division to Singapore, just in time to go into the Jap 'bag', thus wasting 20,000 men as well as a large quantity of equipment. Added to this had been the transfer of the 9th Australian Division to the Pacific, following their heroic defence of Tobruk. But replacements were on their way – though there was a big discrepancy between Churchill's optimistic assessment of their availability for action in the desert and Auchinleck's more realistic reckoning of their readiness for battle. Being on the spot he realised that acclimatisation and training were essential for newly-arrived reinforcements, far better than statisticians in Britain, who tended to tot up the number of tanks and guns available and to demand immediate action on the strength of their calculations.

The Gazala line, despite its name, was by no means continuous. It consisted, rather, of a series of heavily defended boxes protected by minefields stretching from Gazala near the coast and thence south-wards for a distance of thirty-five miles down to the fort of Bir Hacheim in the open desert in the south. The boxes or forts were surrounded by barbed-wire and were from one to two miles square. They were provided with enough food, water and ammunition to withstand a siege. There were narrow lanes through the minefields to provide access for supplies and reinforcements, and also to permit the coming and going of tanks and armoured cars. The guns in these boxes faced outwards in all directions, ready to engage the enemy tanks, should they choose to infiltrate past or in between them over the unoccupied desert.

The northernmost box was at Gazala, where General Dan Pienaar and his 1st South African Division were in occupation. A few miles to the south were two boxes held by the 50th (Tyne and Tees) Division, with the Guards Motorised Brigade holding the patch of previously anonymous desert to the rear, which was now appropriately known as 'Knightsbridge'. Furthest to the south were the Free French under

General Koenig, whose Teutonic-sounding name was explained by the fact of his Alsatian birth. Then, further to the rear at El Adem, south of Tobruk, there was a box held by Indian troops. Tobruk itself with its harbour served as a large base box and was defended by the garrison-commander Major-General Klopper's 2nd South African Division, with units of the supply lines, as well as a large quantity of stores. Free to be deployed as and where required were three tank brigades at General Ritchie's disposal. In control of all this, General Ritchie had his Eighth Army headquarters at Gambut, alongside Air Vice-Marshal Coningham, chief of the air arm, whose close co-operation was vital.

As the two armies faced each other the tension mounted. In the build-up of matériel Rommel had the advantage in that equipment could reach him more quickly from the factories than Ritchie's round-the-Cape supplies could possibly arrive – though one vital convoy of tanks had been rushed through the Mediterranean to help him. To offset Rommel's advantage, however, was the welcome fact that the formidable Grant tanks were arriving from America, which had, as the result of the Japanese assault on Pearl Harbour, changed from being a friendly neutral to helping as an active ally. The Grant tanks were a great improvement on any previous makes available in the desert, such as Valentines, Matildas or Honeys, all of which were under-gunned and out-ranged. The Grants had a 75-mm gun in addition to a 37-mm. Their emergence was to cause considerable consternation among Rommel's hitherto all-powerful panzers. Likewise in the air, Coningham's Beaufighters, Blenheims and Wellingtons were now being supplemented by the more effective Spitfires and Hurribombers to offset the numerical superiority of the Axis planes.

With the stage thus set, both sides were poised to attack – Rommel in the knowledge that it would be unwise of him to delay until the enemy had built up stronger forces, and Auchinleck under the constant demands that he was receiving from Churchill for immediate action and success. This time it was Rommel who struck first.

CHAPTER NINE

Fateful Decision

During the last week of April 1942, the personnel of the 32nd Army Tank Brigade left Palestine by train and returned to base camp at Amiriya, just outside Alexandria, to collect their tanks. The replacement for the 4th Royal Tanks vehicles were not to be the formidable new American Grants, nor the British Matildas with which they were familiar, but the other lighter and slightly smaller British infantry support tank, the Valentine, which was highly rated for its reliability. Both the Matilda and the Valentine had proved the scourge of the Italians in the early desert fighting, thanks to their solid armour and their then adequate two-pounder guns. But since the arrival of Rommel's Afrika Korps, both had been found to be less effective, especially against the deadly 88-mm anti-tank gun, which the Germans used to such good effect. None the less, with no Grants available, the 4th Royal Tanks were soon ready to do battle in their replacement vehicles, which they soon learned to handle efficiently, despite their limitations in speed and range in comparison with their German counterparts, the Mark III and Mark IV panzers.

For Pip Gardner there was to be no Valentine. Instead, as a brigade liaison officer his duties would call for maximum mobility and speed about the desert, and he was therefore provided with a jeep. These excellent small vehicles were ideal for buzzing about the desert at high speed and, unlike the conventional staff cars, were able to negotiate the sometimes variable surface of the desert without getting stuck in patches of soft sand, which involved endless digging-out and pushing. Pip had with his jeep a radio truck to keep him in contact with brigade and divisional headquarters. Of course dashing around the desert at high speed in an open vehicle had its appeal for Pip, who had always had a liking for fast cars. It was also far more comfortable than being inside a tank. But the open jeep certainly had its hazards, especially when

bullets were flying, in comparison with the greater armoured protection
afforded by a tank. On the other hand the superior mobility of a jeep
rendered it a less obvious target for the dreaded German 88-mm anti-
tank guns. Also, despite the comparative comfort of his jeep, Pip missed
the camaraderie of a well-trained tank crew to which he had become
accustomed.

In early May, Pip moved up with the 32nd Army Tank Brigade
Headquarters on the coast below Halfaya Pass, the scene of his first
battle in June 1941, in which he had won the Military Cross. The
brigade was as yet not involved in any fighting, but there was an air
of expectancy which was increased when they were ordered forward
to Tobruk, where they had been for the last two months of the siege
during the previous year, before the break-out in November, in which
the whole brigade had distinguished itself under Brigadier Willison, and
Pip himself had gained his Victoria Cross. Now they all felt that they
were heading in the right direction, moving west to deal with Rommel's
forces in the near future.

Before long Pip was sent forward to report to the 50th Division near
Gazala, where he found himself close to the liaison officer of a South
African armoured-car unit. While waiting for action to start, he found
time for some satisfactory tobacco trading. As invariablly seemed to be
the case with troops on active service, other people's rations always
appeared to be more desirable. For instance, whereas to the British and
Australian troops, who had endured a monotonous surfeit of their own
bully beef, German bully (rudely and contemptuously referred to by
the Afrika Korps as 'Alter Mann' – 'Old Man') was a welcome change
of diet. The same went for the Italian variety (sometimes referred to
as 'Asinius Mussolini' – 'Mussolini's Backside'). The British bully was
regarded as such a luxury in wartime Germany that the soldiers of the
Afrika Korps even contrived to send some home when they could
capture any. In addition to their liking for German bully, the British
troops relished the lime-juice that was very sensibly issued to the Afrika
Korps to make up for the lack of fresh fruit, which caused a certain
amount of problems with boils and desert sores among the troops of the
Eighth Army. Pip's tobacco trading with his South African allies consisted of fixing a mutually acceptable rate of exchange for the scarcer
Players against the more abundant but, to him, perfectly smokeable
Springbok cigarettes. Everyone seemed satisfied.

Rommel made his move on the night of 26th May 1942. His order of the day to all German and Italian troops under his command had announced that they were about to carry through a decisive attack against the British forces in Libya. His first aim was to defeat the British armoured units and capture Tobruk. His failure to achieve the latter objective during the previous year clearly still rankled – in fact it had become an obsession with him.

His plan was to make frontal attacks, mainly with his Italian troops in the northern and central sectors of the Gazala line, against General Pienaar's 1st South African Division and the British 50th Division under General Ramsden, in order to engage their attention, while he sent his panzers down to the south to Bir Hacheim. Leaving the Italian Ariete Armoured Division to encircle and attack the Free French in the fort of Bir Hacheim, Rommel planned to send his 15th and 21st Panzer Divisions round the southernmost extremity of the line in order to force their way northwards again, behind the enemy positions – ever a favourite ploy of his. This they successfully did and thrust their way menacingly northwards in the direction of Acroma and El Adem, to the west and south respectively of his ultimate target of Tobruk. They were soon confronted by elements of General Ritchie's armoured forces, and their way was blocked by the 201st Guards Motorised Brigade in the Knightsbridge box, in an area referred to by the British as the 'Devil's Cauldron', and by the Germans as the *'Hexenkessel'* or 'Witches' Cauldron'.

For several days a series of fierce armoured battles ensued over the area from Acroma in the north to Bir Hacheim in the south, and from El Adem in the east to the British minefield in the west. Rommel had succeeded in driving up behind the Gazala line, to the west of which lay the minefield stretching down from the coast. By attacking with Italian units in various places in sufficient strength to occupy enemy troops there, he was able to carry out his plan to engage the enemy armour and reduce its numbers over a period of several days, notably in the Devil's Cauldron.

At one time, however, it seemed that he had been trapped by his own outflanking movement, and was in danger of running out of supplies – just as he had at Sidi Rezegh in the previous autumn. His forward troops took a tremendous pounding from the guns of 150 Brigade of the 50th Division and from the RAF planes operating from Gambut. But relying, not for the first time, on his conviction that in war fortune favours the brave, Rommel eventually broke through and overran 150 Brigade and managed to hold the ground gained against General Ritchie's piece-meal and unavailing counter-attacks. This paved the way for a series of armoured battles during the second week of June during which repeated losses in British tanks were inflicted, which enabled the German and Italian armour to gain control of the battlefield.

Even the fort of Bir Hacheim, which had been supplied by air, was ordered to evacuate its remaining defenders by night on 10th June, when eventually the problems of supply by air had become insuperable. After sixteen days of gallant resistance by General Koenig and his Free French troops, under constant dive-bombing from Stukas and intense artillery fire, a large part of the garrison managed to obey orders to force their way out and join the Eighth Army to the east. This sustained and heroic resistance in defence of Bir Hacheim marked the first significant resurgence of the French spirit that had been temporarily crushed in 1940. General Koenig had scorned repeated attempts by personal messages from Rommel to induce him to surrender, usually with the rejoinder *'Allez au Diable!'* and a suitable Gallic gesture. Koenig had been ordered to defend Bir Hacheim, and despite the continual pound-ing from all sides, he was determined to carry out his orders – a performance that was to earn him the title of 'The hero of Bir Hacheim'. This title was to stay with him throughout the rest of his service, which included the command, two years later, of the Forces Françaises de l'Intérieur in the liberation of his country.

The fall of Bir Hacheim released a considerable number of enemy guns and troops, and the fighting round Knightsbridge grew in intensity as it moved further north to Acroma and El Adem.

General Ritchie had now lost far too great a proportion of his armour to be able to hold Rommel's panzers, which were bolstered by timely reinforcements as well as by their resourceful recovery units, which were able to operate behind their tanks as they advanced across the desert. The result was that by 18th June, the British and Common-wealth forces were being withdrawn from Acroma and El Adem, and the forward troops of 50 Division near Gazala were forced to make their way eastwards in great haste and at times through the enemy. By now, of all the boxes in the Gazala 'line', only the base-box at Tobruk remained in British occupation – General Ritchie having decided to

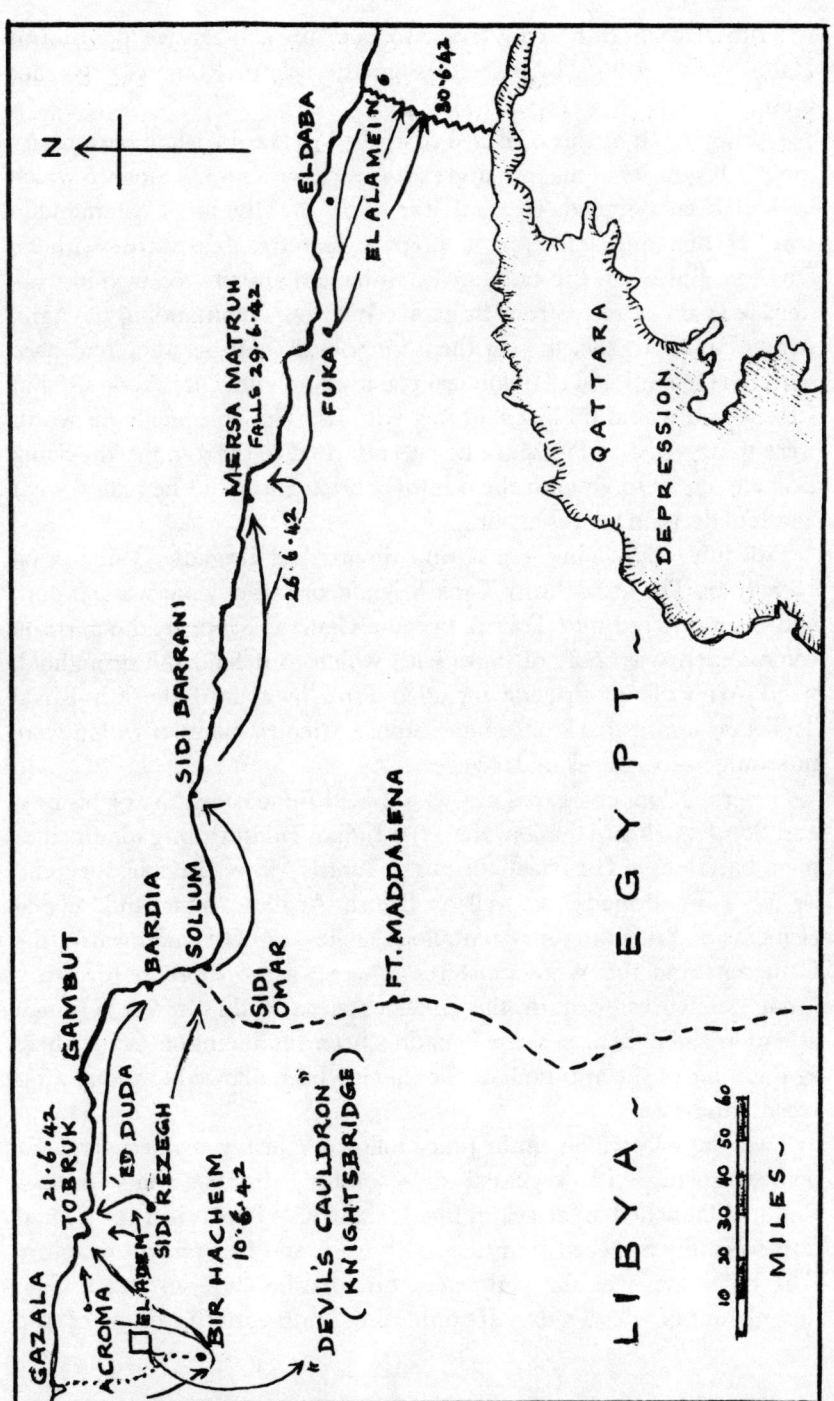

Rommel's Dash to El Alamein, June 1942

withdraw his Eighth Army back to take up a defensive position at
Halfaya and Sollum in order to stem the tide of Rommel's advance
there.

During much of this confused fighting, Pip Gardner had been carrying out his duties in his jeep and radio truck with 50 Division, to which
he had been assigned. General Ramsden, the divisional commander,
sent for him and told him to prepare to retreat eastwards with 50
Division. But when Pip explained that he had already received instructions over the wireless from Brigadier Willison, commanding the 32nd
Army Tank Brigade, to join them in Tobruk, whither they had been
sent, the General said : 'If you feel you must go into Tobruk, do so! But
I think you would do better to stay with us.' How prophetic his words
were to prove! But Pip, since he was attached to the 32nd Army Tank
Brigade, chose to go with them into Tobruk. Little did he realise what
a fateful decision he was making.

Pip duly arrived in Tobruk and reported to Brigadier Willison on
18th June. The 32nd Army Tank Brigade, or rather what was left of it,
had been ordered into Tobruk because General Klopper, the garrison
commander, was short of tanks with which to defend the stronghold.
32nd Army Tank Brigade included Pip's own unit, the 4th Royal
Tanks, so he was back once more among friends, many of whom were
no strangers to Tobruk under siege.

General Klopper's garrison was a mixed force consisting of his own
2nd South African Division, the 11th Indian Infantry Brigade (including a battalion of Gurkhas), the 201st Guards Motor Brigade, the 32nd
Army Tank Brigade, as well as British Artillery units and several
elements of British infantry battalions such as the Green Howards, the
Camerons and the Worcestershires. There was no shortage of men –
though defences used in the previous siege hadn't received much
attention since then, because it hadn't been the intention to use them
again, some of the anti-tank ditches having been allowed to silt up after
recent sandstorms.

Two days later, on 20th June, following heavy artillery and air
bombardment, with repeated dive-bombing from wailing Stukas,
Rommel launched an attack in force at dawn. Whereas in 1941 he had
unsuccessfully attacked from the south-west, and had failed to capture
Fort Pilastrino near the perimeter, this time he chose to attack from
the region of Ed Duda, opposite the south-eastern sector of the

perimeter – forcing a gap through the very area whence Pip Gardner's regiment had made their original break-out to end the siege in November 1941. This time the area was held by Indian troops, and despite an attempted counter-attack in support by the 4th and 7th Royal Tanks the Germans proved too strong and were able to infiltrate with their tanks of the 15th and 21st Panzer Divisions and their lorried infantry, through the minefields of the inner defensive ring to a distance of eight miles. By nightfall they had reached the harbour and virtually the whole of the eastern sector of the Tobruk stronghold was in enemy hands, though the South Africans, who had been stationed in the western sector in order to repel an attack from the west, were still in position, but not dug in to face an attack from the east.

This time Rommel was determined to make no mistake over Tobruk, and had no intention of letting himself in for another long and tiresome siege. He was bent on capturing Tobruk totally and without delay, and without again leaving this irksome thorn in his flank to hamper his eastward progress.

Klopper, on the other hand, after contact during the night with Eighth Army headquarters, seemed to decide that it was no longer possible with the resources at his disposal to withstand Rommel's panzers once they had forced their way inside the perimeter from the south-east. As there seemed no immediate prospect of relief being sent to him, he intended to fight his way out to the west, with the aim of working his way round to the rest of the Eighth Army eventually. But much of the available transport vehicles had been destroyed or captured, and only a few troops, headed by the Coldstream Guards, succeeded in forcing their way through the enemy who were rapidly moving in on the beleaguered garrison. On the morning of 21st June 1942 General Klopper surrendered his garrison, in order to save unavailing bloodshed. It was a day which those who were instructed to lay down their arms were most unlikely to forget. At the time they also found it utterly incomprehensible.

Pip Gardner had gone into Tobruk in the knowledge that it had been held continuously since January 1941, and that the siege had lasted for two hundred days. Furthermore he himself had taken part in that epic siege and this time the garrison had more troops, ammunition and supplies than there had been on the previous occasion. In addition, Churchill had recently announced that Tobruk would be defended. He had received telegraphed news from General Auchinleck that the defences were in good order, the garrison adequate, and that there were ninety days' supplies for the troops to enable them to withstand a siege once more.

Accordingly it came as a great surprise to Pip and his fellow tank officers when it was announced early on 21st June that General Klopper had felt obliged to surrender the garrison, which numbered over 30,000 men. Pip was not alone in his dismay. Churchill, who was at that moment staying with President Roosevelt at the White House for important discussions, was likewise dumbfounded – and extremely embarrassed.

In the midst of the general bewilderment, the least surprised person appears to have been Rommel himself. Both at the time and in retrospect, he reckoned that the situation in Tobruk, despite the greater number of garrison troops, was far less favourable for the defenders than it had been in 1941. He believed that General Klopper had no alternative but to surrender – and had been at pains to leave him none. But on that fateful day in June 1942, Pip Gardner and thousands of his colleagues, including the disgusted 2nd South African Division, were far from reconciled to the fact that they had been ordered to surrender – in many cases without being allowed to fire a shot in their sector of the perimeter. Rommel, on the other hand, was riding high. He had not only captured Tobruk in the space of little more than twenty-four hours – thereby realising his obsessive goal. He had also been promoted by Hitler to the elevated rank of Field Marshal for doing so.

Those unfortunate enough to find themselves captured inside the Tobruk perimeter, like Pip, thought at the time that the Eighth Army had merely withdrawn to their previously fortified positions on the Libyan–Egyptian frontier – a thought that made their surrender all the more galling. They had been prepared to ride out the siege of Tobruk until they were able to link up with their own forces, as had happened in the previous autumn. In fact it was a mere two days before Bardia, Sollum and Sidi Omar were all evacuated and the rest of the Eighth Army went helter-skelter back to the point to which the Italians under Marshal Graziani had advanced way back in September 1940, and from which Wavell's push had started in December of that year – namely, just to the west of Mersa Matruh.

It was at this stage, on 25th June, that GHQ Cairo announced the continued withdrawal, at the same time stating that the command of the Eighth Army had now been assumed by General Auchinleck himself, in succession to General Ritchie whose army was in full retreat. The latter was considered by some to have wasted most of his armoured resources in small batches in action against the enemy, instead of keeping his units together in larger concentrations and inflicting collective damage on Rommel's tanks.

The retreat, however, continued. Mersa Matruh fell on 29th June, despite a brief but gallant defence by General Freyberg's New Zealanders, who had been rushed from Palestine in time to add further laurels to their previous fine record in the Western Desert and elsewhere in the Middle East. By their rugged resistance they succeeded in gaining a couple of precious days, which enabled a few thousand Indians, South Africans and Australians, together with the determined remnants of the British 50th Division, and what was left of the 1st and 7th Armoured Divisions, to take up previously prepared positions at El Alamein. This was where Auchinleck had elected to make his stand and ward off Rommel, where the distance between the sea and the impassable soft sand of the Qattara Depression to the south is at its shortest, thus creating a bottle-neck that could be defended.

Rommel was now within sixty miles of Alexandria and not much more than that from Cairo and the Nile Delta. Only General Auchinleck and his depleted Eighth Army now stood between Rommel and his ultimate goal – the Suez Canal. Pip Gardner's guiding star was unfortunately pointing him in the opposite direction.

Back in Tobruk, Pip Gardner was not the only Royal Tanks VC to reach the end of his desert campaign, with no more tanks from which to fight. Another was Lieutenant-Colonel H. R. B. Foote, who was commanding the 7th Royal Tanks, alongside the remnants of the 4th Royal Tanks, in this final desperate fling against the insurgent 15th and 21st Panzer Divisions, which between them mustered a hundred panzers for the incursion into Tobruk. Lieutenant-Colonel Bob Foote (eventually Major-General H. R. B. Foote, vc, cb, dso) had already been awarded the DSO when, for his outstanding valour and leadership in the brave but costly attack by the 32nd Army Tank Brigade on Sidra Ridge near Gazala he also won the VC. In Tobruk his 7th Royal Tanks was reduced to one serviceable Matilda tank in this last bold but unavailing counter-attack, alongside the 4th Royal Tanks under

Lieutenant-Colonel W. R. Reeves, DSO, who were in much the same state – a sad end to a long and glorious desert campaign for both regiments.

Brigadier Willison, commanding the 32nd Army Tank Brigade, decided that all surviving tank personnel, who had been obliged to assume a defensive role as infantry when their tanks had been put out of action, should, despite the official surrender, be allowed to endeavour to pass through the lines of the encircling enemy and make their way eastwards in the hope of reaching their own troops. As yet he had no idea just how headlong the 'Gazala Gallop', as it became derisively known, had been. Accordingly, Pip found himself in company with Brigadier Willison and Lieutenant-Colonel Reeves, who had taken over command of the 4th Royal Tanks, as they made their way under cover of darkness through the German and Italian lines, in the direction of Ed Duda ridge.

They walked for three days, moving by night and hiding in wadis by day. They tried unsuccessfully to find some food and water from the abandoned vehicles that they passed on their way. But nearly all the vehicles that they came upon were burned out, and by the end of the third day they were completely out of food and water. Far from catching up with their own troops, as they had hoped, the three escapers found themselves on the fourth morning being excitedly ordered to clamber aboard a truck by a group of gleeful Italians who had been given the task of combing the desert and rounding-up any would-be escapers from Tobruk.

Thus Pip found himself a prisoner and obliged to raise his hands to an exultant Italian corporal, before being packed into a truck with other rounded-up prisoners and ignominiously driven back to captivity in an unsavoury prisoner-of-war cage inside Tobruk. He was still unaware that the Eighth Army troops, towards whom he had been optimistically trudging, were by now back at a small railway halt called El Alamein, over a hundred miles away.

For Captain Philip Gardner, VC, MC, the wheel of fortune had revolved. For better or for worse, he was now a prisoner-of-war, and life 'in the bag' was about to begin.

CHAPTER TEN

'Vinceremo!'

Capture by the enemy is a traumatic experience under any circumstances, but when, like Pip, one is in the crowded company of 30,000 other unfortunates, the present nightmare is bound to be intensified – whatever the future may hold in store. The fact that the vast majority of those cooped-up inside the wire enclosures of Tobruk had received orders from a high-up source to lay down their arms, did little to improve matters.

Indignation was now rife, coupled with bewilderment and anger. Everybody knew that the Australians, Indians and the British had held out for two hundred days in the previous year, and yet here were great hordes of able-bodied men obliged, against their will, to cease fighting. It seemed incredible. Looked at subjectively, anyway, that was how it struck them.

Those who had fought elsewhere with distinction – some of them right amongst the enemy, with 'Jock columns' – felt the ignominy of the Tobruk surrender most keenly. But for everyone it was a shattering experience.

Pip Gardner was no exception. He shared this general feeling of having been let down. He had always been prepared to fight his way out of trouble, trusting to Fate. Yet here he was, now feeling that, despite his bold but abortive attempt to escape in order to fight another day, he was out of the fighting at a time when he was needed most. It was a great anti-climax.

The general feeling of those captured could in some ways be compared with the large numbers of British prisoners left behind at Dunkirk and St Valéry in 1940, or the masses of British and Commonwealth prisoners lost at Hong Kong and Singapore earlier in 1942 – or, for that matter, with the hapless Germans who were eventually surrendered en bloc under Field-Marshal von Paulus in February 1943 at Stalingrad. The sheer weight of numbers, when such great quantities of captives are taken, inevitably means that the initial handling is bound to fall far short of anything laid down in the Geneva Convention and its provisions for the treatment of prisoners-of-war, even when the conquering side has been a signatory to the agreement.

Almost immediately, it had become obvious that, though the majority had been captured by Germans – Pip on his escape being a notable exception – they were all to become the prisoners of the Italians. The Germans were urgently needed for the fighting that had moved swiftly to the east. The Italians revelled in reversing what had previously been their usual role, as they set about disarming the British and Commonwealth prisoners and herded them into the prisoner-of-war cages that their compatriots had been made to construct for themselves when they had been captured in large numbers with Marshal Graziani's army during Wavell's push.

After Pip's recapture, he was put into one of the packed enclosures. There was very little food and water, and many of the prisoners were hungry and exhausted. In their state of shock they mostly spent the time catching up on sleep, lying in the blazing summer sun. The majority of them had managed to take into captivity with them a few essential belongings in their haversacks, such as razors and toothbrushes. Many still had their water-bottles with them, and some of them managed to hang on to their wrist-watches, which were always liable to confiscation, usually being considered fair game by the victors in war.

The officers were soon segregated from the men, and were placed in separate compounds. Random interrogations were carried out, although the circumstances of their mass capture were such that there was not much to be gleaned by the enemy as to the order of battle of the other side that wasn't known already. The scoop had been on such a wholesale scale, with complete battalions being captured and easily identified.

Amusement was caused, however, when a particularly snooty officer was singled out for a spell of confinement in a small building in company with a decidedly scruffy and easily-rumbled Italian airman, posing as a shot-down RAF pilot cursing his luck – and the Italians. He would have looked more at home among the Mafia, and in any case he was wasting his time. The haughty officer with whom he was supposed to start a profitable conversation gave him the cold shoulder, and no information whatsoever. As a brother officer remarked, when the stuffy British officer returned to the compound and reported what had been tried on him, issuing a warning to the others to beware, the English-speaking Italian stooge could hardly have been given a tougher assignment. Even if he had been a genuine RAF officer he would have met with no more success against the notoriously stiff upper lip of his intended source of information.

Another officer was interrogated, very courteously, by a pompous middle-aged Italian officer with the air of a head-waiter, as he ushered in his subject for questioning and offered him a seat. He deprecatingly explained that he disliked his present job of interrogating prisoners and that he would far rather be up with the front-line troops for their final drive to Alexandria. He added, with a visionary gleam in his eye : 'But Cairo is my dream.' 'Dream is about right!' commented the officer under interrogation. For a few moments the visionary gleam remained – only to change rapidly to a look of daggers-drawn, when the penny suddenly dropped. The friendly atmosphere quickly evaporated and the interrogation was soon brought to a frosty close.

On 28th June, a week after the surrender, some of the more fortunate officers, including Pip, were moved on. Judging from the alarming news that was being supplied to them by the exultant Italian guards, to the accompaniment of shouts of 'Vinceremo!' ('We shall win !'), thereby reiterating one of Mussolini's favourite boasts, there was little hope of rescue, recapture or escape from where they were. It seemed better to move on to somewhere else, where they hoped that more food and water – and hygiene – might be available. As it turned out, they were heading towards no great improvement in the immediate future, but they were lucky in comparison with the majority of the rank and file, who mostly had to endure (and in some cases sadly succumb to) the dirt and deprivations of another four months in the ghastly prisoner-of-war cages along the North African coast. They suffered great pangs of hunger, which drove some of the weaker ones to swop their army boots for food with the guards. They nearly all became lousy and afflicted by dysentery and other debilitating diseases caused by the conditions and under-nourishment which they had to endure.

Pip and several truck-loads of officers were glad to leave their insanitary compound in Tobruk, the squalor of which anyone who experienced it would vouch for. The journey in the tightly-packed lorries was mercifully fairly short – a mere eighty miles up the coast to Derna. Anything further would have been sheer hell. As it was, the prisoners soon found it very cramped and uncomfortable in the back of the trucks, and their backsides began to ache more and more. Guards armed with sub-machine-guns and rifles were stationed in each lorry, with instructions to shoot anyone who tried to escape. In any case there seemed remarkably little point in escaping on foot into the empty desert – empty, that was, except for an intermittent stream of Axis transport hurrying eastwards in the opposite direction. There were diesel lorries, making their own peculiar chugging noise, laden with troops or stores, as well as some formidable-looking German guns with alarmingly long barrels being towed menacingly along to the east.

As the trucks conveying the prisoners neared Derna, the airfield was visible on the right. It seemed to be very busy with aircraft landing and taking off. The lorries, instead of descending right down to the centre of the coastal town, stopped at a large fort on a hill outside the town. There the prisoners dismounted stiffly and were led into a long bare room. They could have been forgiven for imagining that they had come there to take part in the filming of *Beau Geste*, such was the Foreign Legion atmosphere and appearance of the white-walled building. There were some wooden bunks for them to sleep on, and they were relieved to find that they were also provided with a tolerably hygienic lavatory – a distinct improvement on anything they had encountered in Tobruk. But they weren't provided with any lavatory paper, and when a request was made to the Fort Commandant for this symbol of civilisation to be provided, the reply was that the Commandant himself didn't use it – so why should the prisoners? There wasn't really much answer to that, except to cannibalise a couple of already much-read paperbacks – one of which, appropriately enough, was none other than *Beau Geste*!

In reaching Derna, beyond Gazala, Pip had now arrived at a point further west than he had hitherto ventured in the Libyan desert. He had always been anxious to see more of the desert, but not under these circumstances. He was interested to notice that from Derna onwards, compared with the barren desert that he knew, there was a certain amount of vegetation and human habitation, as they skirted the high ground of the Jebel Akhdar.

The stay at the fort outside Derna was only for the night. Next morning the prisoners were moved as far as Barce where they spent a single night in a camp that was little more than a cage for prisoners-of-war, with few comforts. The following day they were transferred the short distance to a most unpleasant camp at Benghazi. The primitive conditions of the camp were made all the more unpleasant by the trigger-happy Senussi guards who were used by the Italians to help guard the enormous influx of prisoners that had accrued as the result of the fall of Tobruk. The Senussi – and the Italians, for that matter – really reckoned now that they were on the winning side, and their cries of 'Vinceremo!' had begun to carry more conviction. They were in no mood to be soft with their prisoners.

However, in order to cheer themselves up the prisoners organised sing-songs in the evenings. The main object was to show the guards that their morale was still high, despite their recent reverses. One night, during a pause in the singing, they suddenly heard one of the Italian guards start to sing part of an operatic aria in a voice that sounded really marvellous. It held them all spellbound. At the end, the applause was terrific and encores were shouted for and readily given. Thus for a short while the prisoners and the guards established a friendliness which struck Pip as quite remarkable under the circumstances.

Less enjoyable for Pip, however, was an outbreak of large boils on the back of his neck which overtook him. They caused him great pain and distress. They were due, no doubt, to the lack of fresh vegetables in his diet. The pain finally became unbearable and he persuaded the guards to let him see a doctor for treatment. After a long wait his request was granted and he was marched into a hut where an Italian doctor told him to lie on his stomach on a table. He then proceeded to carve into Pip's neck without any form of anaesthetic. The pain was excruciating. However, the agony at the time eventually gave way to relief and the boils disappeared for good as a result of this rough and ready treatment.

Unlike many of the later prisoners from Tobruk, who were destined to be herded into and out of a series of unsavoury camps along the North African coast over the next few months, before being loaded into the dark hold of a ship going via Greece to Italy, Pip and a batch of forty officers were flown direct from Benghazi to Italy. The plane which conveyed Pip was a very old Savoia, whose passengers were mainly returning Italian soldiers, going home on leave. Some of them hadn't been home, it seemed, since the start of the war in Abyssinia in 1936. Now they were being used for escort duty for the journey. The prisoners were spaced out among the soldiers in the plane, at the ratio of five soldiers to one prisoner.

It was a strange journey – with the Italians obviously excited at the prospect of going home, whereas the prisoners had grave misgivings. It was certainly a relief to turn their backs on the misery of the prison camp in Benghazi and its filthy conditions, but on the other hand everything now looked so final. They immediately asked among themselves whether anyone could fly the plane, if they could manage between them to overpower the escort. This idea was quickly abandoned because there were no airmen amongst them, and in any case it was a very tall order.

When the plane took off, it soon became unpleasantly cold as the machine gained height, in order to avoid British fighters, they were told. For Pip and several others, who were dressed in the shirts and shorts in which they had been captured, the journey became something of an ordeal. The only escape the prisoners could hope for now was to be shot down over the Mediterranean and dramatically picked up by the Royal Navy before they drowned. When they were midway across the ocean, one of the aircraft's crew suddenly manned a machine-gun sited in the fuselage and pointed it through an aperture. He swivelled it around feverishly and the prisoners' hopes (and fears!) were briefly raised. But nothing further happened and with a shrug of the shoulders the machine-gunner left his post and returned to the cockpit.

After this brief interlude, the Italians soldiers on board were so relieved that they produced from their haversacks some of their rations. It wasn't long before they offered some to the prisoners, who were eyeing them hungrily. The guards were amazed at the voracity with which the prisoners devoured the bulky Italian biscuits, which looked for all the world like dog-biscuits. The Italians were by no means enchanted with them, but the ravenous prisoners found them most satisfying. This prompted some of the Italians to provide some red wine out of their water-bottles, to wash down the nourishing meal, which was an unexpected bonus.

The Italians were pleased to be nearing home and when one of them looked out of the window and actually sighted land, he yelled out:

'Italia! Italia!' The rest could hardly contain themselves for joy. One of them even kissed the prisoner next to him enthusiastically on both cheeks.

The plane landed with no fuss at Lecce, on the very heel of Italy. The prisoners hadn't been picked up in the Mediterranean after all – they had been safely deposited on terra firma. Fresh woods and pastures new awaited them.

*

At Lecce the prisoners were handed over to a fresh escort, who were distinctly less friendly, but by no means unpleasant. They announced that the prisoners were to be taken by rail to a prisoner-of-war camp at Bari, up the Adriatic coast. They were taken by lorry to the station, where they aroused slight curiosity but no hostility among the local civilians, before being installed in second-class carriages with the guards on watch in the corridor.

As they left for their destination, it was still light. They stopped at several small stations, where passengers got on and off, as well as the big port of Brindisi. By the time they reached Bari, darkness had descended.

They were marched from the station for about two miles, to the outskirts of the town, until they came to the entrance to Bari POW camp. Here they were met by a South African major, who told them that they would be housed in the quarantine hut and that some hot skilly would be provided from the cookhouse. They were led to a long barrack built of breeze-blocks and cement, with a red tiled roof of the kind that is universal in Mediterranean countries.

They hadn't been there long before the Italian camp commandant arrived to address them in person. He was a tall stately middle-aged man in a cloak. He was accompanied by an oily and obsequious Italian lieutenant who acted as his interpreter. The obsequiousness seemed to be catching, for the South African major, who had at first seemed nice enough, chucked up what the new arrivals considered to be an unnecessarily keen salute to the commandant. There were audible murmurs all round. So far none of the new prisoners had found it necessary to salute anybody since their capture, and they resented this subservience, which they reckoned to be a form of toadying. Only later did they learn that

CHIETI. P.G. No.21.

G.J.W

the accepted custom was for prisoners to salute officers of the detaining power of senior rank. Their present attitude would have landed them in severe trouble had they been in Japanese hands, of course – and it was shortly to cause quite a scene in Italy.

Through the interpreter, whose English was a trifle stilted and gave rise to barely suppressed mirth, the commandant explained to his new guests that Bari was only a transit camp, and that after a short period of quarantine and documentation they would soon be sent on to a permanent camp, where they would find better facilities and regular Red Cross parcels. It was a cheering prospect, even if all that was available now was some Italian skilly.

Next morning they were given Red Cross postcards to send to their next-of-kin, and this gave Pip his first opportunity since capture to report his altered status – and his safety – to his wife Renée. Since Pip had left for the desert, Renée had moved back to her native Doncaster, their house in Norwood having been let for the duration of the war. Her contribution to the war effort had been to run a canteen providing refreshments for servicemen. When Pip had won his VC, she was much photographed doing so, by the press. She had wanted to be free to join Pip, should he get a posting back to Britain. On receiving official War Office news that Pip was missing on active service, she naturally hoped that he was alive and safe among the large number of prisoners reported to have been taken at Tobruk. The arrival of Pip's postcard came as a relief, depressing enough though the brief news was.

The news also brought about an instant decision that, rather than hang about at her parents' home indefinitely, she would volunteer for one of the women's services during Pip's absence. Apart from the fact that she liked the idea of joining the senior service, her main reason for becoming a 'Wren', rather than anything else, was the not unknown feminine preference for what she regarded as the smartest uniform. So the WRNS it was. She soon received a posting as a driver, which suited her admirably, at Arbroath on the east coast of Scotland.

Pip's stay at Bari only lasted for a couple of weeks, which was fortunate. Every time the prisoners asked for anything, the answer was that they must wait until they reached their permanent camp. When they asked when this would be, the reply was one to which they were going to grow only too accustomed – 'Domani' ('To-morrow'). Pip was fortunate in that for him Domani came sooner than it did for some of those who followed him to Bari Transit Camp. The permanent POW camps hadn't yet filled up to full capacity with the influx of prisoners. Some of those who reached Bari later, found themselves hanging around there for months in transit, getting hungrier, thinner and colder, as winter arrived. They even had to use the two bed blankets with which they were each provided as a sort of makeshift kilt and cloak by day, as their khaki shorts in which they had been captured in the desert began to disintegrate.

While Pip was there, however, it was high Italian summer. But he was glad to depart for pastures new on 28th July 1942, along with sixty other prisoners, mostly from Tobruk. Included in the party was his friend Percy Gers, of the 4th Royal Tanks, who had been with him since Tobruk. They set off early in the day to Bari station and, travelling once again in second-class carriages, they reached Chieti POW Camp before dark.

Their journey took them further up the Adriatic coast, as far as Pescara, before they turned inland across the coastal plain to Chieti, which lies at the foot of the Abruzzi mountains. From the camp itself, the summit of the Gran Sasso d'Italia (9,584 ft.) was easily visible, towering above them to the north-west. It formed a scenic enough background but the camp itself was far from pleasant. Despite the glowing terms in which the Bari guards had described it, Chieti wasn't a good camp to be sent to. But for Pip there was a pleasant surprise awaiting him. Among the prisoners already there he found several friends, including Captain George Hurst, the Quartermaster of the 4th Royal Tanks. From Pip's first arrival in the desert in 1941 George Hurst had gone out of his way to be friendly and helpful to him, and now, still a quartermaster at heart despite being captured, he managed to fix him up with a toothbrush, a shirt and some soap from his own private 'quartermaster's store' that he had gathered about him. It was a practical gesture much appreciated by Pip, and typical of George Hurst.

Chieti had several drawbacks. For a start, food was short – at any rate for newly-arrived prisoners whose stomachs hadn't yet adjusted to meagre rations. The irony was that the prisoners actually had to pay for the privilege of being half-starved. By arrangement with the British government, prisoners-of-war were charged by deductions from their army pay for the meagre rations provided in the Mess. In the case of

subalterns, this accounted for almost their entire pay, and the position
was made all the worse because a ridiculously unfavourable rate of
exchange had been fixed for the duration of hostilities, taking no
account of subsequent inflation which reduced the value of the Italian
lira drastically. In other ranks' camps the rations were worse, but at
least the prisoners didn't have to pay for them! The supply of Red
Cross parcels, which meant everything to prisoners-of-war, was at that
stage improving but still erratic. Their first parcels were, of course,
welcomed by the prisoners, of whom those who had just arrived from
Bari had begun to think that Red Cross parcels, of which they had
vaguely heard, and to which in some cases they had actually contributed
before they were captured, were purely a myth.

Likewise cigarettes and tobacco were in short supply. People who
were addicted to nicotine found the going particularly tough when their
supplies ran out. A very humiliating occurrence both at Benghazi and
Bari had been the sight of quite senior officers trying to beg cigarettes
or tobacco off the Italian guards. It struck others who were not
afflicted by this craving as decidedly infra dig. When Red Cross
cigarettes, supplemented by private parcels from home, began to arrive
at Chieti, the situation became less desperate for compulsive smokers.
But even so cigarettes remained in short supply and later became a form
of currency in most camps.

There were three recognised methods of approach to one's cigarette
rations when smokers received them. The first was to smoke the cigarette
and save the stub, which could then be rolled into another cigarette,
made with the aid of cigarette papers which were usually obtainable
in the canteen in exchange for special camp 'money', which was value-
less outside. The second method was to cut the cigarettes in half, thus
doubling the number of smokes – and using the stubs, of course. The
third method, favoured by a few devotees, was to break open the
cigarette immediately and re-roll double the number straight away –
also using the stubs, as in the first two methods.

Smoking became quite an obsession with some POWs. In Pip's case,
though he liked a smoke and found that it helped to reduce the pangs
of hunger, he was luckily not a compulsive smoker, ever craving for
a draw – unlike a certain officer in his block at Chieti. The latter used
to patrol the passages between the sleeping bunks each morning, to see
whether anyone had been improvident enough to drop a stub on to the

floor. He even used to grovel on all fours and search under the beds, until one day he became the victim of a humiliating practical joke. One of the occupants of the bunks, with nothing better to do, decided to bait a trap for him. He attached a tempting cigarette butt to the end of a piece of thread, and as the cigarette scrounger reached under his bed to grab his booty, the man on the end of the thread gave it a jerk and snatched away the prey – amid howls of amusement from several onlookers, and considerable embarrassment to the officer under the bed, who looked far from dignified as he emerged empty-handed. He didn't reappear in that quarter!

Added to the shortage of cigarettes and sustaining food – the Italian rations of skilly, macaroni and small white bread-rolls being palatable but not sustaining – there was also a shortage of water. Owing to the vagaries of the plumbing system there were often only two taps out in the open, between some two-hundred-and-fifty prisoners during Pip's first couple of months there. Later the water supply improved and, joy of joys, the prisoners were even allowed a hot shower. At long last they were able to keep clean and those who had picked up lice on their travels through various camps and compounds now had a chance to rid themselves of their unwanted guests.

To add to their general discontent, the Italian commandant was a most unpleasant man, in the prisoners' eyes. He was labouring under the impression that Italy was going to be on the winning side in the war, after the recent victories of the Axis powers in the North African desert. He didn't take kindly to the truculent attitude of his prisoners who, despite recent reverses, were of the opposite opinion.

One day the commandant took it into his head to smarten-up the prisoners on parade for roll-call. He arrived on his rostrum accompanied by a bugler, and flanked by his security officer, Capitano Croce. The idea was to instill a little discipline into the casual prisoners lined up in front of him. He ordered the bugler to sound a call, which in the Italian army meant that they must stand to attention. Having explained what he wanted them to do, he made the bugler repeat the call. The prisoners, reckoning that, though they might for the time being be lodged in a former Carabinieri barracks, they wanted no part of Italian army drill to music and ignored the call. After several repetitions the total number of prisoners who had stood to attention – possibly from force of habit – could be counted on the fingers of one hand. A battle of wills soon developed. The commandant was prepared to keep the prisoners waiting in the hot sun indefinitely.

Extra guards were summoned from their barracks. This gave rise to hilarity and mirth among the prisoners, as the guards marched in file to the scene. They didn't exactly match the soldiers of the Brigade of Guards in stature or precision, and soon their march was to the accompaniment of whistling to the tune of 'Heigh-ho, Heigh-ho, as off to work we go', from *Snow-White and the Seven Dwarfs*, amid mock applause. When the tune came to an end, there was a quick switch to 'We're off to see the Wizard, the wonderful Wizard of Oz.'

All this fun was too much for Capitano Croce, who ordered an individual subaltern to stand to attention, and promptly despatched him to the cooler, amid cheers from the others, when he refused to comply. But the lesson went unheeded. The commandant's next move was to attempt to split the South Africans from the rest of their allies, by offering them the chance to come to attention and be dismissed – 'Divide and rule' being a popular but misconceived tactic of the Italians at that time. The South Africans made suitable gestures and elected to stay on parade. The sun grew hotter and the day wore on.

Then, when the newly arrived squad of extra guards was marched between the ranks of the prisoners, an inadvertent boot tripped one of them up. This immediately started a fracas. The owner of the offending boot was struck on the head by a rifle butt and was left lying on the ground. The prisoners started to advance towards the guards, and Bill Bowes, of Yorkshire and England, as if dealing with a tail-end batsman, removed the offensive weapon from its diminutive wielder. At this the guards took umbrage and began firing their rifles into the air and shouting at the prisoners in quick-fire Italian. This caused the now purple-faced commandant to join in the shouting, in a desperate attempt to regain control of his angry guards.

Fortunately he was more successful than he had been in his attempts to inculcate discipline into his unreceptive prisoners and order was restored before further bloodshed. By now he was ready for a compromise. The prisoners for their part were prepared to come to attention – on the order of the Senior British Officer. A certain amount of honour was thus preserved on both sides, and the marathon roll-call came to a close. Thereafter the services of the bugler were dispensed with.

However, roll-calls continued to be conducted at all times of the day and there were periodic searches by the guards, who seemed to delight in pulling everything off people's beds and generally turning the place upside-down. It seemed fairly certain, from the way they went about their task, that they were acting on tip-offs received from one or more camp stooges, who had told them where certain things were hidden. There was always a danger of this, as Pip was to discover to his cost.

The guiding hand behind these searches was the camp security-officer Capitano Croce. His name, meaning 'Cross' in Italian, resulted in his being known by the prisoners as 'Double Cross'. He was a tall sinister figure with a black moustache and a goatee beard to match, and he towered over the more rotund and somewhat coarse-featured commandant. Croce was responsible for the security of the camp, and as such was a constant thorn in the flesh of the camp tunnellers. He was also responsible for some priceless announcements in English, which he had half-learned in his pre-war career in shipping. One of his gems was a notice attached to the trip-wire which ran some ten feet inside the barbed-wire perimeter fence, which could not be crossed with impunity by the prisoners. The notice ran : 'Passage or demurrage no [sic] allowed.' Croce didn't understand why his prisoners found it necessary to laugh when they stood and read his notice – any more than the commandant could understand why the prisoners in his charge were so anxious to escape when they had the glorious Italian sunshine to enjoy beneath the breath-taking scenery of the Gran Sasso mountain !

Despite all the interruptions and irritations, Pip settled down to the routine life of a prisoner-of-war for the present. He attended a course in accountancy, which was given by a subaltern in the Royal Artillery called John Furman, who had qualified at an early age as a chartered accountant just before the war. He is destined to reappear later in Pip's story.

As in most officers' camps, where the inmates were neither required nor allowed to work, an amazingly wide selection of lectures was on offer. The subjects available ranged from gunnery to farming, from Urdu to bridge, or even musical appreciation to criminal law. The choice was wide and many of the lecturers excellent, which reflected most creditably the latent talent that was cooped up at Chieti and other camps. Pip Gardner chose accountancy with an eye to the future – and also as something to keep his mind off his present empty stomach.

He also became a member of a team of tunnellers. He and some friends started to excavate a tunnel which began under a giant pile of carrots and potatoes in the camp cookhouse store. In order to dispose of the soil, they used to put it into a Red Cross parcel cardboard box, which aroused no suspicion on the part of the guards, who were used to seeing officers walking from hut to hut with these boxes tucked underneath their arms. Then, when the attention of the guards was distracted elsewhere, the soil would be thrown down a well in the compound. After a while, however, this dumping was accidentally discovered. A workman's hammer, borrowed by the prisoners, was said to have fallen down the well and couldn't be returned. The commandant was disinclined to believe this story of an accident, and leaned towards his own theory that it had been hidden for subversive use by the prisoners. He called in the local fire-engine, with orders to pump out the water and look for the missing hammer. When the firemen ran out their hose and started to pump, several interested spectators among the throng of prisoners, armed with razor blades, cut the hose-pipe in a number of places. The water spurted out in all directions – to the frenzied annoyance of the guards, and the child-like amusement of the prisoners. The firemen eventually retrieved the hammer, but at the cost of a tool-kit spirited away from their fire-engine and some gashes in their hose. On these searches the Italians usually ended up by losing more than they found!

But in the course of the search down the well, the inordinate amount of silt at the bottom was discovered. This led in turn to a search for the tunnel which, possibly with the help of a stooge of theirs within the camp, the guards were not long in finding. It had been good experience while it had lasted – and there was always another day.

The weather had been fine and warm at first, which was fortunate for the lightly-clad prisoners from the desert. As winter approached and colder weather began to arrive from the mountains, so too did some excellent news for which they had all been waiting. In North Africa the tide was turning at last, starting with the decisive battle of El Alamein which began on 23rd October 1942.

CHAPTER ELEVEN

Goods News from the Desert

Although what is generally known as the Battle of El Alamein started on 23rd October 1942, there were really three Battles of El Alamein. The first took place from 30th June to 27th July, after the retreating Eighth Army turned and fought the Germans and Italians who were in hot pursuit. This battle, which denied Rommel his hoped-for prizes of Cairo and Alexandria when they seemed within his grasp, was skilfully fought under General Auchinleck, who had assumed responsibility and taken command of the Eighth Army from General Ritchie, whom he had appointed in the previous winter. Ritchie had met with initial success, but after the defeat at Gazala and the surrender at Tobruk, Auchinleck acted swiftly and urgently. Not only did his re-grouped forces manage to hold Rommel at El Alamein – they moved to the attack and inflicted losses on the victorious Axis troops to such an extent that Rommel was obliged to halt his advance and yield important ground in places.

Rommel used his Italian infantry to hold a line from El Alamein station in the north down to Ruweisat Ridge, and further south to the high ground on Quaret-el-Himeimat on the edge of the Qattara Depression, thus using and wearing out his panzers to bolster up the line where needed, in order to prevent a breakthrough by the revitalised Eighth Army. Meanwhile he did his best to hurry up tank reinforcements. Now it was his turn to cope with the difficulties of extended lines of communication – a factor that had been uppermost in Auchinleck's mind, when he chose to make his stand at El Alamein, perilously close to the Nile Delta though it was. Though he wasn't yet in a position to advance, until promised reinforcements arrived, Auchinleck had succeeded in saving the desperate situation.

But General Auchinleck was not to be allowed to reap the benefits of his strategy. This reward fell to his successor as commander of the

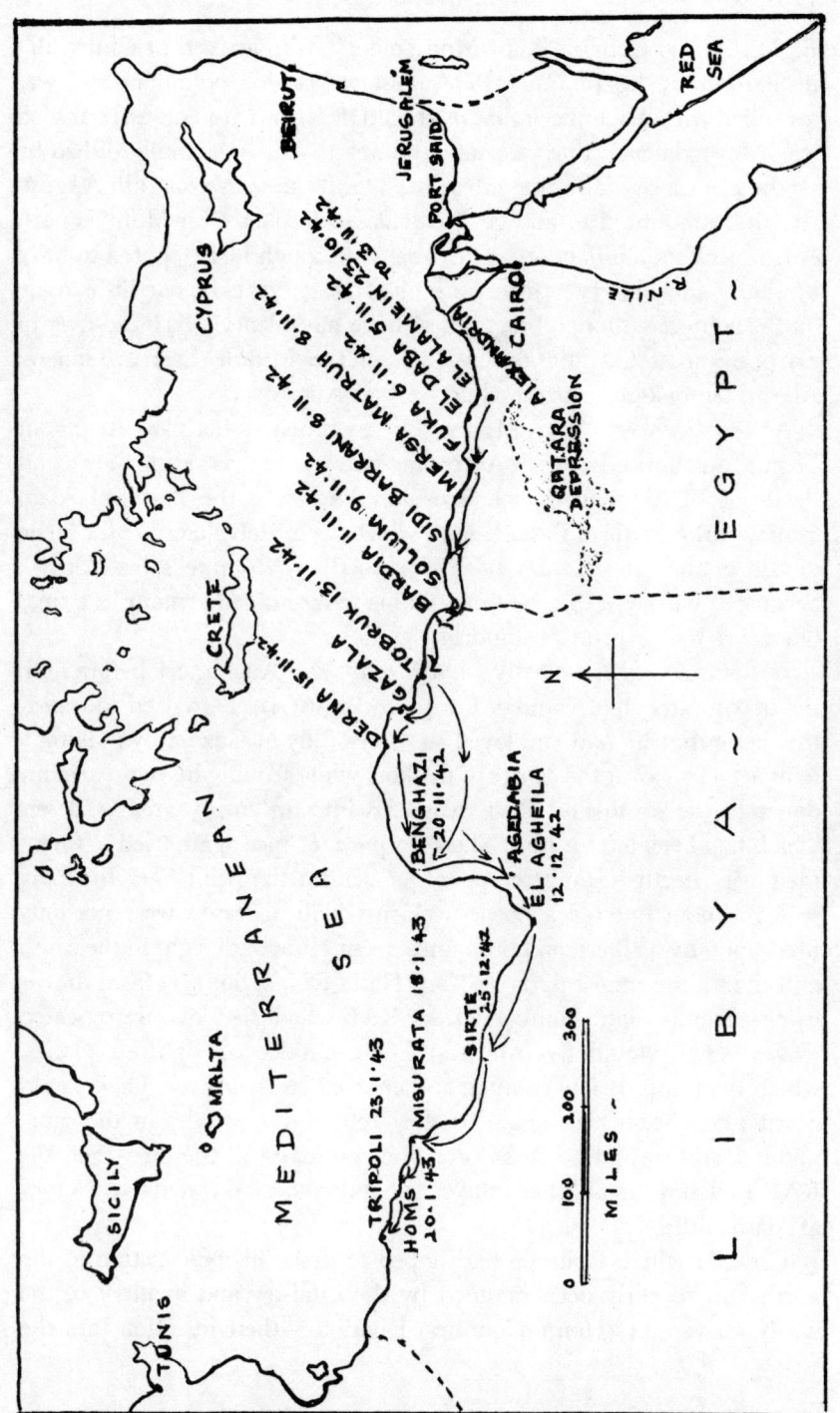

Montgomery's Advance from El Alamein to Tripoli, 1942/43

Eighth Army, General B. L. Montgomery, who arrived at Churchill's instigation in Egypt on 12th August to assume command. It was arranged with Auchinleck that he should do so on 15th August, but such was Montgomery's hurry to take the helm, that he actually did so by sending out a signal to that effect from GHQ in Cairo on 13th August. At what amounted to an act of calculated insolence on Monty's part, Auchinleck took no action at the time – although he is reputed to have been extremely angry, not surprisingly. In later years he had little to say on the subject – though biographers have had plenty. His hand-over of his position as Commander-in-Chief of the Middle East to General Alexander took place on schedule, on 15th August.

A mere few weeks later, Monty, the new broom in his Tank Regiment beret as an alternative to his Australian hat, was orchestrating the second Battle of El Alamein, which is usually known as the Battle of Alam Halfa, or the Battle of Bare Ridge – which accurately describes the scene of the action. It has also been described as 'Rommel's last throw', because it was here that he threw in his re-assembled armour in a final bid to reach Cairo and Alexandria.

In doing so, he did exactly what Monty (and Auchinleck before him, for that matter) had wanted. On 30th August 1942 he tried to repeat the tactic that he had employed so successfully at Gazala by making a feint attack against the centre of the line, while sending his main armour down to the south and then eastwards into an empty area of desert which had been left for him. There his panzers once again tried to thrust their way north in an attempt to get behind the front line. In doing so his armour entered a bottle-neck in which his tanks were not only fired upon by artillery on both flanks, from Himeimat right in the south and the southernmost parts of Alam Halfa Ridge, but also from the air by the Boston Light Bombers of the RAF which flew over in repeated waves. They would fly overhead in formations of eighteen planes, which the troops below counted and cheered on their way. They would count and cheer them again as they returned – usually in the same number and formation as before. The command of the air which the RAF had now established played a vital role in the decisive victory at Alam Halfa.

The box where Rommel had hoped to make his penetration to the north had recently been manned by the infantry and artillery of the newly-arrived 44 (Home Counties) Division – their insertion into the line being one of Montgomery's first moves on assuming command. He had been their Corps Commander a few months previously in Kent, where they had combined coastal defence with Monty's increasingly strenuous training schemes. Now they had a grandstand view of desert warfare, without their perimeter being actually breached by Rommel's probing tanks.

By 4th September Rommel was obliged to call off his costly attack and withdraw his armour, leaving behind in the desert no man's land a trail of burnt-out or immobilised tanks. This time the German recovery units were not able to tow away any that could be used again. In fact, it was left to patrols of 44th Division to go out and survey the carnage – and also help themselves to tins of bully beef and service biscuits with which the Germans had stocked their tanks from captured British supply dumps at Tobruk.

This defeat of Rommel at Alam Halfa, or the second Battle of El Alamein, paved the way for the third and final battle that was to follow seven weeks later. But first Monty's build-up of strength had to continue before he would commit his forces to attack at El Alamein. He was determined to make no mistake by moving over to the attack too soon. Although Auchinleck had been sacked by Churchill mainly for failing to undertake to mount an attack before the end of September, Monty nevertheless resolutely refused to be stampeded into premature action and chose 23rd October as his earliest possible date.

Meanwhile, masses of equipment had been arriving to tip the scales in his favour – notably large numbers of impressive new American Sherman tanks, in addition to more Grants, which had already proved formidable against their German counterparts. Valuable manpower reinforcements in the form of the reconstituted 51st Highland Division were also at his disposal. Their predecessors had been almost entirely killed or captured at St Valéry in 1940, but their reputation as doughty fighters still remained. Guns, too, had arrived in greater numbers than it had ever been possible for Auchinleck to deploy. Monty's assumption of command had indeed proved timely for him.

The result of this purposeful build-up, the intent of which was communicated to the troops, was that at 2140 hours on 23rd October 1942 the greatest artillery barrage hitherto mounted by a British army was unleashed on to the Germans and Italians who had been dug-in in depth along the El Alamein line. By the time the Australian, South

African, British and New Zealand infantry had moved in with the
bayonet, using tracks through the minefields which had been rapidly
cleared by the Royal Engineers, many of the numbed Axis troops were
in a dazed condition and ready to surrender. It was noticeable to those
rounding up the prisoners how the Germans in their Afrika Korps caps
kept well away from their Italian allies. They stood sullenly aloof. The
Italians, on the other hand, seemed to regard their capture as the signal
for the immediate production from their breast-pockets of countless
photos of their wives and bambinos, each vying with the next in the
quantity of photos produced – and the number of children sired, for
that matter!

However, much sterner opposition was yet to be encountered, when
the Germans threw in the 21st Panzer Division to counter-attack
strongly in the north. The third Battle of El Alamein, which opened
on 23rd October, remained in the balance for several days and
developed into the battle of attrition for which Montgomery had
bargained. Finally, on 3rd November the breakthrough was achieved
and Rommel, who had been rushed back from sick-leave, withdrew
his forces before they were all wiped out. Once again the race across the
desert was on – towards the west this time.

Pip and his fellow-prisoners listened to the heartening news with very
mixed feelings. On the one hand it was wonderful to hear the rapid
advances being made by the Eighth Army, with the recapture of many
familiar places – not least that of Tobruk, which held bitter memories
for many of them. This time, on 13th November 1942, Tobruk was
entered by General Dan Pienaar's 1st South African Division, who were
delighted to find a number of South African coloured auxiliary troops
who had been captured there five months previously. On the other
hand, Pip and his friends couldn't help feeling regret that they themselves were not there to join in the pursuit, as the tide turned once more.
They all firmly believed, and rightly, that this time it would be for the
last time.

On 20th November Benghazi changed hands for the fifth and final
time, and all eyes now turned to El Agheila. British and Dominion
forces had reached this point twice before – and twice they had been
held and then driven back right across Cyrenaica and beyond. Surely
this time history wouldn't repeat itself? Would the pendulum swing
back once again?

(*Left*) Major Sam Derry, M.C., in Cairo in 1942. (*Right*) Lt-Col. John Furman, M.C., O.B.E., in Rome in 1984 for a Rome Escape Organisation reunion, forty years after Liberation.

Three prominent survivors of the Rome Escape Organisation visiting the graves of others less fortunate, at the Reunion forty years on. L to R: Bill Simpson, M.C., with Sam Derry and John Furman.

(*Above*) Monsignor Hug
O'Flaherty, C.B.E., (left
appearing on 'This Is Y(
in honour of Colonel Sa
Derry, D.S.O., M.C., J.F
(centre), with Eamonn
Andrews in 1963.

(*Left*) John Furman and
Derry in St Peter's Squa
Rome in 1984, for an Ar
TV interview on June 3r
at 7 am—hence the lac
people and pigeons.

The answer this time was that Monty, who had been knighted on the day that Tobruk was retaken, for his victory at El Alamein, was systematically massing his forces for the renewed assault that was to carry him past El Agheila on 12th December and thence inexorably along the Libyan coast to Tripoli, which was entered on 23rd January 1943. This time there had been the supplies to carry the push right through to Tripoli, and Montgomery had made the most of his good fortune.

Rommel's retreat, frequently a fighting one, was hastened by the most opportune timing of the landings on 8th November 1942 of the Americans at points along the coast of Vichy French Algeria, with the British First Army in support under General K. A. N. Anderson. This added to the jubilation and optimism that pervaded the camp at Chieti. As Christmas 1942 approached, the good news continued to arrive. Prisoners whose command of Italian was minimal suddenly found themselves becoming surprisingly adept at translating the Italian news-bulletins that were received in the camp. The vocabulary used tended to be rather repetitive. Despite valiant attempts by the Italian newspapers to dwell on the enormous numbers of enemy planes shot down by *'nostri aviatori'* – one wondered how on earth the RAF managed to keep flying in the face of such astronomical losses! – it was impossible to disguise the scale of the defeat being suffered by the Axis powers in North Africa.

On the strength of the good news from Africa, many prisoners in Chieti and elsewhere in Italy ventured to hope that Christmas 1942 would be their last in captivity. A few of them were right – but for the majority, including Pip Gardner, Fate was to direct matters otherwise.

*

The good news continued into the New Year, as the prisoners at Chieti watched the Allies' progress in North Africa from the sidelines. The advance of the Eighth Army continued past Tripoli into Tunisia, while the First Army and the Americans were struggling hard to link up from the other direction. It looked all over bar the shouting to anyone who wasn't there. But for those engaged in the fighting, it was clear that the Afrika Korps wasn't done for yet. For the Eighth Army there remained the formidable Mareth Line barring the way in the south of Tunisia, and for the Americans in the high ground in the west there was much hard fighting to be undertaken, including some alarming reverses to suffer. But the end of the road for the Afrika Korps now seemed inexorable.

As spring arrived at Chieti, the thoughts of the prisoners, including Pip Gardner, inevitably turned to escaping. They had already had enough of captivity, meagre rations and an erratic water supply. Furthermore they realised that it was the duty of every officer to escape if he could contrive a method of doing so. But the wire was well-guarded and the Italian guards remained vigilant under the beady eye of the unpleasant commandant. The best prospect of escape seemed to lie in the long-established prisoners' art of tunnelling.

Pip joined a team of tunnellers again and set to work. But before the tunnel had reached the wire, it was discovered under suspicious circumstances, which pointed again to the presence of a stooge within the camp, whose identity, however, was not definitely known. The upshot of this discovery was two weeks' solitary confinement in the cooler for those involved in the tunnelling. Pip's confinement was made more tolerable by the slight increase in daily rations that the British kitchen orderlies were able to contrive. They also managed to smuggle in a few welcome cigarettes to those who were locked up.

Soon after Pip was returned to the compound, after serving his sentence, there followed the news that he and his fellow-tunnellers, along with some other 'undesirables' (from the sorely-tried commandant's point of view), were going to be transferred to a camp further north, where there was known to be a punishment camp near Genoa – a sort of Italian version of Colditz Castle in Germany.

Thus on 12th April 1943, which was Renée's birthday, Pip and his party of *pericolosi* ('dangerous ones') as they were now termed, were taken from Chieti by train to an undisclosed destination in the north of Italy. Their feelings were that the camp would probably be worse than Chieti, which was not a cheering prospect. In the event they were in for a pleasant surprise. After travelling all day in second-class carriages once more, they arrived, not at Genoa as feared, but at the small town of Fontanellato, which lies a few miles to the north-west of Parma in the Lombardy Plain, with a population of just over 6,000.

From the station they were marched a short distance to a tall three-storey building with an imposing classical façade. This turned out to be Campo di Concentramento Number 9, and it was to prove vastly preferable to Number 21 at Chieti. The new arrivals soon felt that the tunnelling and other misdemeanours that had landed them there had turned out to be well worth while after all.

The camp at Fontanellato was in the small town and the prisoners were housed in a building that had been started before the war as an orphanage. But before it could be filled with orphans, it had been taken over as a camp for prisoners-of-war, who thus found themselves using 'squatter' lavatories with small foot blocks intended for children. But apart from the slightly precarious lavatories, the building made a far more comfortable POW camp than Pip and company had so far experienced.

The sleeping quarters were a great improvement on what they had known at Bari and Chieti, where they had slept in wooden two-tier double bunks – forming blocks of four beds. If one of the inmates had accumulated lice, the occupants of the other three beds could expect nightly visits from the hungry insects in their search for fresh food. At Fontanellato, where the prisoners had separate wire beds, there was no such problem. What was more, the prisoners were even provided with sheets, which were regularly laundered by nuns in an adjoining nunnery, whose inmates were never actually seen by the prisoners, but to whom the latter were most grateful for their new standard of comfort and hygiene.

Likewise the food at Fontanellato was a vast improvement on anything they had hitherto come across. For the first time since capture, Pip enjoyed the luxury of a regular supply of Red Cross parcels, and food ceased to be the obsession that it had inevitably become elsewhere. Drink, too, was available in rationed quantities. This was in the form of a very pleasant white Vermouth, as well as a rough red wine. Some people chose to mix the two in a big jug, around which they would sit at a table in an improvised bar on the top floor of the building. The fact that the drink was strictly rationed didn't prevent some cheerful parties from taking place on any given day which seemed to call for a celebration. By a little mutually-advantageous arrangement it was possible to organise a sufficient quantity of drink for a convivial evening. One simply had to give one's ration to some willing accomplices for a few days in advance in order to collect a significant quantity in exchange, for consumption on the appointed night. This was found to be better than trying to accumulate one's own wine in a container,

because the wine turned the inside of the container an alarming shade
of purple or green! Better still, one might be lucky enough to find a
fellow-prisoner who didn't like wine, and arrange a private contract
of supply.

For exercise there was access to an enclosed field from which it was
also possible to view the girls of Fontanellato as they made their way
to the town cemetery. This gave the prisoners a distant glimpse of
normal life which was denied to them from the orphanage building
itself. Those who had ventured to lean out and peer on to the street
at passing girls from the bar window had been met with shouts from the
guards, swiftly followed by a fusillade of bullets through the window,
some of which lodged in the ceiling. The peering game was clearly not
worth the candle.

There were also weekly escorted parole walks, for which a quick way
out from the town was taken. It led into the fertile and productive
countryside of the Po valley which, though full of crops, proved remarkably devoid of inhabitants. The routes were carefully chosen to avoid
contact between the prisoners and the populace. Nevertheless the walks
were much appreciated and were always fully subscribed.

Pip was delighted to come upon old friends and acquaintances from
the desert and elsewhere in Fontanellato. Among them was Jack
Kempton, whose path now merged once more with Pip's. They had
come across each other twice previously: before the war, in pursuit
of the same girl in Bedford (where Pip's black MG had given him an
unfair advantage!), and in 1938 at the medical examination in London
for admission to the Westminster Dragoons. Now they had ended up in
the same Italian prisoner-of-war camp for a while, though their paths
were destined soon to separate again.

All in all, Fontanellato contained a most interesting cross-section of
prisoners – many of them from famous cavalry regiments, having been
cut off and captured in the fluid fighting that was peculiar to desert
warfare. Included in their number were two particularly resourceful
officers: Captain Tom Tufnell of the Royal Tank Regiment, whom
Pip had known in the Westminster Dragoons, and his partner Captain
John ('Crump') Colbeck, a Marine Commando captured on the raid
on Rommel's headquarters in 1941. Like some of the other prisoners,
they were constantly on the look-out for ways of escape from the camp,
despite the relatively high standard of prisoners' living that Fontanellato

provided. Their searches took them down into the drainage system and in the course of their probings they found that the 'squatter' lavatories had yielded a rich harvest of coins, rings and other objects which had landed into the flushing stream, resembling a miniature River Po, that ran swiftly below the juvenile foot-blocks on which the prisoners had to balance in order to perform. With the aid of an improvised rake which they had procured, the firm of Tufnell and Colbeck went into the salvage business and set up a recovery service. For a small number of cigarettes, which had more or less become camp currency, they performed this unsavoury but useful service and carried out some profitable salvage. They fished out a variety of objects that had fallen from people's pockets, and even managed to return a set of false teeth to their distraught but grateful owner.

Spring turned to summer and the good news from North Africa continued. By 16th May 1943 the last Axis troops had been driven out of Tunisia, and the Western Desert campaign was finally brought to a close by the surrender of the German and Italian forces, respectively under General Baron Sixt von Arnim and Marshal Giovanni Messe, the latter having been left in command of all Axis forces after Rommel had been recalled to Germany during the battle of Mareth. Rommel's days as a soldier were not yet over, but the legend of his invincibility had finally been dispelled by Monty's triumphant victory.

Now the prisoners at Fontanellato studied their maps more keenly than ever, trying to work out where the victorious Allies would next attack. They didn't have long to ponder, for on 10th July 1943 the Allied landings on Sicily took place, thus bringing the war unmistakably in their direction. By 17th August, Sicily too had been cleared of Italian and German troops, including men of the Hermann Goering Parachute Division dropped as reinforcements, and the way now seemed clear for an Allied invasion of the Italian mainland. It could only be a matter of time. Nobody knew where the landings would take place, but the prisoners at Fontanellato noted with some concern that they were situated much further north than they would have liked. But doubtless the Allies would be planning amphibious operations at various points up the coast of the Adriatic and Ligurian seas. Surely they wouldn't start in the south and slowly fight their way northwards? Speculation was rife in the camp and optimism grew apace.

Their hopes had received a boost on 25th July when Mussolini was deposed and in his place a government led by Marshal Badoglio assumed control. At first the situation in the camp remained much the same, except that the guards became more overtly friendly, and tore down the pictures of the Duce that had for long adorned their living quarters. They also lost the urge to fire shots in the direction of anyone who ventured to peer out of the window and call to passers-by. On the debit side, as far as the prisoners were concerned, was the cancellation of parole walks outside the compound. A general air of expectancy pervaded the camp, and officers in groups or individually began to make final plans for their imminent release or possible chance to escape.

At Fontanellato, where there had been many blessings to count in comparison with most other POW camps in Italy, the prisoners were additionally fortune to have at their helm a wide-awake Senior British Officer, Lieutenant-Colonel de Burgh, whose alertness and gumption was to play a big part in the immediate future of the prisoners in his care – in sharp contrast to most less fortunate prisoners elsewhere. Colonel de Burgh warned his prisoners to be ready for any emergency that might result from the fall of Mussolini. His first step was to form the prisoners in his charge into companies, so that if a break-out or a walk-out were to happen, they would start off in controlled parties and not in a mad stampede in all directions. Pip and his friend Percy Gers decided that, when the time came, they would team up together in an attempt to reach the Allied landings that most people confidently expected. They prepared their light luggage and hard rations saved from their Red Cross parcels, and awaited events.

The hot Italian summer continued through August and into September. Then on 3rd September the first Allied troops landed in Calabria, the southernmost province of mainland Italy. This was the news that they had all wanted, and everybody now confidently awaited news of progress and other landings up the coast.

Then dramatically on the warm summer's evening of 8th September 1943 a really sensational announcement was made by the Senior British Officer, Colonel de Burgh. The Badoglio government had agreed on an armistice with the Allies. At Fontanellato the balloon was about to go up.

CHAPTER TWELVE

Walk-out

Like nearly all Senior British Officers in other camps, Lieutenant-Colonel de Burgh had received orders passed to him through the channels of MI9, to the effect that the prisoners-of-war in their charge were not to be let loose to roam the countryside, possibly indulging in freelance sabotage and generally causing administrative chaos and confusion. They were to stay put in their camps, under discipline and control, until the relieving Allied forces arrived in their area to rescue them in an orderly fashion. This directive, circulated on General Montgomery's instructions, left little room for doubt or questioning, and nearly all SBOs in charge of other camps carried it out to the letter – with, of course, disastrous results for those in their charge. Not so Lieutenant-Colonel de Burgh. Realising that since the publication of those strict orders, the situation on the spot might alter significantly, he wisely made contingency plans, while still intending to implement his instructions if feasible.

Accordingly he gave orders that everyone was to remain in camp, and that there was to be no fraternising with Italians. These orders surprised nobody and Colonel de Burgh was intending to adhere to the directive he had received, unless events should require alternative action. He also said that he would address all officers and men the following morning at 1115 hours.

The sensational news received on that warm evening set everyone talking. After one, two and, in some cases, three years in captivity the prisoners were free at last. Or were they? Some remained sceptical. Earlier that day some fully-armed German troops had been seen marching past the camp in a southerly direction, which hardly seemed to indicate that they were in any great hurry to pull out of Italy, now that their ally had made a separate armistice. It appeared unlikely that the Germans would in any case allow five hundred British officers to slip

135

through their fingers. Anyhow the prisoners at Fontanellato had received their instructions to stay put, while those in charge kept a vigilant watch on events. A special Intelligence section had been set up and they managed to convince some of the prisoners that the Germans would be far too busy and worried, dealing with impending Allied landings by sea and air, to pay attention to a few hundred unarmed and not very valuable prisoners-of-war.

Meanwhile, despite the colonel's orders of no fraternising with the Italians, shouting and waving from the windows soon took place, to a crowd of friendly civilians who had gathered outside the camp. So excited were they that one would have imagined that their country had just won the war, rather than withdrawn from it. There were shouts of '*Armistizio! Armistizio!*' in case the prisoners hadn't yet grasped the fact – which seemed to bring equal joy to either side.

When the news spread that wine in the camp bar was now off-ration people gravitated in that direction, mugs in hand, either to collect their wine and take it away to consume it in their rooms, or to drink it while propping up the bar counter in excited conversation. Celebrations in the bar were soon in full swing and two separate schools of thought emerged. Optimists were busy calculating how long it would take for them to be back home. Some suggested two weeks, while others were inclined to allow a little longer. Others were less euphoric and couldn't ignore the recent sight of German troops moving southwards and seemingly in no hurry to pull out. They felt strangely uneasy about the situation and were soon branded as pessimists.

The revelry and the discussions continued unabated, however, and both the day and the bar closed without further incident. The prisoners trooped off to bed, with shouts of '*Armistizio!*' still ringing in their ears, and thoughts of home running through their minds. Pip's thoughts naturally turned to Renée, from whom he had now been separated for over two and a half years. For most of them exhaustion took the place of excitement and they eventually fell asleep.

The next day, 9th September, started somewhat ominously. Colonel de Burgh, who had originally arranged to address the camp at 1115 hours, sent round word that he was now calling a meeting for 0900 hours instead. He informed the assembled gathering that Germans were now said to have established themselves in the district. Although they had so far made no move to approach the camp, it was nevertheless felt that they might well make an attempt to collect the prisoners and transport them hurriedly to Germany. This was a contingency for which Colonel de Burgh was prepared to disregard his instructions to stay put, and he was ready to take avoiding action. The prisoners were warned to pack their haversacks, or some similar home-made hold-all, with their small kit, including tooth-brushes and razors. They would also be issued with a Red Cross parcel each. The idea was that they would march out of camp in organised companies to an area away from the camp, which the Italians had reconnoitred for them. He didn't expect them to have to stay out for more than twenty-four hours, by which time it was considered likely that the period of danger would be over. It was the intention of the Italians to bar the way of the Germans, should they attempt to enter the camp.

Colonel de Burgh added that the Italian commandant and his staff had sent out patrols to keep an eye on any move the Germans might make, and report immediately back to the Senior British Officer. Thus they would receive warning if the camp appeared to be the Germans' objective – though nobody could know how long that warning might be. They were therefore ordered to be prepared to move at fifteen minutes' notice.

The prisoners, now feeling far less optimistic than they had the previous evening, spent the next couple of hours in preparations and packing, amid further speculation. They had just gone into the Mess for lunch at noon, when an urgent message came through. They were to parade by companies on the football field immediately. A mad rush ensued, with everyone imagining that the Germans had arrived at the door.

Pip Gardner and Percy Gers had just grabbed their kit and were passing through the door leading outside, when a shout of alarm was raised. A German bomber was heading straight for the camp. It came roaring over at a height of no more than 300 feet. They all expected to be bombed, but the plane passed harmlessly over. Perhaps it was merely on reconnaissance – which, of course, could be ominous. The sooner they got away the better.

After this disturbance, the prisoners formed up on the football field in their pre-arranged companies, platoons and sections. Pip and Percy were in the same section, intending to stay together if at all possible. The companies made an orderly exit from the camp, with the Senior British

Officer taking the salute. For one officer who had broken a bone in his leg, a horse was procured, with an Italian soldier at its head to lead it. The whole procedure was a trifle unreal, but it was certainly a disciplined departure.

The mid-day heat was fierce and many of the prisoners, especially those who had been in captivity the longest, began to feel weary, as they marched three miles out into the country. Italian soldiers led the way. Their hiding-place had been selected among vineyards which were in full leaf and laden with grapes, plenty of which were ripe enough to eat. The vineyards lay well back from a road and were concealed by a row of poplars and some bushes. It was a well-chosen site and the prisoners were soon dispersed in company areas, with the SBO and his Intelligence headquarters in the middle.

The march had been carried out in perfect order, except for one alarming incident. Another German plane appeared on the scene and caused everyone to make a wild dash for any cover they could find on either side of the road. Once again nothing came of this second visit from the Luftwaffe, but the plane's sudden arrival and departure left the prisoners with an uneasy feeling about their situation. Had their walk-out been spotted?

The road ran east–west, just south of the vineyards, and guards were posted to keep a watch on this highway. Extreme caution seemed to be called for and they talked in whispers, so as not to give away their position to any passers-by along the road. It was feared that the Germans might approach along this road in their efforts to track down their vanished quarry.

Percy Gers found himself doing the first two hours' guard duty for his section. Nothing happened for the first three-quarters of an hour, but then he was startled to see three German motor-cyclists travelling in a westerly direction. They were followed by tanks, motorised infantry and lorries bringing up the rear. Percy's first reaction was one of panic. He felt like running like hell in the opposite direction, spreading the alarm as he went. But he quickly realised that the Germans were completely oblivious of the presence so close to them of several hundreds of escaped prisoners-of-war. From a concealed position behind some bushes Percy estimated the strength of this warlike column to be about twenty-four tanks, three to four hundred infantry and forty covered lorries. He reckoned that they must be on their way to the Genoa area, to confront the Allied landing which had already been strongly rumoured. Nor was Genoa the only place mentioned in connection with an Allied landing. Other seaborne landings were also reported, as well as airborne landings which were rumoured to have taken place near Rome and Milan. It was even said that American parachutists had been dropped to block the Brenner Pass in the north. These rumours, exciting though they were at the time, were to prove a great delusion and a nuisance in the weeks to come, when escaped prisoners had to base their decisions on false premises.

The only other Germans to pass along the road were a few despatch-riders, who rode straight past at speed. News was received from the Intelligence section that about an hour after the departure of the prisoners the Germans had indeed turned up at the camp in considerable strength, reputedly seven hundred of them. This was borne out as the escaped prisoners spent their first night in the open, hidden under the vines. They could hear the sporadic crackle of rifle fire, punctuated by the occasional rat-tat-tat of a machine-gun. There were explosions at intervals and bright flashes could be seen in the neighbourhood of the camp.

The prisoners got very little sleep – the situation was too tense for relaxation. In the dark, imaginations were running riot. Trees and vines took on all sorts of queer shapes in the moon's rays. However, nothing disastrous occurred and the new day, 10th September, broke fine, if a little misty at first. But what had the next twenty-four hours in store for the prisoners in hiding? It seemed that it would now be hopeless to attempt to return to the camp and no alternative solution came immediately to mind. It was decided to sit tight for the present.

During the morning, news came through from the Intelligence section that the Allies had made landings at La Spezia, Livorno and Genoa on the Ligurian coast to the west, and at Trieste and Rimini on the Adriatic to the east. This meant that there could be a good chance of linking up with their own troops somewhere not too far from their present position.

Everyone's spirits rose considerably and hopes remained buoyant until an Italian civilian wandered into Pip and Percy's section area. They questioned him about the news of landings that they had just received. He denied all knowledge of any such landings, and added that as far as he knew the nearest point at which the Allies were to them was at Salerno, some six hundred miles to the south. This information was passed on to the Intelligence section, who replied somewhat haughtily : 'On no account will information brought in by Italians be treated as authentic. The only authentic news will be distributed by this headquarters. We confirm our previous report re the landings.'

That seemed to be that! But Pip and Percy and those round them had their doubts and began to make their own plans to get going and make for their own lines. It would surely be better than this endless waiting and uncertainty.

An incident that occurred late in the afternoon helped them make up their minds to leave the area. Pip and Percy were lying under a vine when they saw a number of men in grey uniform making a dash for the bund, which was a high bank along a canal. All those in their section went into hiding in the first undergrowth they could find. After lying low for a quarter of an hour, they decided to investigate, and found that the men who had dashed for the bund were some RAF types, whom they had mistaken for Germans. This had raised the alarm, and that settled it. They were all getting too jittery to remain any longer where they were.

As Pip and Percy set off, a Canadian lieutenant who had been attached to the 4th Royal Tanks asked if he might join them. Though Pip and Percy had originally considered two a better number than three, for escaping purposes, they agreed to let him accompany them. He was shortish and rather a quiet type. His name, coincidentally, was Jimmy Gardner. They held a quick conference and decided to head east. They would have made for the Apennines to the west, but the fact that one of the companies had previously elected to go in that direction meant that the area to the west would be too crowded with escaping prisoners-of-war, without any further additions to their number. This seemed the logical decision, and they waited impatiently till dark before setting off.

At 8 p.m. the three escapers, Pip Gardner, Jimmy Gardner and Percy Gers, set off with full haversacks, carrying tins of bully beef, service biscuits and slabs of chocolate with them, as well as one water-bottle between them. It was already dark by the time they started, for which they were very thankful. They were still very jittery and moved with extreme caution.

The first major obstacle they imagined would be the crossing of the road along which the German troops had passed the previous day. Every time anyone made the slightest noise, they all went to ground and lay listening intently for danger. In the end they managed to cross the road without any difficulty at all. They had decided to avoid all roads and to make their way across country. They found it very heavy going over ploughed fields, with their boots becoming progressively heavier as they became caked with mud.

By 1 a.m. they found themselves near a farmstead and they debated whether to look for shelter there and then, or wait until daylight first before asking permission to hide in a farm building. They decided on the latter course and tried to settle down for a few hours' sleep. A vine offered them sparse shelter from the light wind that was blowing. As they had only one greatcoat between the three of them, they found it difficult to keep warm and could only manage some very fitful slumber.

Dawn broke fine once more and there still appeared to be no signs of life at the farm. Leaving Pip to guard their few belongings, the other two reconnoitred. They approached a cowstall, where they found a farmer busy milking his cows by hand. At the first sight of them he appeared considerably shaken. But when they explained that they wanted to shelter in his barn, he immediately gave permission, enquiring at the same time whether they were escaped English prisoners-of-war. There was no sense in denying this, and anyhow he seemed pleased to see them. He supplied them with as much milk as they could drink – warm and fresh from the cow. He also fetched them some bread. Percy and Jimmy were tucking into the bread when they suddenly realised that the unfortunate Pip was still out in the vineyard, faithfully guarding their possessions. Percy dashed out to fetch him and explained their luck as they walked back to the cowstall.

This farm was to be their home for the next five days, and their friendly hosts were kindness itself. Renewed rumours were received that the Allies were now moving east from Genoa, and this news, coupled with what they had previously heard from their own Intelligence section, persuaded the three escapers to lie low where they were, in the area around Parma. Their present refuge seemed as good as any, and they didn't expect to have to wait there more than a couple of weeks, before the Allied troops arrived.

However after a few days their host began to get the wind up. He said that he had heard that the Germans were going to conduct a systematic search of the countryside for escaped prisoners and that anyone found sheltering fugitives would be shot out of hand. When a further piece of unwelcome news arrived, to the effect that the Germans had offered 1500 lire – a lot of money in those days for a peasant – for any information leading to the recapture of a prisoner-of-war, their minds were made up. For the sake of the farmer and his family they simply must move.

The eve of their departure was a good excuse for a farewell party, coupled with the fact that it was also Percy Gers's birthday, 16th September. Their host, whom they had nicknamed 'George', to avoid using his proper name in case they were caught and questioned, certainly rose to the occasion by providing six bottles of good wine and plenty of food. The party lasted until midnight, and the only reason for breaking up then was the fact that the three fugitives were due to leave at two o'clock in the morning and they wanted to snatch a couple of hours' sleep before leaving.

The night was black and dismal, and the escapers were in two minds whether to move or not. It was consideration for the farmer's fears that made them stick to their original plan and leave without delay. With their motley collection of belongings packed into their army haversacks they set off once more on their adventurous journey. They had marched out of camp in battledress, having no civilian clothes. During their stay at the farm, the farmer's wife had kindly dyed their khaki clothing in order to give the fugitives more of an appearance of Italian farm workers or soldiers returning home after the armistice.

Pip and Percy had also decided to remove their moustaches, as they were not commonly worn by Italians. The prickly operation took place in a hut in the middle of a field, and the result caused much amusement. Neither Pip nor Percy had seen the other without a moustache and the transformation looked decidedly odd. They felt, however, that this facial adjustment increased their chances of merging with their present environment.

Their journey started with extreme caution; they took fright at the slightest rustle and dived for cover. The first obstacle on their way was a small bridge which carried the road over a very deep river cutting. They expected to find it guarded and approached it warily through some trees, until they were within twenty yards of it. Even then they weren't satisfied that the coast was clear.

A hurried conference took place in the dark. In low whispers it was decided that one of them should move up to the bridge and cross it if possible, while the other two watched results and followed if all was well. They hastily drew lots with some small twigs – one of them being shorter than the other two. Jimmy Gardner, the Canadian, it was who drew the short twig and was thus selected to act as a sort of guinea-pig or decoy. Leaving his kit with the others, so as not to be encumbered if he ran into trouble and had to beat a hasty retreat, Jimmy moved off after good-luck handshakes from the other two. Pip and Percy watched his dark figure moving slowly on to the road, before he disappeared for a few moments among the shadow of some trees. Then he reappeared moving carefully towards his objective. He had just reached the road noiselessly and was walking stealthily towards the bridge, when suddenly he turned and made a frantic dash for the cover of the trees which lined the road. He reached them and disappeared from view. The others waited with bated breath, wondering what was going to happen next. Nothing could be seen or heard of Jimmy – nor was there anything to account for his sudden action.

Pip and Percy had just decided to make an exploratory move towards the bridge themselves when they were startled to hear the engine of a motor-cycle starting up; then another, and another – until there seemed to be some ten or twelve machines roaring away somewhere on the road. They didn't have long to wait before they saw the dim blue lights of five of the motor-cycles which came dashing over the bridge, past them and away into the night. Their hearts beat frantically, as they wondered what was in store for them next.

Jimmy was nowhere to be seen and it seemed that they had lost him for good. They kept their eyes on the bridge, despite the discomfort of their position. The undergrowth was soaked with rain that had fallen earlier in the night, and they felt cold, wet and miserable. They kept up their vigil for a good ten minutes before Jimmy reappeared on the road, walking cautiously towards the bridge. He reached it, quickening his pace to almost a run and was lost to view once more.

Now it was the turn of the others, and they hurriedly drew twigs to see who should lead. This time it was Percy Gers. Pip was to wait until Percy had reached the bridge and then he was to follow about ten yards behind with Jimmy's kit as well as his own. Off went Percy at a brisk pace and rapidly approached the bridge. He was soon on it and quickly

(*Left*) Chieti 1943. Pip Gardner and Percy Gers. (*Right*) Before the bombing at Brunswick in 1944. A group of POWs, with Pip Gardner and Tug Wilson in front (centre).

Hungry but happy. Brunswick Camp at the time of the liberation, on April 12th, 1945. L to R: War Photographer W. A. ('Click') Vanderson, Pip Gardner and Lieutenant Lewis Wiard of the Royal Tank Regiment.

Welcome Home! Pip Gardner being received by some of the work-force at the Beckenham factory of J. Gardner and Co Ltd in May 1945.

VC's inspection. Captain Pip Gardner, V.C., M.C., being honoured by ex-servicemen at the family engineering works in 1945.

across to the far side – though at the time it seemed an eternity, and one of the tensest moments of his life. On reaching the far side, he heard a faint call from the trees. He moved quickly towards the sound and heaved a sigh of relief as he rejoined Jimmy. Pip caught them up a few moments later.

It was then that they heard Jimmy's explanation for his strange behaviour. Just as he was about to cross the bridge, he had seen a dim blue light appearing in the dip about twenty yards the other side. He recognised it as a military vehicle of some sort – and how right he had been!

They later heard that the Germans were greatly perturbed at the number of Italians who were deserting from the army since the armistice, and they had sent out patrols on most roads with the intention of rounding them up and giving them the option of taking up arms against the Allies, or being deported to Germany as forced labour. It was doubtless into one of these patrols that the escapers had so nearly bumped.

Leaving the road and going through the trees they walked for four hours across open agricultural country of various types. The going was inevitably slow in places, but they reckoned that they had covered about eight miles when they decided it was time to find some sort of shelter. It was now nearly broad daylight and they were still suffering from fright after their experience at the bridge a few hours before. Pip and Jimmy went off to make enquiries at a farm nearby, but drew a blank. The farmer was not at all well-disposed towards the British – in fact Pip and Jimmy, with the limited understanding of Italian which they had picked up in camp, were left with the impression that he was a Fascist sympathiser. They thought it best to give him and his farm a wide berth.

They carried on their way for another two miles to another farm where, in sharp contrast, they were greeted with great courtesy and were allowed to spend two days in a barn, along with their friends the rats and mice. The Italian rodents seemed to be very tame – some of them too much so, when at night they chose to crawl up the fugitives' trousers legs while they were asleep. Despite the rats, the escapers were in no hurry to leave, because they were still under the impression that it was only a matter of time before the Allied troops began advancing in their direction. The main thing was to lie low until they arrived.

But after two days at the farm, putting their kind hosts at risk, they felt bound to move on and seek shelter elsewhere. Accordingly, they spent the next six days wandering around by night and hiding by day, until they arrived back at their original haven, the farm belonging to 'George'. Here they received a great welcome and they remained with 'George' and his family for another six days. Then the old fear began to surface once more, with 'George' informing them that the Germans had not only put a price on the heads of all escaped prisoners-of-war, but had also added a special bounty on officers, graded according to rank. He repeated that anyone found attempting to conceal or help Allied servicemen on the run, did so under penalty of death. His story was soon borne out by the appearance of three German motor-cyclists along the road that skirted his farm. This was enough for the three escapers, who decided to move off the next morning at 2.30 a.m., and make for the British lines down south, until they reached them – a distance according to the Italian radio of six to seven hundred miles. They couldn't put their kind and gallant hosts at risk any longer.

Hospitable to the last, 'George' laid on a special farewell party for his likeable but dangerous guests. His wife shed bitter tears at the thought of the fugitives leaving, and explained that, had it not been for her children, she would gladly have had them stay until the Allied troops arrived. It was a touching farewell, but they had made up their minds to move south as fast as they could.

Thus it was that, after waiting in vain for the arrival of the Allies, which rumours had led them to believe to be imminent, Pip, Percy and Jimmy started out on what was to prove a most arduous and exciting journey for them all. The time was 2.30 a.m., the date was 30th September 1943, the direction was south, but the destination was unknown.

CHAPTER THIRTEEN

Heading South

It was cold and wet when the three escapers set off into the night. But, despite the weather, they left with light hearts, feeling that at last, after so much indecision and waiting, they now had a goal to aim for – albeit at possibly 700 miles away.

Soon after the start of their journey they came once more to the bridge that had given them so many palpitations before. This time it fell to Percy Gers to be the first man across. Rather than mess about drawing lots with twigs at critical moments, they had come to an amicable agreement that they should each take daily turns at being responsible for spying out the land and taking the lead when necessary. It was Percy's turn for that day. At the bridge they carried out the same procedure as before. This time there was no hitch and not a sound of a motor-bike to be heard. Percy in the lead started cautiously, before dashing across the bridge and diving into the nearest undergrowth. Pip and Jimmy both strolled casually across after him and were amused to find him still panting from his efforts on their behalf.

The going became very heavy, owing to the fact that it was raining hard and that they kept well off the roads whenever possible. All of them fell down in the mud at one time or another, which didn't improve their tempers or their already dishevelled appearance. They covered about five miles in three hours before deciding to look for a place to hide for the day. They had no intention of walking by daylight until they could procure some civilian clothes.

They were unsuccessful at first in their search for shelter. Nobody seemed prepared to harbour them even for one day, which was hardly surprising in view of the risks involved. They spent two hours looking for a kindly soul to take them in. Meanwhile it had become light and the rain, far from easing off, came down in bucketfuls. A bridge crossing a stream provided them with shelter from the rain for a while. As they were refreshing themselves with the small supply of bread and salami that they had with them, they received one of the shocks which they were beginning to associate with bridges that they came across.

A convoy of lorries passed above them and soon after these were safely over, they heard the sound of marching feet in the distance, accompanied by unmistakably German voices raised in song as they marched along, as is their wont. Soon the steps and the Teutonic voices drew closer and closer, until the leaders were overhead as they crossed the bridge. The fugitives' hearts pounded away and they were even afraid to swallow, for fear of making a noise. Fortunately none of them needed to cough or sneeze. The marching continued for what seemed a lifetime, before they heard the last footsteps over the bridge.

A quarter of an hour elapsed before the escapers made any sound or move, not knowing what to do, in case there were some stragglers or even another company of marchers still to come. Finally it was decided that Percy, as leader for that day, should spy out the land above them. He crawled out of their hiding-place and clambered up the bank in order to have a cautious look around. There was no sign of the Germans and their noise had faded into the distance. Percy went along the road in the same direction as the Germans had gone, until he came to a T-junction where he went into a field in order to get a good view from a vantage spot with some bushes for cover. The coast was clear in all directions so he ran back to his companions, who by now were shivering with cold and wet. They were much relieved to learn that it was now safe for them to come out of hiding.

They were standing by the side of the road, discussing their next move, when a man approached them along the road and asked if they were escaped prisoners-of-war. Without thinking, they affirmed that they were. The man's reaction was astonishing. He grasped them each in turn by the hand and kissed them all on each cheek, at the same time inviting them to his farm for food. This seemed too good an offer to refuse and the three escapers set off with him along the road and then up a track to his farm. There they ate an unusual but welcome breakfast, consisting of walnuts, grapes, bread and cheese, with wine to wash it down. The wine nearly proved their undoing because it was very strong and went to their heads alarmingly.

Pip pointed to their muddy clothing and asked if he could fix them up with some civilian attire to wear instead of their dyed army battledress, as whenever they got wet they went blue from the dye. At first the man wasn't sure, but when Pip offered him his wristwatch his initial hesitation left him. He produced an assortment of old workmen's clothes into which they climbed, amid much laughter at the transformation.

The subject of staying the day was mooted, but the farmer seemed very nervous at the thought of having them around for the whole day. As he had at least set them up with food and clothing, they didn't feel inclined to press the point, but thanked him warmly and went on their way at about 11 a.m. As they went out of the house the effect of the wine really hit them. It gave them 'Dutch courage', and they walked along the road – a risk that they hadn't at any time taken before. Striding nonchalantly along, they felt ready to confront the entire German army if necessary! Percy Gers, feeling extremely aggressive, actually said: 'Show me a bloody Hun – wheel one in', looking challengingly around him as he voiced his alcoholic sentiments.

What he saw shook him considerably. There was a German riding a bicycle towards them from behind. Percy, lowering his voice to a whisper, warned the others: 'Don't look now but I think we are being followed by a bloody Hun!' They nearly upset everything by breaking into a run instinctively, but fortunately they gathered their wits about them sufficiently to keep walking along, like three unconcerned Italian farm-labourers. At any moment they expected the German to pass them and possibly stop them. At last Percy ventured a glance back, but his Hun was nowhere to be seen. The question was now, had he gone off post haste to summon help, or had he merely gone into one of three cottages by the roadside? The three escapers didn't wait to find out the answer, but rushed for the fields and went floundering across a sea of mud as fast as their legs could carry them.

When they were well away from the road, they took refuge in some bushes far from any human habitation. They thanked their lucky stars that their over-confidence, induced by the wine and the civilian clothes, hadn't after all landed them into serious trouble. They managed to sleep for the rest of the day and woke up sober and considerably chastened.

When darkness fell, they resumed their southward journey. As yet they hadn't gone very far on their march south, but from this point onwards they fell into something of a routine and began to make

slightly faster progress. In avoiding the roads they were obliged to wend
their way up and down more hills and valleys than they would have
liked, but each day they were able to get shelter in barns, and usually
a little food from kind Italian families, for whom they sometimes
performed menial chores, such as chopping swedes.

On one occasion they were able to spend two days at one farm, by
helping with the grape harvest. At the end of the day they joined in the
treading of the grapes in large wooden vats in their bare feet, which
rapidly turned red with the juice. In return for their labour, they were
asked into the farmhouse and their day ended with a very cheerful party
with their friendly hosts and their daughters. The latter produced an
ancient gramophone with a huge horn to which they danced. At first
they danced in their heavy army boots, but later, at the suggestion of
their bruised partners, they took them off and danced barefoot – with
grape-stained feet.

Their route lay along the foothills of the Apennines. By keeping the
main Milan–Bologna railway on their left, and the high mountains on
their right, they steered a course that was leading them more or less
to the south-east, and was reasonably easy to follow without a compass.
They skirted Modena and Bologna, before turning due south and a bit
higher into the hills. They were making for Florence, which they hoped
to skirt when they reached it. By covering on average about ten miles
a day, as the crow flies (though a good deal more by the up-and-down
route that they were obliged to take, in order to keep clear of trouble),
they had reached a point between Bologna and Florence in three weeks.

By this time they had become tired of walking by night and decided
to journey by day, having grown more confident in their peasant attire.
One Sunday they found themselves walking along a path near a large
village. Though they resembled walking scarecrows in their tattered
clothes, their attire probably wouldn't have drawn much attention on
a week-day. But the Italians were in the habit of dressing up in their
best clothes on a Sunday and parading in public. This especially applied
to the womenfolk, who after dressing and working as peasants in the
fields during the week, somehow contrived, even in wartime, to look
really smart on Sundays. The men, too, mostly wore suits. The three
escapers pressed rather self-consciously on, hoping to get past the
Sunday strollers without comment or involvement.

Suddenly a man came up and walked beside them. He said : 'You're

British soldiers, aren't you?' to which Pip replied, in bad Italian, 'No, of course not. We're just Italian soldiers returning to our homes.' The man knew of course by their looks, and from Pip's broken Italian, that his guess had been correct, and said : 'Look, I can help you but for heaven's sake get off this path, or someone will send for the Fascists or the Germans and you will be caught.'

Having little option, they followed his advice and he led them across the fields to a large farm, where he took them into a cow-shed and told them to wait.

They had no idea whether he was really being friendly, or whether he was sending for the Germans in order to claim a reward. But they decided to wait where he had put them, ready to bolt, if they saw anyone coming over the fields. After a short while, a young maid, dressed in a black-and-white domestic uniform, arrived with a card table and laid it with a white table-cloth and some beautiful silver and glass. She then served them with an excellent meal, as well as several bottles of wine.

A little later their new friend arrived with a bottle of brandy and said that he would like to help them further in any way possible. He suggested for a start that they should go over to the farmouse, which turned out to be a very lovely home. There they were introduced to all the family and were invited to tune in the radio to the BBC, so that they could listen to the English news. By this time they had become pretty friendly with their host, who suggested that he should give them some money to buy some respectable clothes. He added that, as their Italian wasn't good enough to go shopping, he would send his wife into the nearest town next day to buy clothes and shoes for them.

The three escapers were quite overcome by his generous offer, but their benefactor hadn't finished yet. He explained that he was a bicycle-manufacturer, and that he would provide them with a new bike each for their onward journey. He provided them with beds in the farmhouse for the night. Next day he was as good as his word, and Pip, Percy and Jimmy set off on their new bicycles looking like well-to-do Italians out for a joy-ride. As if their unknown host, whom they referred to amongst themselves as 'Vanderbilt', hadn't already done enough for them, he thrust into their hands a wad of lire each. Their gratitude knew no bounds.

Thus transformed, and not a little cheered, they didn't bother about making a detour round Florence – they cycled slap through the middle

and crossed the bridge over the Arno in style. In this way they made
much faster progress, of course, and from then on they always found
some kindly Italian to put them up for the night, and they never went
hungry or thirsty. The journey wasn't, however, without incident.

On leaving Florence in the afternoon, it was Jimmy's day to lead
and they came to a steep hill, leading down to a bridge at the bottom.
The other two warned him not to take it too fast, but he lost control and
crashed heavily at the bottom, hitting the kerb very hard. When the other
two followed him down, they feared that he might have hurt himself
seriously but, though shaken, he was able to pick himself up in one piece.
Apart from a little grazing on both hands, he wasn't seriously damaged.
But the bicycle hadn't got off so lightly. The front wheel was badly
buckled and their attempts to mend it proved unsuccessful – as well as
attracting undue attention. However, one of the bystanders led them
off to a bicycle shop. The owner didn't say much, but made a good
job of repairing the buckled wheel. When Jimmy tried to pay him, he
absolutely refused to take any money. Instead he gave them a knowing
wink and wished them a safe journey. Once again an unknown Italian
had shown them kindness, for which they were extremely grateful –
even if once again they had been rumbled all too easily.

Their bicycles led them into another tricky incident. One day they
were toiling up a hill on the way out of a village, when a lorry full of
German troops passed them and stopped. The three escapers thought
that after all their hard slog, their freedom was about to come to an
abrupt end as the lorry pulled up. But all that happened was that the
driver got out and came up to the cyclists and, in Italian as bad as theirs,
said : 'I will tie a rope to the back and will tow you up this steep hill.'
The cyclists grabbed the rope, one behind the other, and had a comparatively effortless ride towards the top of the hill, peeling off and
disappearing down a side-turning just before the top, with a wave of
hands, rather than get further involved with the helpful Germans.
Once again luck had been with them and they didn't want to push it,
just for the sake of politeness.

The quicker progress that the bicycles enabled them to make soon
took them up into the mountains, and when this happened the bicycles
became less of a boon, as they frequently had to dismount and push
them up the hills. It wasn't really bicycle country any more, and the
travellers began to feel out of place as they rode or pushed them up

and down the hills. Yet they were reluctant to part with them, after they had given such good service; any anyway their fancy Italian shoes with thin soles were by now in poor repair for walking all the way.

The solution to their problem presented itself one evening at a village where they were being put up for the night in the local *osteria*, or pub. The owner made a suggestion that they should swap their bicycles for some suitable mountaineers' walking-boots. These, like bicycles, were in short supply, but their host said that he could probably procure three pairs if the escapers would be willing to exchange their bicycles for them. They hesitated before agreeing. It didn't seem a very good bargain from their point of view. Yet it might well pay them to be properly shod, rather than hang on to the bicycles, which certainly made them feel more conspicuous the further up into the hills they went. So they decided to accept the offer provided that they could find three pairs of walking-boots to fit them. They succeeded in doing so after trying out several pairs that various inhabitants of the village produced for their inspection, and the deal was clinched.

Next day they set out over the mountains, which were steeper than anything they had so far tackled, and they were soon glad that they had acquired some stout boots and left their bicycles behind. It was by now late October and the weather had already grown appreciably colder – so much so that they began to wonder at times whether they could exist at that height when winter came in earnest. But they were determined to continue their journey south to the Allied lines.

One day they were walking along the road, when two rough-looking men sprang out from the trees near the road and, brandishing pistols, said: *'Mani in alto!'* – 'Hands up!' The surprised travellers rapidly did as they were told. They had been arrested by partisans – the first they had encountered so far. However, they turned out to be friendly and led the escapers to a small village called Bacugno, situated on the side of a hill, whence it was possible to see German transport moving along the valley below.

Bacugno seemed to be inhabited mainly by Italian pastry-cooks who had fled from Rome when the Germans had occupied the city a few days after the armistice in September. Although they now had little means of subsistence in their country refuge, they fed and housed the escapers for the night, in separate small houses. In the evening they took the three soldiers down to an *osteria*, where they all drank quantities of vino. As the evening wore on, the partisans discussed a plan to attack a German convoy on the road below, with guns that they claimed to have hidden somewhere for just such an occasion. The three escapers rashly volunteered to lead the proposed attack. Although they all arranged to meet the next evening to carry out this raid, before finally dispersing for the night, that was the last that was seen of those particular partisans – which was doubless just as well, as they would in all probability have been outnumbered and badly shot up.

After spending two nights in Bacugno, they moved on to the next village along their route. Here they met some more partisans, who were equally friendly but less belligerent. They took the three escapers to a house in the village, where food was provided round a warm fire in a large communal room. When the time came for bed, they were shown to sleeping bunks that lined the walls of the room. Sleeping, too, was evidently to be communal – a bit too communal, they were soon to discover!

Hardly had they dropped off to sleep, when they heard the front door being opened. To their surprise a young couple walked in and sat on a rug in front of the fire, after chucking some more wood on to the dying embers. They went into a clinch, apparently oblivious of the fact that they had an audience. It wasn't long before they took off some of their clothes and went into action in full view, lit up by the flickering flames of the fire. Nobody said a word. The young couple then put their clothes back on and spent the rest of the night curled up near the fire. Only in the morning, as it got light, did they seem to realise that they were not alone. By then it was too late for anything but an exchange of sheepish grins all round!

When day finally broke, the three guests were given some hot polenta and acorn coffee for breakfast. After that, it was suggested that they should take refuge in a shepherd's hut up in the mountains, as there was too much danger for their hosts to harbour them in the village. Apparently there were some other escaped prisoners-of-war already in hiding up there, and the three travellers felt in need of a few days' rest.

Accordingly they set off with one of the partisans acting as guide to show them the hut. At first they gained height through the trees, but were rather shaken to find that the hut itself was above the tree-line, and that at that height the snow had already fallen. They didn't realise it then, but it wouldn't be long before they were virtually snowed in.

THE OSTERIA AT BACUGNO ~

G.J.W.

Sure enough they found three more escapers, who had been there for a couple of days – two South Africans and a New Zealander, who had also walked a long way down Italy, with the intention of finding and crossing the Allied lines. They made the new arrivals welcome – more bodies would mean more heat!

The hut was built against a slope and was in two storeys. The bottom section had recently been used for sheep at night, and the escaped prisoners slept above the sheep pen. They kept close together at night, for warmth, although this seemed to appeal to the lice, which Pip and his companions didn't know whether to attribute to the recent presence of the sheep below or their present bed-fellows alongside them. In any case it wasn't long before they were all lousy.

Each day one or more of their partisan friends would arrive up the steep climb to the hut with food and any news of the position of the Allied troops, who by now, in mid-November, seemed to be bogged down in the mud to the south of Cassino. Meanwhile, with winter setting in, the prisoners felt more and more disinclined to leave their hide-out and venture forth into the snow which had now descended well below them. They had long discussions about what to do, huddled round a fire which they managed to keep going during the day by cutting down trees and bushes with an axe provided by the partisans.

After two weeks of this existence in the hut, they received a surprise visit, from a partisan whom they hadn't met before. He asked which of them was Captain Philip Gardner, and handed Pip a note. To his amazement it was from a British Army major, Sam Derry by name, whom Pip had known at Chieti Camp. The note said that if they wished to have food and shelter in Rome, the partisans would arrange to escort them there. This sounded an ideal solution to their present predicament. Once they reached Rome, they could then make a plan to carry on down to the Allied lines. Pip knew Sam Derry well enough to be confident in following any plan that he suggested. But there was one immediate snag. The partisan could only undertake to escort one of them now. He would have to arrange to collect the others in the near future.

After some discussion, it was arranged that Pip should go first, leaving the others to follow later. Little did any of them realise quite what a momentous decision this was going to prove, as they bade each other farewell, to the accompaniment of : 'See you in Rome!'

CHAPTER FOURTEEN

'When in Rome . . .'

The partisan escort explained to Pip that he would be spending the night in the village, ready to board a bus in the morning in which they were going to travel all the way to Rome. He was taken to sleep in the same house that he had slept in before, with his partisan friends. Once again he found himself in a bunk in the large communal room – but this time there was no 'cabaret' in front of the fire for them to watch!

Before he was taken to board the bus, he was told that he was supposed to be a relative of the partisan who was escorting him to Rome for an operation on his throat. He was told that under no circumstances must he speak during the journey. A second-hand bandage was put round his throat, to lend credibility to the whole idea. The instructions to remain silent suited him admirably. He was put into a seat next to a window and left alone with his thoughts throughout the journey, which took seven hours. They made frequent stops of several minutes' duration, when a few of the civilian passengers got off and others would take their places. Some of the stops were long enough for Pip to get out and relieve himself, accompanied by his 'cousin', which they did on a couple of occasions. The driver certainly seemed in no great hurry.

Pip had been alarmed at first by the large proportion of soldiers in uniform, presumably Fascists, on the bus. None of them seemed to leave the bus at the early stops. He felt sure that they, like him, must be going all the way to Rome – which turned out to be the case. But at no time did they pay any attention to him, and they only exchanged a few words with his escort. Presumably the escort's short explanations were adequate, because thereafter the two travellers were left in peace.

The peace, however, was rudely interrupted when a low-flying American fighter whizzed over them with its machine-guns firing. The bullets flew well beyond the bus and kicked up the gravel on the road ahead of them. It was all over in a flash, but the delayed reaction of the passengers, soldiers and civilians alike, was quite extraordinary. When the plane had gone by in a flash, there was a frenzied stampede for the door of the bus and they all ran to shelter in the trees near the road – probably out of fear of a return visit from the fighter or a swoop by one of its colleagues. But nothing more appeared out of the sky and after about five minutes the passengers began making their way back into the bus, with Pip among them, trying his best to look ill and not in need of conversation.

After that excitement, they settled down to an uneventful journey. Pip's thoughts carried him back to Renée, with whom he had naturally lost all contact since he had walked out from Fontanellato, more than two months previously. He wondered how long it would be before he saw her again. He was still determined to make his way to the Allied lines and freedom. He reflected that his life since he had left Britain had contained some remarkable peaks of achievement and elation, offset by some troughs of frustration and discomfort. His own personal peaks included, of course, his winning of his VC and MC in the desert. His troughs had included his capture at Tobruk and the early days of captivity, notably at Benghazi and Chieti when the war in the desert had not yet swung back finally in the Allies' favour.

Now he was in limbo. He was neither captive nor free – just a fugitive, whose whereabouts was known to nobody at home. He was sorry to be separated from his friend Percy Gers, with whom he had been for so long, both before and after capture. But Percy had insisted that he should accept Major Sam Derry's offer out of the blue and go on ahead. Anyway, they would soon be reunited in Rome, which was only ninety miles away.

Then Pip's thoughts turned to the present and the immediate future. How on earth had Sam Derry heard of his whereabouts up in the mountains? Perhaps they weren't as completely in limbo as they had thought, in the solitude of their shepherd's hut. He wondered how Derry himself had got to Rome and what exactly he was doing there. Above all, he felt sure that Sam Derry wouldn't have sent an escort for him personally unless he had something in mind for him in Rome. Pip had always reckoned that Derry was an outstanding soldier, who could be relied upon to help them on their way to the Allied lines. Time would soon tell.

Finally his thoughts were lost in a long deep sleep, as they journeyed for hours through the mountains. When he finally woke up, they were beginning to lose height and he realised that they were nearing Rome. As they approached the outskirts they came to a road-block, manned by Fascist soldiers, but the sentry merely waved the driver through, as if he were an old friend of his. This was a relief, though there had scarcely been time to become apprehensive.

On arrival in the suburbs of Rome, they got out of the bus and Pip's escort took him straight on to a crowded tram, which conveyed them into the centre of the city, where they got out. Without hesitation Pip was led into a basement cellar, which was full of partisans, most of whom greeted the escort and patted him on the back. They were obviously glad to see him return. Pip was now at liberty to speak again – hard though it was to get a word in edgeways amid all the excitement. They all seemed intent on playing around with loaded pistols and talking of killing Germans and blowing up trains. He was glad when the hubbub subsided and he was allowed to doss down for the night on a mattress in a corner, after he had been given some pasta to eat. The cellar emptied appreciably and the noise died down. He slept like a log.

Next morning he was taken on foot to a respectable and spacious flat on the sixth floor of a building near the Vatican, which was owned by a Signor Nebulante. The latter had originally come to Rome from Florence and was obviously a cultured man, who also spoke good English. He welcomed Pip to his flat and immediately introduced him to a British officer who was also staying there, Captain Robert Wilson by name, who was not surprisingly known as 'Tug' – the fate of most Wilsons in the army. Tug Wilson was the same height as Pip, and of slight and wiry build. The two men clicked right from the start.

Tug Wilson had been in Nebulante's flat for nearly a month. He, like Pip, had been at large in Italy since the Italian armistice on 8th September – or, rather, soon after it. On the day of the armistice he had been a prisoner-of-war at Bologna Camp where, unlike Fontanellato, there had been no walk-out of prisoners. The Senior British Officer at Bologna, a brigadier, had carried out his instructions received from Britain and ordered the officers and men in his charge to stay put, unless the alarm was sounded. The alarm was sounded all right, just before dawn the following morning. But though the prisoners started pouring out of the camp compound and surged along a path towards the main gates, they were confronted there by an enormous German tank blocking the exit, with the menacing barrel of its gun pointing straight down the path, right at the advancing prisoners. They fell flat to the ground. A few of them managed to slink away and escape by a back exit, before that too was sealed off by another tank; in addition, a few independent spirits, revealing a mixture of indiscipline and initiative, had disobeyed the original order to stay put and had cleared off the previous night, while the going was good. The total that escaped probably numbered no more than twenty. Thus almost all the prisoners-of-war at Bologna, with Tug Wilson among them, were scooped up by the swiftly-acting Germans. But Tug Wilson wasn't among them for long.

Three days later they were taken in covered trucks bound for Modena Camp, so they were told. On arrival at Modena, they were rushed instead to the station and rapidly bundled into some waiting trucks lined-up ready for them. Having no wish to be transported through the Brenner Pass to Germany, Tug Wilson was one of the first to find a way of leaving the train. He managed to leave the train before it had even started – with the aid of a friendly railway-worker, coupled with his own opportunism.

Opportunism came naturally to Tug Wilson. Despite being an army officer, he had had a remarkable war with the Royal Navy! After returning safely from Dunkirk in 1940, he was one of the first to answer Churchill's call for men prepared to 'set Europe ablaze', by volunteering for service of a hazardous nature. He was soon recruited as a founder-member of Number I Special Boat Section of the Commandos, and carried out his folboat training in Scotland. At the beginning of 1941, Number I Special Boat Section was sent out to the Middle East as part of Layforce, consisting of 7, 8 and 11 Commandos, under the command of Lieutenant-Colonel R. E. Laycock. By April 1941 the SBS was put under the Royal Navy and thus it was that by the summer of that year Tug Wilson was embarking, together with his chosen folboat partner, Marine Hughes, aboard Royal Navy submarines on a series of daring and successful sabotage operations on the shores of Sicily, Italy, Greece and North Africa. His spectacular run of success had earned him promotion to the rank of captain and also won him the DSO.

Finally, in August 1942, his luck ran out and his submarine failed to pick him up. He thus found himself a prisoner-of-war in Italy. Wilson already had one ingenious but abortive escape to his credit, in company with Captain Guy Greville of the Royal Tank Regiment, from Sulmona Camp. After recapture and the customary spell in the cooler, they were both moved to Bologna. Guy Greville, after witnessing Tug Wilson's adroit escape at Modena station, managed to emulate him by bringing off an amazing feat of daring, which released not only himself but also most of the prisoners in his cattle-truck. He and a Commando friend of his, Lieutenant Sherard Veasey by name, made a hole in the floor of the cattle-truck with an iron bar that Veasey had managed to smuggle aboard, down through which Greville squeezed in order to hoist himself on to the running board of the truck and reach up to release the catch on the outside of the sliding door. Twenty of the prisoners in the truck were able to jump to freedom. Many of them, including Guy Greville and Sherard Veasey, managed to reach Switzerland eventually.

Tug Wilson, on the other hand, had headed south from Modena. He had fallen unwittingly into the hands of an escape organisation and was escorted by train to Rome by two Roman Catholic priests at the end of September 1943. There he had been billeted in a safe flat, but when it later came under suspicion he was moved to Signor Nebulante's flat, where Pip Gardner had now joined him. Pip found him well settled in and seeming to know the ropes, which was a great help to both of them.

When Major Sam Derry, who had taken over the running of the Rome Organisation from its founder Monsignor Hugh O'Flaherty, had heard that Pip Gardner had turned up amongst some partisans near Bacugno in the mountains, he had sent a reliable partisan helper from Rome to fetch him, if he wanted to come, having known and liked him at Chieti, where Sam Derry had been head of the escape committee. The Rome organisation, under Derry's admirable administration, not only looked after escaped prisoners who had reached Rome, but provision was also made for many more who were in hiding in farms and villages far outside the city. In fact, when Rome was finally reached by the Allies on 4th June 1944, there were 3,925 escapers and evaders of various nationalities on the books of the Rome Organisation, of which for security reasons only 200 were billeted actually in Rome itself.

When Sam Derry was wondering where to billet Captain Pip Gardner, VC, MC, his mind quickly turned to Captain Tug Wilson, DSO. He asked Tug if he minded having Pip, whom he hadn't previously met, to share his flat. Tug raised no objection, and that was how these two highly-decorated officers on the run came to share the same hide-out in Rome.

Sam Derry's own arrival in Rome had been most resourceful. At Chieti he, like everyone else, had been ordered to stay put and wait for the Allied troops to arrive and release them. There they had remained, amazingly enough, in this unsatisfactory state of suspense for thirteen days. Two officers who had had enough of waiting managed to climb over the wire, but were caught and returned to the 'cooler' – to be dealt with when the Allies arrived! Instead of the Allies arriving, the Germans turned up with covered trucks to take them off to Germany. They took the prisoners first to Sulmona Camp, before herding them into a train consisting mainly of cattle-trucks, with an ordinary carriage on the back. It was from the latter that Sam Derry managed to bale out and escape. He decided to make his way south on foot and, after walking for several days, he came to a village north of Rome, where he found a large number of other-rank escapers scattered around on various small farms. They looked to him for a lead.

Derry succeeded in getting to Rome in the back of a peasant's cart laden with reeking cabbages. This involved burying himself among the overpowering vegetables in the back of the cart, while the driver took it through the check-point at which all traffic into the city was stopped. He arrived in Rome smelly but undetected and was taken to a building which he imagined to be part of the Vatican. He was shown into the room of a most remarkable man, Monsignor Hugh O'Flaherty, who, as an Irish neutral, was free to come and go as he pleased in the streets of Rome. He was actually working in the Collegio Teutonicum, which was an extra-territorial property of the Vatican, with direct access to the streets of Rome. In the Collegio Teutonicum his daily food was served by German nuns and Derry was introduced to them as an Irish writer. Derry was given a much-needed bath before donning one of the Monsignor's cassocks – fortunately the two men were the same size, broad-shouldered and well over six foot in height – so that they could go together along an internal passage into the Vatican itself, to meet the British Minister in residence, who was operating a skeleton staff there. He was particularly anxious to meet Major Sam Derry.

The Minister was a grey-haired diplomat called Sir D'Arcy Osborne, and the reason why he was so keen to see Derry was that the escape organisation that Monsignor O'Flaherty had been running to help fugitives from Nazism, had now been swamped by the sudden influx of escaped prisoners-of-war who were roaming Italy since the armistice. It had grown to a volume that the Monsignor and the priests who were helping him could no longer cope with on their own. It was, in fact, two of O'Flaherty's priests who had fetched Tug Wilson from hiding in Modena. Sir D'Arcy Osborne was anxious to put a British officer in charge of the Rome Organisation, which located, guided, checked, hid, clothed, fed and found safe lodgings for wandering escaped Allied prisoners-of-war. It would require a man of great drive and organising ablity.

Sir D'Arcy Osborne quickly sized up his man and decided that Derry was the person for the job – though this didn't prevent him from making thorough checks on Derry's background with the War Office, Scotland Yard and even Derry's father in Newark in Nottinghamshire, in order to be sure of his bona fides.

Sam Derry felt that he must accept the assignment. At the time he was the only officer of field rank whom the Minister had met in Rome. Acceptance meant, of course, that Derry would have to abandon all plans of going further south himself towards the Allied lines, and he would have to remain in Rome until the Allies arrived – and they were still to the south of Cassino. Derry was to organise the administrative side of the Rome Organisation, as it was later known, though at the time its name and activities were kept as secret as possible, while the Minister set about providing the considerable amount of funds required. This he was able to do via his links with neutral Lisbon and the British Treasury.

That was how it had become possible to billet escaped prisoners-of-war and other evaders in houses and flats in Rome and to provide funds for their maintenance. With the Organisation's tentacles reaching far and wide into the country, and even into remote villages such as the place where Pip and his companions had been found, it had been possible to take action. When Sam Derry heard that Pip and his friends were snowed-up in the Apennines, he had immediately arranged for one of his trusted partisan helpers to go and fetch him – and here he was, safely installed in a comfortable flat in Rome.

Pip soon settled into his new, and much improved, way of life. Taking his cue from Tug Wilson, who appeared to be nicely adjusted to his changed circumstances, their policy was 'When in Rome, do as the Romans do'. This meant circulating confidently in the streets, rather than lying low and getting depressed in the flat. To this end, Tug had fixed himself up with a season ticket on the buses and he soon procured one for his new flat-mate. One of Pip's first outings was to report to Sam Derry in Monsignor O'Flaherty's room in the Collegio Teutonicum, to which Derry had summoned him. Both Derry and O'Flaherty were anxious for him to take refuge in the Vatican, in the knowledge that once in there he would be safely interned until rescued by the Allies. Many prisoners had made for the Vatican for sanctuary, and early on a few had been admitted. But when they suddenly began to arrive in such large numbers as to endanger those already inside, it was reluctantly decided to issue orders to the Swiss Guards outside to admit no more. If necessary they were to be kept out by force. But as non-posthumous VCs were something of a rarity anywhere, especially on the run in Rome, it might be possible to persuade the authorities to make an exception in Pip's case.

But the idea didn't appeal to Pip, any more than it had to Tug. They both wanted to carry on further south with the intention of reaching the Allied lines. That was why they had come to Rome – not in order to be interned in the Vatican. But Pip's visit to Sam Derry wasn't wasted. It was reassuring to meet an old friend and it was also a delight to meet the impressive grey-haired Monsignor for the first time. Furthermore he was able to cash a cheque through the Vatican, which not only provided him with funds to spend in Rome, but also had a useful sequel, of which he only learned later. When the cheque was presented to his bank in England, Renée received her first news of her husband's whereabouts since his walk-out at Fontanellato in September 1943, when the bank manager passed the news about the cheque on to her.

Back in Nebulante's flat, Pip and Tug had several discussions as to what they should do. Having ruled out refuge and internment in the Vatican, they searched for alternatives, and it proved hard to find any concrete ideas. Reports received by the Organisation of attempts to reach the Allied lines by groups or individuals weren't encouraging. Some had been reported dead or recaptured, and of others there was no news of any safe arrivals. The weather as well as the terrain was against them. The autumn rains and slush were beginning to give way to winter's frost and snow. Nor did there appear to be any organised escape lines for them to travel. It was all rather depressing.

There had also been talk of reaching either the Adriatic or the Tyrrhenian Sea and boarding a boat at night, to ferry them further down the coast. There were vague reports of both success and failure of parties that had made these attempts by sea – but nothing definite seemed on the go at present. Pip and Tug thought it best to bide their time and wait for better weather to enable them to attempt the journey on foot, unless some better proposition presented itself.

Rather than let their lack of further progress get them down, Pip and Tug decided to make the best of their present good fortune and count their immediate blessings. Food was getting scarcer in Rome for the civilian population, and for the troops for that matter. But for Pip and Tug there were two factors in their favour. The Rome Organisation was paying the householders who were looking after escaped prisoners-of-war money towards their upkeep, which enabled them to supplement their rationed food with items from the black market. Secondly, the prisoners were able to report to the Swiss Legation at intervals to collect Red Cross parcels. The same sort of parcels as had saved the lives of many of them in camp were now proving a great boon to those of them who were still at large. The parcels from Geneva, in the absence of any Italian POW camps to receive them, had accumulated at the Swiss Legation in Rome and were coming in most useful.

The collection of these parcels was staggered so that there wouldn't be too many escapers hanging round the Swiss Legation at any one time. The parcels were handed to each ex-prisoner in a thin paper wrapper in order to camouflage the tell-tale markings on the cardboard box. Normally there was no snag, but one day it was raining when Pip and Tug collected theirs, and when they were on the way back to the bus-stop the heavens opened and they and their precious parcels received a real soaking. By the time they had climbed on to the bus and taken their seats, Pip noticed that the paper wrapper round Tug's parcel had melted in the rain, and staring him in the face on the box were the words '*Prigionieri di Guerra*'. A furtive glance at his own parcel revealed the worst – his was just as incriminating. They had to sit for the rest of the journey trying to cover up the boxes as much as they could, like a couple of broody hens spreading their wings over a nest. However, nobody on the bus made any comment. In those days of the black market, it was not unusual for people to be seen carrying strange-looking boxes and parcels, and it was best not to probe.

As well as food, sometimes items of clothing were issued to ex-prisoners in need. Both Pip and Tug possessed reasonably smart town suits, but Pip had no pyjamas to sleep in. He asked for a pair from the Red Cross clothing store, but the best that could be offered was a pink lady's night-dress. As someone remarked, there couldn't have been many VCs around sleeping in women's pink nighties – but he found it very warm and comfortable!

To help pass the time and to get a change of scenery, Pip and Tug used to go to cinemas, where they were inconspicuous. They also used to go to quiet cafés for a drink now and then. An awkward episode occurred at one particular café that they had visited more than once. The place seemed to be safe and free from anyone in uniform, but on one occasion they were in for a fright. The owner, who had always appeared friendly and discreet, suddenly produced a pistol from his pocket and said, *'Mani in alto!'* ('Hands up!'). Pip and Tug were taken aback and went white with shock – until the café proprietor broke into a smile. He had been having a joke at their expense with a toy pistol, knowing them to be *'Inglesi'*. Pip and Tug regained their composure and just managed to laugh – but they hoped that the fellow would in future refrain from jokes of that type!

Christmas came and went, but still there was no sign of the arrival of Pip's friend Percy Gers or his near-namesake Jimmy Gardner. A crisis had developed in the Rome Organisation, with the fear of worse trouble to come, when some of the partisans recently arrested began to talk under duress or torture. The plan to fetch Gers and Gardner had to be postponed until things quietened down in Rome. It was getting hard enough to house some of the ex-prisoners already in billets, without adding to their number. For the present Percy and Jimmy would have to remain where they were, up in the mountains with partisans to look after them. This worried Pip a lot, but there was nothing he could do about it. As will emerge later, he needn't have worried over them – in comparison with him, they were the lucky ones.

To celebrate New Year's Day 1944, two girls of Yugoslav birth, whose territory had been annexed by Italy, whom Pip and Tug had met in Signor Nebulante's flat, obtained seats for the opera and the two British officers escorted them to the famous Opera House. They listened to Beniamino Gigli and his daughter Rina singing *La Traviata* – seated in the sixth row of the stalls, surrounded by German and Fascist officers and their womenfolk. There was also an unmistakable presence of Gestapo officers hanging around in the vestibule of the enormous Opera House, in their customary civilian clothes. In order to reach the auditorium, after buying a programme from an attractive girl in uniform without any trouble, the party had to enter by one of the large doors, each one of which was guarded by two Italian policemen resplendent in purple-lined black cloaks and wearing swords, which made Pip feel that, should they be detected now, their way of escape was effectively barred!

In their sixth row seats, they found a couple of German other ranks immediately on their left, and to the right two German naval officers. In fact the whole place seemed to be stiff with German and Italian officers and their girl-friends. But Pip and Tug were not dismayed. In their 'gents' natty' Italian suits, they sat back to enjoy the opera. During the first interval they repaired to the bar for cups of coffee and were amazed to find a total of eight other British officers, similarly clad to themselves, all talking to each other and their girl-friends in excruciating Italian, accompanied by many gesticulations with the hands, all the time surrounded by Germans talking Italian to their girl-friends equally incorrectly. All the Italian women were exceptionally well dressed and Pip looked forward to the day when he could go to the opera in his service dress.

Among the British officers to whom they actually spoke were two of Sam Derry's chief helpers, both lieutenants in the Royal Artillery, Bill Simpson and John Furman. They had been at Chieti, and it was John Furman who had given lectures on accountancy which Pip had attended there. Simpson and Furman were responsible for distributing money to buy food, and properly accounting for it, to the Romans who were housing escaped prisoners at such great risk to themselves. They also arranged the billets into which new arrivals were placed, changing them when complications or danger arose. They performed a remarkable job for the Organisation, circulating at great risk among the citizens of Rome in order to carry out their important duties – duties that were to land them both inside the dreaded walls of the prison overlooking the River Tiber, the infamous Regina Coeli.

The night at the opera on 1st January 1944 was a memorable evening for Pip and Tug and their escorts. But it nearly ended in disaster on the bus on the way home. One of the two Yugoslav girls was so carried away by the singing of Gigli and his daughter that she unguardedly said in English : 'That was an excellent opera. Did you enjoy it?' Fortunately most of the other occupants of the crowded bus were talking excitedly at the same time, and the girl's words were lost in the general buzz of conversation. The other three looked away from her.

Thus 1944 narrowly missed starting with a disaster – but unfortunately, as far as Pip and Tug were concerned, there wasn't long to wait for one to happen.

CHAPTER FIFTEEN

'Queen of Heaven'

On 8th January 1944 Pip's four months of freedom came to an end. There had always been a chance that the presence of two escaped British officers sheltering in Signor Nebulante's flat would eventually be discovered by the Gestapo or the Fascist police; but the end came about in a strange manner.

Since the armistice, though the Fascists had crawled out of the woodwork and had begun to assert their authority once more, the Germans had soon found it necessary to move into Rome and take control of the city. The bulk of the population, particularly the communists, remained strongly anti-Nazi and anti-Fascist. Subversive activities, usually attributed to the communists, often resulted in explosions in the night and had rendered the city by no means easy to control. The Fascist police and the Gestapo, acting often in collusion, began to step up their search for communists and partisans. They were also out to suppress and arrest black-marketeers who were wrecking the economic stability in the city, and undermining the already tottering rationing system.

The arrest of Pip Gardner and Tug Wilson came about as a result of this clamp-down on communists. Trouble started just before Christmas with the arrest of Signor Nebulante's brother-in-law. It was a foregone conclusion that he would be beaten up and, if necessary, tortured. This was confirmed when one day, on 7th January, an unknown visitor arrived at Nebulante's flat, purporting to have been in gaol with the brother-in-law. He reported that the latter had indeed been beaten up, but that there was a plan to spring him from Regina Coeli. Very much against the instincts of Pip and Tug, Nebulante invited the stranger to stay to lunch. It was an uneasy meal, as the newcomer put forward a plan of rescue which would involve several people, including his present hosts. The man, who claimed to be a partisan (but was in fact

169

a Fascist agent), arranged to return with the final details the following day, 8th January. Pip and Tug rounded on Nebulante for taking such a risk with a stranger, but Nebulante insisted that it was justifiable if it could lead to his brother-in-law's rescue.

Next morning two plain clothes Gestapo men burst into the flat as soon as Nebulante opened the door. Brandishing their Lugers, they shouted at Pip, Tug and Nebulante to put their hands up and stand on a sofa facing the wall. In that position they were quickly searched for weapons, which none of them were carrying. There was just time for Tug to whisper to Pip : 'Let's rush them and get their guns', when, before Pip had time to reply or react, in rushed six uniformed SS soldiers. Thinking that they were rounding-up a nucleus of Italian communists, they pushed and kicked them unceremoniously out of the flat and down the stairs to a waiting police truck below. The three captives were driven fast along the bank of the Tiber to a forbidding building overlooking the river. They had been taken to Rome's main prison, the dreaded Regina Coeli, from which there was said to be no escape. As the main prison doors were closed behind them, their hearts sank. Their freedom had come to an abrupt end, after four months on the run. It all seemed so final.

The euphemistic name of the Regina Coeli (Queen of Heaven), chosen presumably on the same principle which had made the old Dutch settlers on the southern tip of Africa change its name from Cape of Storms to Cape of Good Hope, was a complete misnomer. Any place less like Heaven would be hard to image – nor was there much evidence of hope within its portals.

After being searched on arrival and relieved of their few possessions – including among them a solid silver compact with Tug Wilson had optimistically bought for his wife, Marjorie, for Christmas, they were led by SS guards to the cells. Fortunately they had had nothing on them in any way incriminating or compromising as far as the Organisation was concerned. They were installed in the German-run wing, which was one of several wings radiating out from a central entrance hall, the wings being three or four storeys high, as far as could be judged. Pip was placed on a higher floor than Tug, and Nebulante was locked up elsewhere in the same wing. It was obviously intended that they should have no further contact with each other. Having been arrested in civilian clothes and in company with a communist or partisan – and the Germans were at no great pains to differentiate between the two – the two British officers were not surprisingly regarded as spies, and were to be treated as such. Their main hope of remaining alive would be to establish the fact that they were escaped prisoners-of-war on the run, and merely sheltering in Rome. They could then invoke the Geneva Convention and seek restoration of their prisoner-of-war status, which they had both gone to such lengths to abandon. Poor Nebulante's prospects were far worse. As a resistance organiser he could expect no mercy, and this was borne out later when Tug Wilson caught a glimpse of his former host hobbling along a passage, barely recognisable and hardly able to walk. It was a sickening sight.

Pip was put into a cell by himself, whereas Tug was in with three other prisoners – two cheerful Italians and a very cowed Russian Jew, who had already been beaten up considerably and was in a pathetic state, with little hope for his own future. With the language barrier, and the reality of the situation, it was impossible to cheer him up. After three days on his own, Pip's cell began to fill up, by the addition of Italian detainees, until there was a total of six people altogether. Though in some ways he was glad to have company, the over-crowding made conditions most oppressive. At night they were obliged to sleep close together on the floor, lying like sardines. The only form of lavatory was a stone pot in the corner, which had to be used in full view of everyone else in the cell. Apart from being embarrassingly public, it was also very unhygienic and liable to spillage. One of the cell-mates had to slop it out along the passage at some time convenient to the guards – and sometimes too late for the prisoners!

The prison 'food' consisted of a piece of dry bread and a mug of ersatz coffee in the morning, and a bowl of greasy water passing for soup after mid-day. That was the ration for the day. However, parcels were allowed into the prison, and these could be shared. Pip was particularly lucky one day when a delicious piece of cake was delivered to him surreptitiously by one of the 'trusties' responsible for bringing round the food. Pip's cake arrived with the compliments of General Gariboldi who had been arrested by the Fascists after Marshal Badoglio's government had left. He was now residing in the cell opposite. Pip never actually met General Gariboldi, but could merely send his grateful thanks back via the 'trusty'.

Altogether there were twelve escaped Allied prisoners-of-war, officers and other ranks, in Regina Coeli, but they were all in different cells and thus unable to communicate with each other, owing to the presence of the guards as well as the general hubbub in Italian whenever the coast was clear. But at night, when many of the guards were off-duty, the prisoners used to call out to each other and boost each other's morale by exchanging news and rumours. The remarkable thing was that, although there were probably more than five hundred Italian detainees and convicts, they would all keep quiet for a while, in order to let the *Inglesi* have their turn to speak to each other. In this way Pip was able sometimes to shout to Tug. Except for one occasion later, this was the only contact that they had in the 'Queen of Heaven'.

Among the voices in the cells was that of John Furman. The arrest of Pip, Tug and Nebulante had produced immediate repercussions. Nebulante's cook, a timid grey-haired old man was easily threatened into accompanying the same Gestapo squad that had just arrested his employer. He led them to another of the Organisation's flats, in Via Chelini, and told them the secret signal that had to be given on the doorbell before it would be opened. The two plain-clothes Gestapo men were thus able to gain access, closely followed by their SS men, and promptly arrested the occupants. Their haul this time included John Furman, Captain Macauley, who was the Organisation's medical officer, and a sick American airman whom he was attending. In addition, they grabbed a Yugoslav communist and an Austrian girl who was working for the Resistance, as well as a couple of British other ranks who were found elsewhere in the same block. For the Gestapo, 8th January had been quite a field day. In trawling for Italian communists, they had netted a useful catch of escaped Allied prisoners-of-war as well. One of the Gestapo men told John Furman with glee that he could now go and join his friends Wilson and Gardner in Regina Coeli.

John Furman was a remarkable man. He had a cheerful, intelligent face, with bright and alert eyes, beneath a head of auburn hair. His build was short and slight – about an inch shorter than Pip Gardner. He had been captured by the Germans on three occasions and had managed to escape twice already. He had, like Pip, been captured in Tobruk in 1942, and had made his first escape shortly after the Italian armistice in September 1943, when the inmates of Chieti had been moved to Sulmona after their disastrous orders to wait for the Allies to fetch them. On the spur of the moment he had tagged along at the end of a fatigue party of orderlies fetching water under guard outside Sulmona camp. Seizing his chance he had hidden in a field before eventually finding sanctuary in a house in Sulmona. There, three weeks later, he was unlucky enough to be caught in a German round-up of Italian workmen and impressed into forced labour on defence lines further south. His knowledge of German enabled him to escape ten days later and get back to Sulmona, which contained several escaped prisoners-of-war in hiding. Early in December, having obtained false identity papers, he travelled to Rome in a party led by two partisan sisters who were in touch with Sam Derry's organisation. Also in the party was his friend from Chieti, Lieutenant Bill Simpson. Together they were soon to play a vital role as two of Sam Derry's main helpers. They both knew Pip from his Chieti days and had bumped into him, in company with Tug Wilson, at the opera only a week before their arrest. The Gestapo had missed Simpson on this occasion, but his turn was to come later.

On 22nd January there was great cheering in the prison wings, caused by a rumour that the Allies had landed at a place called Anzio on the coast and were about to advance on Rome. Pip had heard all too often of Allied landings up and down the coast of Italy before, but was nevertheless heartened by the news. Next day the guards were in a flap, and the unpleasant SS men were replaced by much less objectionable convalescent soldiers, hurriedly rushed from hospital to take over. They were aided by the 'trusties', one of whom Pip managed to persuade to let him out of his cell and take him down to talk to Tug on the floor below. They hurriedly discussed the possibility of soon being able to get out and meet the advancing Allied forces; but they were still securely guarded in Regina Coeli. However, hopes of an early release were rising.

It was also on 23rd January that John Furman, with typical thoughtfulness and efficiency, managed to send a message to Sam Derry. The note was smuggled out by an Italian barber who was allowed into the prison to shave the prisoners, who weren't permitted to have razor blades with them in the cells. The note gave a list of all the British ex-prisoners-of-war being detained in Regina Coeli, including the names of Pip and Tug.

But two days after that, on 25th January, the dreaded SS guards returned to duty in the prison, with the bad news that the Allied

landing at Anzio had been contained and that the advance on Rome
had been checked. Though Pip didn't foresee it at the time, it wasn't
in fact until 25th May that the troops of the Anzio bridgehead were
able to link up with the main forces and even then it took them another
ten days to reach Rome.

The hold-up at Anzio was indeed depressing news, but Pip didn't
have long to brood on it. Along with the other British prisoners he was
warned to be ready to leave almost at once. There was, however, just
time for John Furman to send another hurried note to Sam Derry,
reporting their imminent departure from the 'Queen of Heaven'.

*

All the Allied prisoners in Regina Coeli, with one unexplained exception, were extracted from their crowded cells on the various floors of
the tall prison and were assembled down in the main entrance hall for
what turned out to be a relatively perfunctory search. They had all been
stripped and thoroughly searched when they were first brought within
the portals of the forbidding gaol.

This done, they were then herded into a coach which was waiting
for them outside the building, before being driven out through the main
prison gates. It was a momentarily exhilarating feeling to drive through
the streets of Rome, which had become so familiar to most of them,
and to see civilians going about their daily business. But the euphoria
didn't last for long.

The transport of prisoners, numbering about a dozen in all, was
under the direction of an SS sergeant-major of a particularly unpleasant
type, who stationed guards with machine-guns at the ready at the back
of the coach, with instructions to shoot any prisoner who made a sudden
move towards escape. The prisoners had already been issued with a
clear warning not to make any such attempt, on pain of dire conse-
quences should any of them fail to heed this advice. Judging from the
general look of the guards, the warning seemed well-founded, and in any
case, though the prisoners were bent on escape if at all possible, at
present it seemed wisest to wait and see whither and how far they were
being taken.

The prisoners, nearly all of whom were in Italian-type civilian clothes
in which they had been picked up by the Gestapo, had very mixed

feelings at this stage, as they thankfully emerged from incarceration in Regina Coeli.

On the one hand it was good to be together and able to converse among themselves, and it was an enormous relief to be out of the over-crowded cells, which they had had to endure for some weeks. Pip Gardner, Tug Wilson and John Furman had been inside for three weeks and this had proved a very cold and hungry ordeal. It had also been an unhygienic and uncertain period for them all, and naturally their immediate reaction was one of great relief at ending their close confinement – if only temporarily.

But on the other hand their prospects still looked undeniably bleak. With the Allied forces drawing gradually, but only slowly, towards Rome, their hopes of liberation had been pinned on their being able to sit out the waiting period at Regina Coeli – without being shot as spies or transported northwards, out of reach of rescue. Now the move in that direction could really only be regarded as bad news. But, as is the wont of prisoners-of-war, they began to clutch optimistically at straws of hope. Perhaps they were merely being transferred to a nearby prisoner-of-war camp, with the threat of being shot as spies now removed? Perhaps they were being taken to another prison where, they felt, conditions could hardly be worse than those experienced at Regina Coeli? Perhaps there might still be a chance of escape?

So it was with such thoughts revolving through their minds that the prisoners were driven out of Rome and were soon heading northwards out of the city via the Salario bridge. They were interested to see several signs of fortifications and defence lines being hurriedly constructed, with the help of Italian civilian labour – doubtless conscripted by the Germans and Fascists. It looked as if the Germans intended to defend Rome against the expected Allied advance, and any retreat would be orderly rather than headlong.

Some thirty miles north of Rome they stopped at a village called Fara in Sabina. There they drew up at a large prisoner-of-war camp, with speculation as to whether this was to be their destination. But after a long wait in the bus – with nobody allowed out to attend to the call of nature, despite impassioned pleas to be allowed to do so – instead of the prisoners in the coach being admitted to the camp, eventually two prisoners were brought out of the camp and installed in the coach, which then resumed its journey north.

The two newcomers were British officers who had been recently taken at Anzio, soon after the Allied landing there. At first they were reluctant to tell their fellow inmates in the coach anything about the fighting – understandably so, in view of the motley collection of 'civilians' among whom they now found themselves. But when they had established to their satisfaction that these 'civilians' were in fact Allied prisoners-of-war, despite their assorted civilian garb, they relaxed their guard and began to converse. In no time they were bombarded with questions about the recent fighting south of Rome, from the old lags who were avid for red-hot news. It gave them all hope that, provided that they weren't whisked away too far and too quickly, they still had a reasonable chance of rescue by the advancing armies.

Their journey continued via the industrial towns of Rieti and Terni, to the north-east of Rome. Progress in the coach was frequently slowed by bomb-craters in the road, which had to be circumvented. The more frequently this happened, the better it suited the prisoners, who were in no hurry to go further north. Better still was an ominous spluttering which developed in the engine of the coach, which finally came to a halt seventeen miles short of Spoleto.

At this juncture there ensued a bizarre incident, involving an unfortunate couple of Italian peasants who were innocently plodding in the opposite direction in a cart drawn by two large white oxen. The SS sergeant-major stopped them and ordered them at gun-point, despite their voluble protests, to uncouple the oxen from the cart and harness them to the coach and tow it to the nearest village some two miles away. Leaving his wife sobbing by the roadside, the hapless husband was forced to goad his over-burdened oxen into towing the bulky coach.

On reaching the village, the sweating oxen and their distraught owner were dismissed and allowed to return to the sobbing wife. The coach was pushed by hand by the guards into a large garage. They wouldn't risk letting the prisoners out of the coach to help push, so the prisoners sat back and enjoyed the sight of their guards straining away – amid a mixture of cheers and jeers. Once safely inside the garage, they spent the night there, with all the doors firmly shut and the guards strategically placed to prevent all escape.

Next morning a relief vehicle was summoned by the sergeant-major, and it wasn't long before an open lorry arrived, with an Italian civilian driver. The latter was ordered to fix a tow-rope and pull the coach, in

Pip Gardner and Sam Derry appearing on the 'This Is Your Life' programme in Sam Derry's honour, in 1963.

(*Left*) Her Majesty The Qu[een] shaking hands with Pip Gardner in the garden of Buckingham Palace, at th[e] presentation of new stan[dards] to The Royal Tank Regim[ent] 1960.

(*Below*) Her Majesty Que[en] Elizabeth The Queen Mo[ther] Clarence House in 1984, [with] members of The Victoria [Cross] and George Cross Asso[ciation] of which she is President[.]

which the prisoners could be more safely guarded. But the driver of the lorry strongly demurred, despite threats and bombast on the part of the sergeant-major. Only when the driver succeeded in explaining that their route lay over a 2,000-feet pass, would the sergeant-major relent and transfer his charges to the open lorry for the continuation of their eventful journey, still accompanied by the armed guards.

The journey took them eight miles beyond the town of Spoleto, to a village rejoicing in the name of Pissignano. Here they were taken to a prisoner-of-war transit camp, which contained an assortment of Allied prisoners, old and new, awaiting transport by train to Germany, so they had been told.

Pip Gardner found several familiar faces, mostly old friends and acquaintances from Chieti and other camps. Most of those who had been at large following the Italian armistice in September 1943, a period of five months, were, like Pip, in some sort of civilian clothing that they had managed to acquire from brave people who had so kindly and dangerously provided them with shelter, pending the arrival of the Allied forces – an arrival which had remained pending for longer than they had expected. A few, still in their original battledress, were by now almost in rags and had had a hard time in the hills as they struggled to make their way south.

Others in battledress were recent prisoners, captured in the fighting round Cassino or at Anzio. They were in much better shape. But a large group of Americans from a battalion which had been captured almost en bloc, at the crossing of the River Garigliano, appeared to be still mostly in a somewhat shocked and unshaven state after their capture.

Among the old lags John Furman found a blond burly six-footer from the Royal Engineers who, like Furman himself, had already escaped from the Germans on two previous occasions – the latter occasion being from the camp at Pissignano itself. He was Lieutenant J. S. (Johnny) Johnstone. He was still bent on escape, but he told John Furman that security round the camp perimeter was now much tighter and that their chances of getting out were very remote indeed. This, however, didn't prevent their teaming up together to explore any opportunity for escape that they might devise. Likewise Pip Gardner and Tug Wilson were anxious to regain their liberty once more and joint discussions were held.

But, before plans could be made, they were told on the morning of 30th January that they were to parade, ready to march to the station. Things looked ominous. They were lined up in fives inside the camp, with 'the Romans', as Pip Gardner's group was known, all together, along with others who had been captured in civilian clothes. It suited them to be all together in a bunch, for escaping purposes, should there be a chance.

Off they marched to the small station nearby. On arrival at a siding beyond the platform they were herded into cattle-trucks, with straw on the floor and a tin can in each for use as a urinal on the forthcoming journey, and issued with a three-day bread ration – if they could make it last for three days. It was clearly going to be a long hungry journey to contend with.

It was while they were being herded aboard the cattle-trucks that Fate took a hand in the proceedings. Quite by chance, Pip Gardner, Tug Wilson and Doctor Macauley became separated from the rest of the 'Romans' and were bundled into the adjoining truck. This chance happening was to have a fateful bearing on Pip Gardner's destiny.

Had he been in the same cattle-truck as John Furman and Johnny Johnstone, as was originally intended, the remainder of Pip's story might have been very different. It might also have been brought to an abrupt ending – far less happy than it turned out for him in the long run. But in the short term this accidental separation meant that Pip was not in the cattle-truck which already contained two knives which the others hoped to use in order to cut their way out. Furthermore the truck was shortly to contain an iron bar which John Furman spotted and took steps to acquire by quickness of thought, coupled with persuasive talk with the surly guards – to the considerable benefit of those in his truck who were bent on escape.

At this juncture, before we accompany Pip Gardner on his depressing journey north, John Furman's initiative and resourceful actions, which were to lead him back south again, warrant our attention.

*

The prisoners were ordered to remove their boots and shoes and hand them to the guards, who put them into sacks for safe custody during the forthcoming journey. Bitter experience with train-loads of prisoners in recent months had induced the Germans to take no chances. With the snow on the ground, it seemed that the removal of all footwear ought to rule out any question of prisoners jumping from the train and taking barefoot to the hills in the deep snow that had fallen in most areas during the cold winter of 1943/4. They had reckoned without the determination of John Furman and the nucleus of all-weather escapers in his truck !

The train waited for some while outside Pissignano, and this delay gave John Furman just the chance he needed. On his way into the truck he thought he saw, at a few yards away, an iron bar lying on the ground, half-buried in the snow that lay around. By dint of persistent banging on the cattle-truck door and using his adequate command of German to reason with the sentry posted outside his truck, he managed to persuade the guard to open the door. Pleading acute dysentery, Furman implored to be let out of the truck in order to relieve himself – in the name of hygiene and for the sake of his fellow travellers.

Ever since his first escape from custody in the previous autumn, the scourge of dysentery was never far away from John Furman, and his sojourn inside Regina Coeli had done nothing to alleviate matters. But now he was able to turn his affliction to his advantage. He managed to convince the guard of his urgency and was allowed down from the cattle-truck, with instructions to perform within view.

This just enabled him to walk across towards the spot where he thought he had seen the iron bar. It was there all right, half-hidden in the snow. In order to perform, he rapidly took off his overcoat and threw it, as if at random, taking care to let it land over the protruding bar.

Having attended to his business, he pulled up his trousers, tucked in his shirt, and proceeded to retrieve his overcoat, to the accompaniment of the familiar shouts of *'Schnell! Schnell!'* from the guard. Furman grabbed the coat together with the bar and hurried back to the truck with his bundle. The bar, a solid piece of iron, was rather heavier than he had expected and it was difficult not to make the overcoat appear unduly heavy as he staggered along, trying to make light of the weight. Things weren't made any easier when the overcoat slipped and part of the bar began to protrude. But he made it safely back to the truck and was helped up, iron bar and all, by his comrades anxiously waiting to lend a hand.

This acquisition put a different complexion on the plan to escape from the train. Their prospects now looked much more promising. With the door securely shut behind them, they got to work on starting a hole at one end of the truck, using the two knives that had been smuggled aboard. They couldn't, of course, start banging with the bar, for fear of alerting the guards. That would only be possible once the train was in motion. But at least they could make a silent start with the knives. They now felt that they were in business, with a good chance of escaping.

They chose the end next to the adjoining truck in which Pip Gardner and Tug Wilson now found themselves, in the hope that they might be able to cut a small hole quickly from the outside and pass the knives and the bar into their friends who had become separated from them. But first they had to make their own exit-hole.

They had made an exploratory slice down the wood panel when the sliding door was opened and a German officer made an interior investigation with his torch to check the prisoners. Just when it seemed that he had noticed nothing amiss he flicked his torch back to the place where the cut had been made in the woodwork. The prisoners nearest to the cut tried in vain to maintain that it was an old scar obviously made by previous occupants of the truck. The German officer remained unimpressed, and with a sardonic smile demanded the surrender of the knife that had made the palpably new mark on the woodwork.

He threatened to turn them all out into the snow and search them and the truck. John Furman, anxious to avoid losing the iron bar and both knives in the search – and, with them, all hope of escape – thought quickly and told the owner of the smaller of the two knives to hand it over to the German officer, in the hope that the capture of one trophy might prove sufficient. The trick worked. Honour was satisfied, the knife was gleefully confiscated and the sliding door was once more slammed along, keeping the light out and the prisoners in. But they still retained in their possession the larger and more serviceable of the two knives, as well as the precious iron bar – ready for a hefty coup de grâce once enough preliminary cutting had been done.

With the final check along the trucks now completed, it wasn't long before the train chugged out of Pissignano and gathered speed for its journey north. Work could now resume on the woodwork at the end of the truck. With the aid of the remaining knife a couple of vertical cuts were made, just above floor level to a height of two feet. All that was needed now was a firm bash with the iron bar, and their exit-hole on to the couplings between trucks would be completed.

But to bash the hole through during the hours of daylight would be inviting detection, should the train stop at a station. It would also be suicidal to leap out in broad daylight, because the train had the usual observation boxes at intervals behind some of the trucks, with sentries posted in them armed with rifles and machine-guns. So the intending escapers had no option but to wait for night to give them a cover of darkness, and a far better chance of success.

Not all the prisoners inside were intending to escape. Several of them were in no physical state to attempt any more bids for freedom, after rough going in the mountains following the arrival of winter and semi-starvation. They felt obliged to remain in custody and to take whatever lay in store. This was a sad but understandable state of affairs for them.

Meanwhile those intending to attempt an escape arranged an order of exit among themselves. John Furman, who had provided the iron bar, and his partner, Johnny Johnstone, who had smuggled the knife aboard, were to be the first pair to jump when the time came. The others also teamed up in pairs and impatiently waited for darkness to descend.

After its delayed start, the train had travelled fast – too fast for the prisoners' liking. Every mile the train covered as it sped north was one mile more to be retraced if they were to make their way back to Rome or to the Allied forces further south. Furman and Johnstone intended to make for Rome, where they were confident that they could go into hiding – and not into Regina Coeli! They had resolved that the fact that they were at present barefoot wasn't going to deter them from making the attempt. It was now merely a question of waiting for nightfall.

As soon as it was properly dark, Sergeant-Major Billet, a South African, gave the woodwork at the end of the truck a mighty bash with the bar. Out crashed the panel which had been previously cut. It flew away and disappeared down the track, leaving behind it a neat exit-hole, big enough for the escapers to crawl through.

Losing no time, John Furman led the way through and perched himself precariously on the couplings. Johnny Johnstone followed him out, finding it rather harder to squeeze his bulk through the hole. It was freezing cold outside on the couplings and obviously this was no place to linger – if only the train would slow down.

It was at this point that John Furman asked Johnny Johnstone for the knife, with which to make a rapid hole in the end of the adjoining truck, with a view to passing the knife and the iron bar onto Pip Gardner and Tug Wilson. But Johnstone, in his anxiety to get through the hole, had left the knife with another escaper who had put it down somewhere in the straw inside the pitch dark cattle-truck. It couldn't be found and Johnstone couldn't now go back through the hole and rummage for it and risk upsetting the plan for their own escape.

Thus it was that Pip and his partner, Tug, had to forgo their possible chance of rescue – not that they knew anything about the plan that the others had devised for them. On such small details men's destiny can sometimes hinge in wartime. But Fate had willed it otherwise.

The train at last began to slow down, as if approaching a station. John Furman and Johnny Johnstone were determined to seize their opportunity. Down they jumped, one to either side of the moving train, and landed safely in the snow beside the track. There was some shooting from the train, but by that time John Furman had run to safety in some bushes in a garden abutting on to the railway embankment. He heard movement near him and froze where he was. The next moment what he took to be the bulky figure of Johnny Johnstone rushed past him in the darkness. Furman emerged from his temporary refuge and followed after him. To his immense relief he caught him up and the two escapers were reunited – breathless and bootless. Phase one of their escape had been successfully and bloodlessly accomplished.

So far, so good! But they wouldn't get far in their bare feet in the snow, and Johnny Johnstone needed some more respectable clothing if he were going to have any chance of passing for an Italian civilian, albeit a singularly blond one! Somehow they must seek help, which, judging from their previous experiences on the run, shouldn't prove impossible to find, especially as John Furman still had with him a wad of lire which he had managed to retain for such an emergency.

How they succeeded in acquiring not only a pair of shoes each and some cleaner clothing for Johnny Johnstone, but also two old bicycles on which to start their long journey southwards back to Rome, is graphically recounted by John Furman in his gripping book, *Be Not Fearful* (published by Anthony Blond in 1959). They travelled via

Modena, Pistoia (which they skirted), Siena and Viterbo, before abandoning their bicycles and avoiding a road-block in order to enter Rome on foot.

They finally arrived back in Rome on 14th February 1944, after completing an epic escape and journey in the space of two weeks.

At the earliest opportunity they caught a tram into the centre of the city that John Furman knew so well. He went straight to the Collegio Teutonicum and found his friend Monsignor Hugh O'Flaherty. The Irish priest was overwhelmed with joy and amazement at seeing John again – the last news of him being that he had been taken off to an uncertain fate in Germany. As soon as O'Flaherty had regained his composure, he arranged for the two escapers to go into hiding in one of the Rome Organisation's safe billets in the city.

So it was that John Furman, against great odds, had made his way back to Rome, thereby escaping from German arrest for the third time within the space of six months. It wasn't long before he was back at work in the Rome Organisation – with his auburn hair dyed black and parted in a different place, and his moustache removed. He still had nearly four months, and several narrow escapes from arrest, to survive before liberation, when the Americans finally entered Rome on 4th June 1944.

Pip Gardner and Tug Wilson, meanwhile, had ordeals of a different kind to undergo, after remaining aboard the cattle-truck on their grim journey north to Germany.

CHAPTER SIXTEEN

'All Hope Abandon . . .'

For Pip the journey north was his first taste of travel in a crowded cattle-truck as a prisoner-of-war, with the door tightly slammed and the tiny ventilator wired up. It was to prove a very mortifying experience. He and Tug knew nothing of what was going on in the next truck, which had contained John Furman and the rest of the 'Romans', until the end of the journey. Tired, hungry and very cold, Pip found the journey a depressing and uncomfortable ordeal as they travelled relentlessly northwards. The train chugged its way up the Brenner Pass and then down to Innsbruck and on through Bavaria beyond Munich. The journey was prolonged by intermittent halts, where they weren't allowed out of the trucks – though they were permitted to empty the foul contents of the can posing as a lavatory. The grim journey lasted for four days.

They were taken right into Germany until they eventually reached their destination at a station marked 'Mühlberg', a place of which none of them had heard, situated on the River Elbe, between Dresden and Leipzig. The weary prisoners, relieved to be out of the trucks at last, were marched to Stalag IV B. Things at once started to look up, after an initial fumigation and de-lousing for them and their clothes separately. Those who were in civilian attire were fitted out with battle-dress from the clothing store, supplied by the Red Cross, and some hot stew, also made from Red Cross ingredients, was produced from the camp cookhouse.

The shower and the food worked wonders for their morale, and Pip reflected that, disappointed though he was to have lost his freedom once more, he was nevertheless thankful to have emerged from Regina Coeli without being shot as a spy, or tortured to give information. After a grim three weeks in his cramped cell, it was almost a pleasure to be shown to some wooden sleeping bunks in a long hut. At least he and

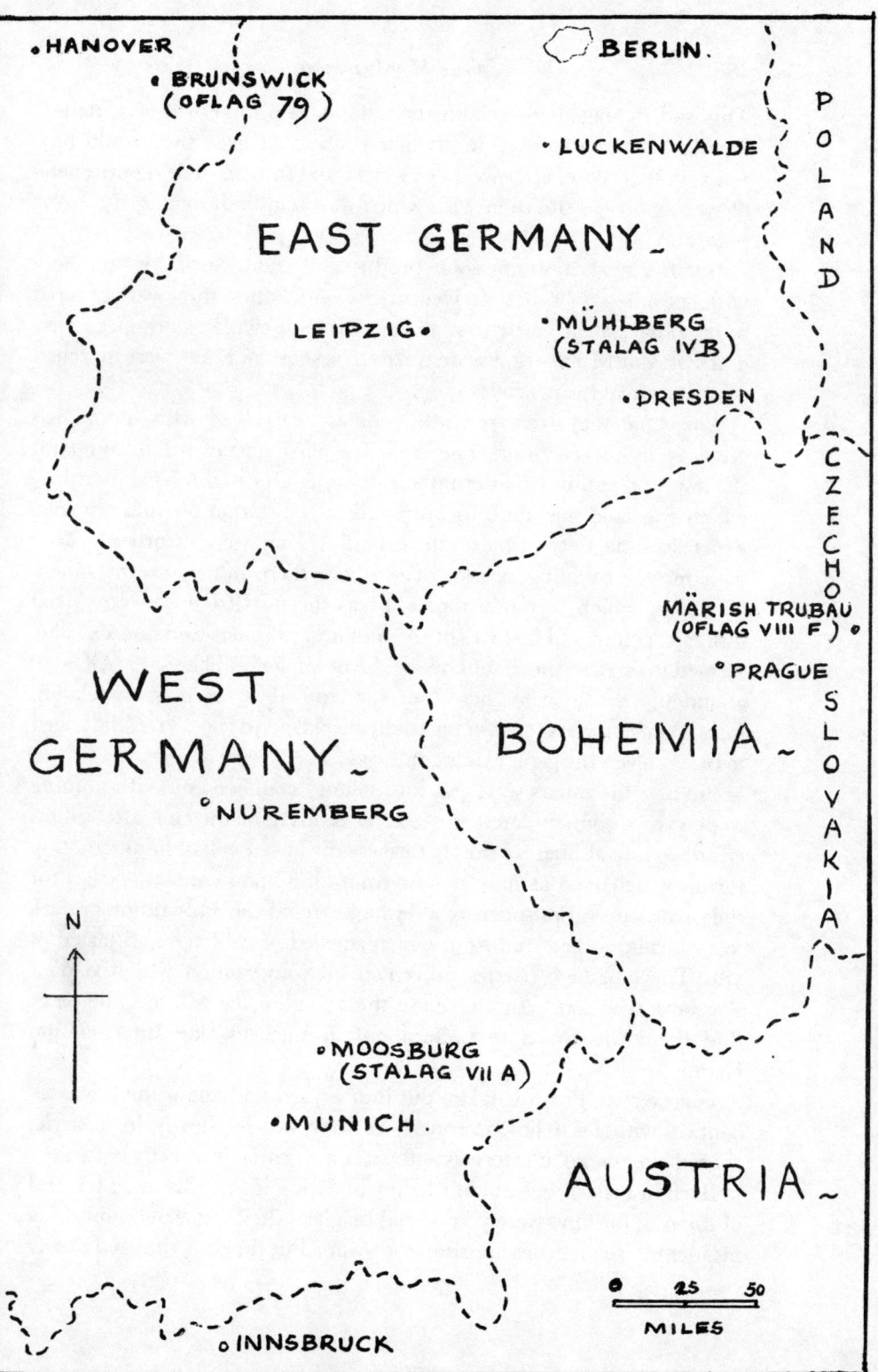

Part of the Third Reich

Tug had managed to reclaim their status as prisoners-of-war, despite having been re-captured in civilian clothes. At least they could now relax on that score, after weeks of worry, and face up to being prisoners-of-war again – a situation with which they had both managed to cope before.

But the next morning soon produced a rude shock. In company with six others who had arrived in civilian clothes, they were ordered to hand back their battledress and put on their civilian suits once more. Their stay at Mühlberg was destined to be short and they were marched off to a train at the nearby station.

This time they were put into ordinary carriages, with the guards on duty in the corridor. The train travelled northwards throughout the day, and continued intermittently through the night. Next morning, which was cold and dull, they arrived at the station of Luckenwalde, which is some sixty miles south of Berlin. They were escorted on foot to a most forbidding prison, over which there hung an atmosphere of gloom, which certainly didn't lift as the puzzled prisoners walked inside its confines. The faces of the inmates, prisoners and guards alike, seemed to offer no gleam of hope to the newcomers. The sign: 'All hope abandon, ye who enter here!' or the equivalent German translation from Dante's *Inferno*, wasn't actually displayed to view – it didn't need to be, such was the general aura of doom!

Pip and the others were put into solitary confinement, with nothing to do except contemplate their fate. Was this to be the end, after all his efforts to stay at liberty? Surely this was the lowest ebb of his fluctuating fortunes, debarred as he was now from all human contact, except for the silent Russian prisoners who brought round the daily ration of dark sour-smelling bread and soup which smelled of cabbage and tasted of salt. The language barrier prevented all conversation with the poor Russians, who seemed to have lost the ability or the will to smile – not that there was much to smile about in Luckenwalde Interrogation Camp.

For exercise Pip was taken out into a yard and again there was no contact with his fellow-prisoners, as they walked slowly in a circle, spaced out at regular intervals with all conversation strictly forbidden.

Back in his cell he couldn't help wondering if this was to be the end of the trail for him. Surely he would be given the chance of establishing his identity as an escaped prisoner-of-war? But the days dragged slowly by and he continued to languish in this ghastly gaol. Even the over-crowded cell in Regina Coeli now seemed preferable to this present isolation.

After what seemed like a month, but was in fact just over a week of this waiting, he was at last called for interrogation by an SS major who, without exactly exuding charm, was by no means unreasonable. He seemed disposed to accept Pip's claim that he was simply an escaped prisoner-of-war and not a spy or *agent provocateur*. As he had been captured nearly two years ago, he couldn't be expected to have much useful information to divulge, and rather than waste time on him, the SS major reached out and passed to him, with a smile, a packet of cigarettes and an American magazine to read in his cell. It was the first smile that he had seen in Luckenwalde – and the first cigarettes that he had smoked there.

Two days later, Pip and Tug plus six others in civilian clothes were marched off under guard to the station and put on to a train. The escort was under the command of a German corporal, who told them that they were being sent to an established prisoner-of-war camp for officers in Czecho-Slovakia. So that the prisoners might have a compart-ment to themselves, the civilians already ensconced in their seats were ordered to move out. This they did without a murmur – doubtless resigned to such evictions at the hands of the military.

The German corporal was very affable and friendly – an attitude that he managed to pass on to the rest of his posse of guards. This made for a pleasant journey. The corporal explained that he had worked in a bar in Hamburg before the war and had picked up some English, as a result of which he was now obviously anxious to try out his linguistic skill on his captive audience. He seemed positively pro-British in his outlook and appeared just as weary of the war as were his charges. After the long days of gloom at Luckenwalde, it seemed as though a threatening dark cloud that had been hanging over them had suddenly dissipated and given way to blue sky – such was the relief at being on the move. As the train travelled through open countryside, the journey took on the feeling of a holiday excursion.

The holiday atmosphere, particularly for Pip and Tug was heightened when they had to change trains at Dresden. When the prisoners asked if they might fill their water-bottles that a couple of them still had in their possession, the genial corporal selected Pip and Tug, who had the smartest clothes of the party, to accompany him to the station restaurant. Once again some long-suffering civilians were ordered to move from their tables, in order to make a place for Pip and Tug, while the corporal went to the bar. He returned with beer in mugs with lids on and placed them before his 'guests'. He then returned to the counter to fill up the water-bottles – not with water, but with beer!

As the two prisoners sat there comfortably drinking, and reflecting on their rapidly altered circumstances, Pip noticed that the room had suddenly gone quiet. He asked his 'host' why this had happened, and the latter casually replied, in between gulps of beer: 'They think you are Gestapo.' Their mackintoshes and trilby hats had evidently given that impression, and Pip felt like bursting out laughing at the thought; but he and Tug contented themselves with a quiet chuckle as they quaffed more beer!

As the three of them were sauntering back along the platform to join the rest of the party, a train-load of troops in cattle-trucks, with the doors open, drew out from another platform. They seemed strangely subdued – almost morose, in fact – and Pip commented on this. The corporal explained that they were most likely leaving for the Russian front – something which evidently was no longer a cause for the jubilation and singing that would have marked such a departure in days gone by. It was, he said, a sign of the times – and for Germany in 1944 the signs were not propitious.

The journey continued until evening, when, in accordance with the friendly corporal's promise, they arrived at the gates of Oflag VIII F at Märisch-Trubau in Czecho-Slovakia. It was a mighty relief to think that they had said farewell to the nightmare of Luckenwalde, where all hope had, indeed, nearly been abandoned, and to see what Märisch-Trubau had in store for them.

CHAPTER SEVENTEEN

Twilight of the Third Reich

Oflag VIII F at Märisch-Trubau could hardly be described as a holiday camp, but for Pip, after the depths to which he had plunged since his re-capture, it seemed pretty much like one to him. For a start he was back among friends and acquaintances from former camps – many of whom had also been on the loose and had interesting tales to tell. He found that he was not the only one to have had some tough times, as well as some amusing episodes. What was more, it was a great relaxation to be able to talk only in English again as he exercised round the compound, chatting with friends.

The camp was a former Czech military academy, which had been converted into an Oflag. It was on the old border between Bohemia and Moravia, which had both been absorbed into the modern Czecho-Slovakia at the end of World War I. It lay in the rolling and partly wooded country 125 miles to the east of Prague. The main building looked like a modern factory, built of grey stone, with four storeys and a basement. The adjoining bungalows were built of yellow sand-stone, which caused the present occupants to nickname the camp 'the biscuit factory'.

It was far better heated than the vast majority of prisoner-of-war camps elsewhere and, while Pip was there, Canadian Red Cross parcels, notable for their bulk and rich contents, were in regular supply. Pip was thus able to build up his strength and energy and to make good some of the deficiencies of his diet during recent weeks in Regina Coeli and Luckenwalde. In Märisch-Trubau, Indian officers, most of whom had been taken prisoner in the desert, actually had their own cookhouse and received special Red Cross parcels containing the necessary ingredients for the making of curries and other dishes to their liking.

One of the first blessings of being safely installed in Oflag VIII F was the return to the routine of writing letters and cards home. Pip was thus able to re-establish contact with Renée. All she knew of his whereabouts was that in early December he was at large in Rome, cashing a cheque there. This news had allayed her earlier fears and worries about his safety which resulted from the breakdown in correspondence after the Italian armistice. But when no more cheques were reported, her worries began to mount once more. She knew that he would be trying his best to complete his escape and she only hoped that his determination to do so wouldn't lead him into danger. Now he was able to write to her from a fixed abode, knowing that in one way she would be disappointed for his sake at his present whereabouts, but relieved to hear that he was now safely accounted for – even if their longed-for reunion was indefinitely postponed. In all there was a seven-month gap in the prisoner-of-war letters received from him, from the time he had walked out of Fontanellato, until five weeks after he had arrived at Märisch-Trubau. Likewise, Pip had to wait another two months for the reply to his letter to Renée. Both letters had to pass through censors before being sent by train and boat via Geneva. A month was considered good going for a letter, though its journey could often take longer. One prisoner-of-war wrote a letter to an American cousin from a camp in Italy in March 1943, and received it back in his new camp in Germany in June 1944, marked 'Unclaimed', and stamped all over with American, Italian and German censorship marks. His letter to the same cousin sent from England after the war did rather better – it arrived, and was claimed, within a week!

As winter relaxed its grip and gave way to spring in Czecho-Slovakia, the prisoners of Oflag VIII F developed the seasonal urge to dig their way out of their camp – ignorant as yet of the fate of fifty of the seventy-six escapers from Stalag Luft III who did so around that time. A lot of tunnelling was in progress, but before Pip became involved with one of the several tunnels under construction, outside events overtook the tunnellers – and doubtless saved the lives of most of them.

As the Russian spring offensive began to gather momentum for a mighty push through the Balkans, the Germans were obliged to prepare for a retreat on their east front. Rather than risk allowing their prisoners in Czecho-Slovakia to be rescued, it was decided to move them right into the heart of Germany itself. Furthermore, there could be, and indeed there was, the likelihood of a mass breakout by the prisoners, with the intention of making a determined dash to meet the on-coming

Russian armies in the east. Any such breakout could probably count on support with food and shelter from the local population, which included a lot of Czechs who had no love for their German occupiers.

Thus it was that, in order to forestall any rescue by the advancing Russians from the east, orders came from Berlin that the prisoners of Oflag VIII F were to be moved. The camp was evacuated in two batches, of which the first containing Pip Gardner and his former flat-mate in Rome, Tug Wilson, departed on 28th April 1944 to a destination rumoured to be near Hanover.

As always when prisoners-of-war were moved, there were mixed feelings amongst them. For some prisoners, the grass was always greener on the other side of the barbed-wire fence, and a change was nearly as good as a holiday. For others, the devil they knew was preferable to the devil they didn't. The latter knew only too well from experience that conditions elsewhere might well be a good deal worse. Anyway the choice wasn't theirs, and the first batch marched cheerfully down to the station, to the accompaniment of encouraging shouts of temporary fare-well from their colleagues of the second batch. The leavers even broke into song on their way to the station – partly to boost their own morale, and partly to put on a bold show for the benefit of the local inhabitants, for whom singing had gone largely out of fashion in their prevailing circumstances. A few of them responded with friendly glances, but they dared not show outward enthusiasm.

But the singing changed to cursing when they reached the station and found what was in store for them. There were guard-dogs and cattle-trucks there to greet them, and this time extra precautions were being taken to prevent prisoners from escaping. They were made to remove all belts, braces and boots, which were put into sacks. Then they were handcuffed and ordered into the trucks. The prisoners were put into one end of each truck, which had been partitioned by means of barbed wire. The sacks containing the boots, belts and braces were stowed under a table used by the guards in the other end of the truck, with fierce Alsatian dogs guarding them. There were eighteen prisoners in the sealed-off end of each truck, with four or five armed guards facing them with weapons handy. The prisoners were provided with benches to sit on – an unaccustomed luxury to most of them – along the end and down the sides and centre of each section, thus enabling more prisoners to be squeezed in, but leaving little room for movement or kit. Much of the prisoners' private luggage was soon hung from the ceiling, despite the difficulty caused by the handcuffs, and lack of space to manoeuvre.

The handcuffs at first proved irksome and restricting. But many of the trucks contained some old lags who had had previous dealings with handcuffs; the wearing of them during the day had been ordered by Hitler, as a reprisal for the temporary use of them on newly-captured prisoners in the course of battle by the Allies on the Dieppe raid in 1942. These old lags, after recovering from their initial shock at this unpleasant reprisal, which came as yet another form of degradation that had followed their capture at Dunkirk or in Greece, had devised ways of picking the locks. The reprisal was gradually abandoned. Now, on their present cattle-truck journey, it had been revived, as a means of preventing escape. But nail files were soon produced and when the guards' attention was elsewhere, or when it got dark, the handcuffs were deftly removed.

Different truck-loads had different ways of dealing with the handcuffs, once they were off. In one truck the method used was to drop them out of the small ventilator, which was wired-up but not shut. In another, where the handcuffs had been removed, they were retained and later handed in solemnly by each prisoner as he jumped down from the truck on arrival at the journey's end to a waiting guard, who sheepishly collected them in his steel helmet. In Pip's truck the favoured method was to deposit them for the night into the pee-bucket, which seemed as good a place as any. In the morning a prisoner advanced to the barbed-wire partition and signalled to one of the guards that the bucket was full and needed emptying. The bucket was passed carefully through to the helpful guard for him to empty out of the sliding door. With a mighty heave he threw the contents of the bucket through the gap, spreading the urine over agricultural Germany. He took great care to hang on to the bucket – but this failed to prevent a bunch of saturated handcuffs from flying out through the door. The embarrassed guard was greeted by his chums with roars of laughter – in which the prisoners joined. It was too late for the guard to do anything about it.

The journey to their destination took two days. On 1st May the prisoners arrived at Oflag 79, five miles away from the town of Braunschweig – or Brunswick as it is called in English. To those who had learned or read Robert Browning's *Pied Piper of Hamelin* the name

Pip Gardner with H.R.H. Prince Philip unveiling a plaque at the Brunswick Boys' Club in Fulham in 1972.

H.R.H. Prince Philip visiting the Brunswick Boys' Club, escorted by Pip Gardner, with Alf Gibbs, M.B.E., (behind), who was for many years Secretary of the London Federation of Boys' Clubs.

H.R.H. Prince Charles talking to Pip Gardner at a Victoria Cross and George Cross Association reunion dinner at the Café Royal.

General H. R. B. Foote, V.C., C.B., D.S.O., and Captain P. J. Gardner, V.C., M.C., looking at an artist's painting of the latter's deed of valour in the Western Desert.

was familiar, appearing in the very first line of his lengthy rodent epic. On closer inspection, Pip was relieved to find himself at a well-run established prisoner-of-war camp, fortunately bearing no resemblance to Luckenwalde. The camp was right on the edge of Brunswick aerodrome and about 500 yards from a large aircraft works, the Luftwaffe barracks having been converted into Oflag 79 – the juxta-positioning of which was destined to prove far from safe in the not-too-distant future for the inmates.

But for the present they were reasonably cheerful, and were shortly to become more so when, on 6th June 1944, the good news broke that the Allies had landed in force and with success on the beaches of Normandy. Pip met more of his 4th Royal Tank Regiment friends, including Colonel Reeves, DSO, with whom he had made their brief but abortive exodus into the desert on foot after the fall of Tobruk; also Major Bertie Roberts, MC and Bar, who had sent him out to win a VC in the desert (as things turned out!); another was Captain Quartermaster George Hurst, the donor of a shirt to Pip at Chieti from his private QM stores; another Quartermaster from the Royal Tank Regiment, Reggie Beales by name, generously re-equipped Pip with a serviceable toothbrush. Little acts of thoughtfulness like this counted for a lot in prison life.

The progress that followed the D-Day landings inevitably seemed slow to the prisoners-of-war in Brunswick and camps elsewhere, as they hovered around in expectation at every censored broadcast from the Oberkommando of the Wehrmacht, which was a daily occurrence. They were itching to hear an admission that the Allies were advancing. They certainly hadn't been driven back into the sea, as the reports first forecast. These reports from the enemy would, later in the evening, be carefully compared with the BBC bulletins which were received on the camp's clandestine radio and passed round the huts at night. Pip never knew who operated the radio, nor where it was hidden. It was best not to know. But the news was the life-blood of the prisoners, eagerly awaiting good bulletins from all the battlefronts. The news from the Italian front had been painfully slow and bore little relation to the fanciful rumours that had abounded at the time of the Italian armistice. But at least Rome had finally been entered two days before the D-Day landings – though the 'D-Day Dodgers', as a lady MP so shamefully labelled them from the safety of Parliament, still had a lot of hard fighting to do in Italy, denuded as they were of the troops that had been needed to ensure the success of D-Day.

Pip settled into a tolerable existence at Brunswick and, to pass the time by doing something useful, he worked in the camp cigarette store. Prisoners were allowed to receive cigarette parcels from friends and relations – and most welcome they were. Sometimes there would be a glut of them and prisoners were allowed to put their surplus tins unopened into store, against the lean times that would inevitably occur. The job suited Pip, because in all his wanderings there had been a hiatus in the sending and receiving of his personal cigarette parcels and he had no cigarettes of his own in store. He was glad to accept the occasional tip, in the form of a few cigarettes from 'well-off' prisoners who came to add to, or draw on, their private supply.

But Pip wasn't only a tobacconist – he was also a part-time barber, in a room set aside for cutting hair. Tips were received in the shape of cigarettes, which, as ever, had become a form of camp currency. Some of his customers were Sikh officers and he even coped with their unusual hair-style. There must be some elderly Sikhs in India to-day (and perhaps in Leicester, too?) who can claim the unusual distinction of having had their hair cut by a holder of the Victoria Cross!

The summer continued on its way and the good news was received that, on 25th August, the Allies had taken Paris. General Koenig, the hero of Bir Hacheim, soon arrived there as Commander of the Forces Françaises de l'Intérieur – a far cry from his desperate days in the Libyan desert during the battles near Gazala in 1942. But the news reached an already stricken Brunswick Camp – on 24th August the camp had been on the receiving end of a big daylight bomber raid by American super-fortresses.

The raid was aimed at the underground engine factory near the camp, but bombs landed on the camp as well. For the prisoners the raid turned into a most traumatic experience. Many of them were outside their huts one morning, watching the American planes coming over in swarms, high up in the sky. The prisoners were cheering them on, when suddenly sticks of bombs were seen dropping from the planes. Several of them headed straight for the camp. By this time Pip and most of the others had made a desperate dash for the cellars underneath the building. He went down the steps ten at a time, followed by several others. They all landed in a heap at the bottom. The earth began to shake, as bomb after bomb landed in the compound, and Pip expected to be killed at any moment. But, not for the first time, fortune was on his side. When the bombing and the ack-ack fire finally ceased, the shaken prisoners emerged to find several buildings on fire and badly damaged, with huge craters in a line across the compound. It was remarkable that even more damage had not been done to the buildings. As it was, the raid resulted in the deaths of three British officers, with eight others seriously wounded, plus another thirty slightly hurt. On the German side, one officer and several soldiers were killed. Though bad enough, the casualties could easily have been very much worse.

From that moment on, life in Brunswick Camp, which hadn't been too bad, suddenly became not so good. Apart from the fact that for a time there was no water, no electricity, no cookhouse and not many windows left, the Germans on both sides of the wire were by no means pleased. The prisoners realised that the war had to be won and that life was bound to become increasingly uncomfortable for them, situated as they were, in the middle of so many bomber targets. All they could hope for was an early end to the war, which, after the liberation of most of France, now seemed distinctly possible.

But after the gallant but comprehensive failure of the airborne drop on Arnhem to hasten the end, by enabling a thrust to be made in the north in the direction of Berlin, it became obvious to the prisoners in Oflag 79 that they were in for a long lean winter, punctuated with frequent air-raids. On 14th October there was another big air raid, this time on the town of Brunswick itself, a mere five miles away.

As the air-raids all over Germany increased in frequency and intensity, the prisoners at Brunswick also found themselves getting progressively hungrier. The bombing not only destroyed German factories – it also caused havoc on the railways, and the supplies of Red Cross parcels from Switzerland began to fail, for lack of transport. As the winter wore on, they were reduced to a mere trickle, before stopping altogether. Most prisoners had lived through hungry times before and now they had to pull in their belts once more. Strangely enough, they didn't feel quite as ravenous as they had in the early days of their captivity. Over the years their stomachs had contracted and the pangs of hunger weren't quite so acute. But they all lost weight that they could ill afford to shed, and their energy diminished accordingly.

It was at about this time that one of the camp padrés startled his congregation one Sunday with his sermon in the camp chapel. He announced that, as the going was getting really tough, he regretted to have to say that too many examples of what he called the spirit of 'Fujima' were occurring – and that he didn't at all care for it. As his baffled audience looked up to hear what he meant by 'Fujima', he went on to spell it out for them : 'F U J I M A'. After a pause, he added, for the benefit of those who hadn't yet caught up with him, that the 'J I M A' stood for 'Jack I'm All Right.' He left the first two letters of this acronym to their imagination. Suddenly the penny dropped and the congregation exploded with laughter and applause. But his words hadn't fallen upon stony ground – his flock took them to heart.

Whether or not the padré's words were behind a remarkable response to a scheme that was born of this time of adversity, remains in doubt. But in this time of great stress from hunger, cold, air-raids and anxiety, it was felt that it would be beneficial for the prisoners of Brunswick if they could try to forget about their own present plight and think of some future benefit for others also in need. Their attention focussed on to boys at home, whose homes had also been wrecked in the London Blitz, which the advent of Hitler's revenge weapons, the V1 and V2 bombs, had re-started. Surely they must be in similar straits – living in bomb-damaged buildings, with nowhere for exercise or recreation.

The idea caught on immediately among the prisoners-of-war at Brunswick with such enthusiasm and interest that cheques came rolling in, written on all sorts of pieces of paper, all of which were duly honoured after the war. Donations were also made in the form of money from the prisoners' pay sent home via the Red Cross. The response was magnificent.

In the camp a special 'Boys' Club Office' was opened daily from 1st February 1945, where National Association of Boys' Club pamphlets and the government white paper 'Youth Services' were available, with a draft of the proposed trust deed there for inspection. Then on 14th February the first General Meeting was held in a basement room to discuss the whole proposal for the foundation of a Boys' Club by the camp, and to approve the trust deed and elect a Board of Trustees. In this way the prisoners-of-war of Brunswick raised the handsome total of £13,000, which in those days was sufficient to buy the necessary site and start the club. The success of the Brunswick Boys' Club, which has continued and prospered beyond its first forty years of existence, in which Pip has played a leading part, belongs to the epilogue of this book.

Meanwhile the war was drawing to its close, and the twilight of the Third Reich had been reached with a vengeance. Over Brunswick during the period from 2nd February to 31st March, there were air-raid warnings every day or night, as bombers made their way to Berlin and elsewhere. Brunswick seemed to be in the direct path of the bombers and the effect on the prisoners' nerves was proving understandably great. But the end must surely be in sight? There was speculation as to who would reach them first – the Americans, British, Canadians or the Russians? In the end, while the Russians were making their final assault on Berlin, and the British and Canadians were forcing their away along the northern coastal area of Germany, it was the Americans who finally arrived to liberate the prisoners of Brunswick, on 12th April.

The prisoners were beside themselves with joy, having stuck it out through the last grim winter of the war, through air-raids, hunger and cold, to survive until this longed-for day. As if to confirm that they hadn't been dreaming it all, they were solemnly told by the BBC that a camp at Brunswick containing two thousand British and Allied officers and four hundred other ranks had been liberated on 14th April. This announcement drew hoots of derision from the prisoners, who had already tasted two days of freedom !

But they hadn't tasted much food since liberation, because even the meagre German rations ceased to arrive. It was left to the prisoners' own enterprise to supplement the bread ration that the Americans managed to issue to them. Pip and some of his friends foraged for eggs and other food from nearby farms. After a few days of waiting, during which their health seemed to pick up considerably, a large number of Dakota aircraft arrived to fetch them from Brunswick airfield, so recently the magnet for the bombs which had spilled over on to the camp.

The flight home was in two hops, and Pip's plane landed at Brussels where a Stirling of the RAF took him on the second leg of his homeward journey. As the plane flew over the English Channel, some of the prisoners were invited to the flight-deck to see the White Cliffs of Dover, followed by the green fields of southern England. The latter were in pleasant contrast to the acres of rubble that they had seen as they flew over Cologne and other flattened German towns and cities. It made

Pip feel very fortunate to have ended the war on the winning side. His own contribution had been in the earlier days in the Western Desert, when the result had appeared very much in the balance. From June 1942 onwards it had been for him a matter of survival, escape and more survival. Two thoughts in particular had sustained him. First, when he was facing up to his third Christmas since his capture, the unfortunate prisoners from Dunkirk and St Valéry were spending their fifth behind barbed-wire. Secondly, thanks to the Red Cross, he had managed to survive, but whatever must it be like for the poor devils who had fallen into Japanese hands, with no Red Cross parcels? They had been prisoners for more than three years already, and weren't by any means free yet. Now he was on his way back to Renée, and feeling very grateful indeed.

The plane landed at an airfield near Oxford, where the ex-prisoners were dusted with de-lousing powder, given tea and buns, and driven off to a nearby reception centre in a large country mansion, which had been used the previous year as quarters for the troops assembling in readiness for the Normandy invasion.

Each prisoner was allowed one phone call. Pip rang Renée at her Naval base in Scotland. She had steadfastly rejected suggestions that she should apply for a commission in the WRNS. Not only would a commission probably have led to an office job, instead of the driving that she so much preferred, but, more importantly, it might have entailed a posting abroad. At all costs, after waiting so long for his return, she was determined to be on hand to welcome Pip back home when he eventually turned up. She caught the first available train down to Oxford, where he would meet her – leave from the WRNS being no problem for the wife of a returning VC.

Pip spent his first night back in England at the reception centre, where he was fitted out with a few respectable items of army clothing, with the help of kind members of the Women's Volunteer Service, on hand to perform any emergency sewing required. Next morning he and Lieutenant Lewis Wiard, a Royal Tank Regiment friend with whom he had travelled back from Brunswick, were driven into Oxford in the staff car of the Colonel in charge of the reception centre. There they eagerly awaited the arrival of their wives.

But first they had to arrange accommodation, and this proved by no means easy. The city seemed to be packed with American troops on leave. However, after at first drawing a blank at the Mitre Hotel, they were finally given preferential treatment. Pip and Renée were to have the hotel's best room, complete with a four-poster bed, reputed to have been slept in by the ubiquitous Queen Anne! Now for two nights it was their turn.

Pip Gardner had returned at last from his desert – exchanging the Pyramids of Egypt for the dreaming spires of Oxford. After all his ups and downs, he was safely back in Renée's arms.

The Brunswick Boys' Club

Though Pip Gardner's war was over on his return from his years in the Libyan Desert and as a prisoner-of-war, both behind barbed-wire and on the run, his military service hadn't quite ended.

On his return to Britain, he was given the customary six weeks of repatriation leave granted to all returning prisoners-of-war, except for an isolated few who faced charges of collaborating with the enemy. He enjoyed his leave with Renée, and they were delighted to find that their relationship carried on just as before – almost as if there hadn't been a five-year interruption. They realised how fortunate they were in this respect, because they noticed that not all couples similarly re-united were able to pick up the threads so smoothly, nor even to make the adjustments and allowances that in some cases were required.

But before Pip could resume his civilian life, he first had to complete his military service. His release was due on 21st November 1945, under the totting-up system of combining age with length of service in order to determine one's release date. At the beginning of July he was invited to take over an exhibition of tanks and armoured corps equipment which was being staged in Stanley Park, Blackpool. He had a most amusing and enjoyable time showing the public the vehicles and weapons that had helped win the war. The whole show was later transferred for a month in the autumn to Brighton, where two of his aunts lived. The display was set up in marquees erected on the car park next to the old ice-skating rink (since demolished in favour of the new Brighton Centre). Again Pip found this a pleasant interlude, with Mayoral receptions to add to the enjoyment.

At last, in November, he was able to return to his family company and was appointed Joint Managing Director with his father. He felt lucky to have his pre-war occupation to return to, and appreciated the great reception accorded to him by the company's workers, to whom he used to write while he was in the desert. They in their turn were proud to welcome back the wearer of the Victoria Cross into their midst.

As well as applying his time and energy to running I. Gardner and

Co Ltd during the transition back from war to peace, Pip remembered his promise to himself and others, made in the dark days of the bombing over Brunswick Camp, and devoted much of his time to the starting of the Brunswick Boys' Club. He was not only a foundation member, but was also a member of the management committee.

The returning ex-prisoners from Brunswick Camp (Oflag 79) lost no time in starting the Boys' Club for which they had raised money so enthusiastically. The enthusiasm was due in no small part to Major Percy Flood, who had had some experience of boys' clubs before the war, and was some twenty years later the subject of an Eamonn Andrews *This is Your Life* programme, in recognition of his great contribution. It is also gratifying to record that the original draft trust deed, drawn up by the solicitors in Brunswick Camp, was approved on the prisoners' return to England and has remained unaltered to this day.

After consultation with the National Association of Boys' Clubs, a site was purchased in Haldane Road, Fulham, London SW6, and in spite of post-war building difficulties the club premises were completed by 1948. These consisted of two large huts containing a club-room, reading-room, library, workshop, gymnasium, showers and a canteen. Outside there is a playground for football, cricket and tennis. It was thus very much the kind of club that the contributors from Oflag 79 had envisaged.

The club was opened in 1948 by HRH The Duke of Edinburgh and has been running at full capacity to this day. The membership is for 120 boys between 14 and 18, and 100 junior boys from 11 to 14. Apart from the physical and cultural recreation offered, every effort is made to ensure that the boys leaving school enter a worthwhile trade or occupation. The club was re-built in 1970 and re-opened by HRH Prince Philip. In 1977 it was extended and opened, on this occasion, by Lord Aberdare.

Throughout its existence the club has been managed by trustees, all of whom were POWs in Brunswick, and is still supported by subscribers, the majority of whom are ex-prisoners-of-war. As the years pass their number diminishes, but the club continues to go from strength to strength. Characteristically, Pip has been closely associated with the club from the start – first as a founder member and then as a trustee, and later as Chairman of Trustees for fourteen years. In 1985 he was elected President, an honour which he greatly appreciates and richly deserves. His appreciation is heightened by the fact that he has succeeded the Club's first President, Major-General W. D. E. Brown, CB,

CBE, DSO, one time Senior British Officer in Oflag 79, whose contribution to the club was immense before his death in 1984, and to whose great efforts the present extensive buildings are largely due.

Brunswick Boys' Club is a shining example of how a period of stress and deprivation for one group of temporary unfortunates has resulted ultimately in benefit for others whose lives have been greatly enriched by the support received. The creation and continued existence of the Brunswick Boys' Club reflects most creditably on all those who made and kept their promises to do something positive, should they themselves be fortunate enough to survive the war and thus be able to implement their altruistic intentions. One of these foundation members, and also a continuing subscriber, is Tom Tufnell, who with his salvage partner 'Crump' Colbeck has appeared in this story in connection with the 'recovery unit' operating in the Fontanellato drains – both of them having reached Brunswick after a taste of freedom and hunger on the loose in the Apennines in 1943.

Another benefit arising out of Pip's spell in Brunswick Camp was his first meeting there with Edward Newbald, MC, who had been captured on the island of Kos in 1943. Edward Newbald is a chartered accountant and in 1955 he became Company Secretary and Financial Director of J. Gardner and Co Ltd. He was also a founder-trustee of the Brunswick Boys' Club.

Sadly, in 1955, Pip received a nasty shock when his father collapsed and died in his arms in his office, thus leaving him as sole Managing Director of the company. Since then, managing his family company has naturally absorbed a major portion of his energy, but he nevertheless accepted an invitation to serve on the board of governors of his old school, Dulwich College – a duty which he performed with enthusiasm for seven years.

Another of his voluntary undertakings has been the honorary secretaryship of the Victoria Cross and George Cross Association. This has kept him in touch with his fellow VCs, including the Association's Vice-Chairman, General H. R. B. Foote, VC, CB, DSO, of the Royal Tank Regiment, their paths having first converged during the fighting in the Western Desert in Tobruk in 1942.

One of the highlights of Pip's involvement with the Association was a trip to Kenya organised by East African Airways – for 10 VCs in a VC10 for 10 days. Their itinerary included some unforgettable visits, of which perhaps the most memorable was a night spent at 'Treetops', the famous hotel built in the branches of some large Cape Chestnut trees, high up in the Aberdare Mountains. It bears the inscription: 'In this Mgumu tree HRH The Princess Elizabeth and HRH The Duke of Edinburgh spent the night of 5th February 1952. While here, Princess Elizabeth succeeded to the throne through the death of her father, King George VI.' Thus Pip added another historic place to the varied collection that he had amassed during his pre-war travels round the world and his wartime adventures in Egypt, Palestine and Rome. Treetops ranks in his memory alongside the Great Wall of China, the Pyramids and the Sphinx of Egypt, and the Opera House in Rome – all of which have appeared in this story.

Several of Pip's friends from his days in hiding in Rome have kept in touch with him during their post-war lives, which all of them at times could hardly have expected to reach. They include: Lieutenant-Colonel Robert ('Tug') Wilson, DSO and Bar, with whom he shared a flat in Rome, as well as some testing times after their re-capture, and to whose story *Special Commando* Pip contributed in no small way; Colonel Sam Derry, DSO, MC, JP, DL, of the Rome Organisation, with whom Pip appeared in a *This Is Your Life* programme in Sam's honour, in which Monsignor Hugh O'Flaherty, CBE, also appeared, just before his death; Lieutenant-Colonel John Furman, OBE, MC, who was in Chieti POW camp and Regina Coeli prison with Pip and emigrated in 1948 to the future state of Israel, has also remained in touch from there.

Percy Gers, Pip's friend in the Westminster Dragoons in England and the 4th Royal Tanks in the desert, before they escaped together from Fontanellato, managed most creditably to find his own way to the Allied lines in 1944, after it had unfortunately, as it was thought at the time, become impossible to escort him to Rome. He was thus already home, on duty at a POW camp, and ready to greet Pip a year later on his return from Germany. It was a happy reunion and they kept in touch thereafter, until Percy's death in 1980.

It is granted to all too few war-heroes to survive to enjoy the well-deserved fame that results from the winning of the Victoria Cross. In Pip Gardner's case, he also had to endure a series of adventures and setbacks as a prisoner-of-war before he eventually reached home safely. Apart from the joy that his survival brought to his family and friends, what a boon it has proved for over forty years to all the youngsters who have been fortunate enough to benefit from the creation of The Brunswick Boys' Club!

Index